The Old Dispensation

The Old Dispensation

Loyalty in Business

John J. Clancy

Madison • Teaneck
Fairleigh Dickinson University Press
London: Associated University Presses

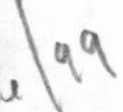

Associated University Presses
440 Forsgate Drive
Cranbury, NJ 08512

Associated University Presses
16 Barter Street
London WC1A 2AH, England

Associated University Presses
P.O. Box 338, Port Credit
Mississauga, Ontario
Canada L5G 4L8

The paper used in this publication meets the requirements of the American National Standard for Permanence of Paper for Printed Library Materials Z39.48-1984.

Library of Congress Cataloging-in-Publication Data

Clancy, John J. (John Joseph), 1937–
The old dispensation : loyalty in business / John J. Clancy.
p. cm.
Includes bibliogaphical references and index.
ISBN 0-8386-3793-0
1. Corporate reorganizations—History—20th century. 2. Business ethics—History—20th century. 3. Employee loyalty—History—20th century. I. Title.
HD2746.5.C54 1999
658.3′14—dc21 98-7073
CIP

PRINTED IN THE UNITED STATES OF AMERICA

Dedicated to the memory of my father,
William Edward Clancy, Sr.

I have fought a good fight, I have finished my course, I have kept the faith.

—1 Tim. 4:7.

Contents

Preface

The Sea of Faith
Was once, too, at the full, and round earth's shore
Lay like the folds of a bright girdle furl'd.
But now I only hear
Its melancholy, long, withdrawing roar,
Retreating, to the breath
Of the night-wind, down the vast edges drear
And naked shingles of the world.

Ah, love, let us be true
To one another! for the world which seems
To lie before us like a land of dreams,
So various, so beautiful, so new,
Hath really neither joy, nor love, nor light,
Nor certitude, nor peace, nor help for pain,
And we are here as on a darkling plain
Swept with confused alarms of struggle and flight,
Where ignorant armies clash by night.

—Arnold, *Dover Beach*

THIS is the story of loyalty-lost, of profound changes in values, of an old American social character overturned. Now, it is a commonplace that there have been momentous changes in loyalty over the last twenty or so years; the very idea of a loyal bond to a corporation seems quaint, archaic—particularly to young people. Loyalty to organizations may still live on in the older generation, but overall it fades fast as their time, and their values, pass. In *Dover Beach*, Matthew Arnold expressed his feelings of loss and dismay as the old Christian orthodoxy—the old dispensation—lost its hold on nineteenth century Britain. Arnold feared the worst; the world without faith is depicted as grim indeed. What will our world be like without loyalty? This work tries to understand loyalty and determine the effects that its general loss will have on our society and economy.

There is general agreement that corporate loyalty—that old dispensation—is dying if not dead, but there is much less agreement about why this is so. Some say that the economy has changed, others that people have changed, and still others that companies are now run differently. Which is right? I think they are all more or less right—but the interesting questions are: Why so? What has happened to the economy, the culture, and the management practices so that loyalty is waning or gone? And, how did loyalty emerge in the first place? Was there a time when the old dispensation was new, when corporate loyalty was waxing?

In this work, I attempt to write a 'natural history' of loyalty, the causes of its flowering and its demise—and, what that demise portends for us all. For this is also a cautionary tale: the 'new dispensation' with its new management ideology, that fierce pursuit of shareholder wealth which has American businessmen in thrall, carries with it great opportunities for productivity and competitiveness, but it is also laden with a heavy cargo of risk—risk to their businesses, risk to their employees, and risk to the society.

History is said to be written by the winners, but I hope to give voice here to the losers as well, the losers in the individual battles for security and meaningfulness that stormed through America from the early 1970s to the present day. I wish to give voice to the defeated ranks of the old corporate loyalists, bravely soldiering on in their diaspora of unemployment, self-employment and underemployment or, warily clinging to any job at all in Corporate America; and to give voice as well to the new professionals who have more or less successfully accommodated themselves to the new organizational realities.

So, this is the story of loyalty-lost, the passing of the old dispensation, a story of hopes destroyed and new hopes inspired, of betrayal and opportunity, of broken dreams, new promise. Like the passing of anything of value, this story can take an elegiac tone, a tone of irreparable loss as a cherished belief has lost its power, a tone Matthew Arnold captured in *Dover Beach*. It may be that the new corporate orthodoxy is that 'land of dreams which lies before us / So various, so beautiful, so new.' But we must understand what we have left behind when the Sea of Faith retreated.

Acknowledgments

A work of this sort is never a collaboration, in the sense of shared responsibility for its accuracy and quality. But it is nonetheless a result of a great deal of assistance from a number of colleagues and friends. I owe a great debt to Professors Nicholas Baloff, Henry Berger, Iver Bernstein, and Gary Miller for their advice, criticism, and unwavering support. Professors Jean Ensminger and John Cross gave critical advice on methodological considerations, and Nicola Gillis and Dr. Harvey Colton reviewed final drafts for me and offered very helpful critiques; I am grateful to all of them.

My dear wife Sue was a constant inspiration as well as lively critic of my ideas as I thought through the issues found in this work. Her support over the years has been irreplaceable.

I must also thank the officers of my research-site company, called "Softmatics" in this work. Without their active support of my research, this work would have been impossible.

And last, and perhaps most importantly, I owe much to the employees of "Softmatics" who took the time to respond to my survey, and took even more time to talk at length with me. This work is in many ways their story, the story of their hopes and fears, their insights into our current condition. I am in their debt.

I hereby acknowledge the Rhoda Weyr Agency of New York for granting me permission to quote two lines of Randall Jarrell from *The Lost World.*

I hereby acknowledge the the New York Times Co. for granting me permission to use material by Walter Kissinger as quoted from the *New York Times.*

The Old Dispensation

Part One
The Old Dispensation: The Oldest Cohort

1
Introduction

> *So many people worked so many countless extra hours without being asked to . . . But then when things really got bad, some of those very same people, came in one Monday morning and were led into their manager's office and were met then with a security guard and escorted out the door. . . .*
>
> —*Bill Abernathy*[1]

I am talking with Bill Abernathy, a bright forty-four-year-old software professional, ordinarily quick to smile, but now visibly upset. I have just asked him about the early days of his career:

> Twenty-one years ago, when I started working, I really honestly believed that I could go to a company, I could put in my 35 or 40 years, I could grow as an individual . . . I would retire and everything would fall into place naturally . . . in the business environment in the U.S. at that time . . . that was the way of things . . . That's how it happened. I mean, as long as you're relatively honest, hard working, loyal, you had a job. You were OK. You'd get by.

Bill had started his professional work life in 1971, and as he talked I recalled my own beginnings in 1960. Without much thought of alternatives, I had joined a large corporation—that is what an engineering graduate did in those days, urged along by strenuous recruiting from the big firms. For us fortunate graduates in 1960, it was a matter of deciding where you wanted to live and then choosing from a number of excellent offers.

I joined a big company, undeterred by a reading of William H. Whyte, Jr.'s *The Organization Man* while I was in college. That popular work described a corporate world of conformity, the betrayal of individualism in the corporation's quest to build a type of *ersatz* community. I never forgot Whyte's book, but my own experience of the large corporation differed in a fundamental way: I found an arena for challenging and rewarding work, and I also found a real community, a true camaraderie of people doing something important together. I was not so obtuse not to see some of the follies and conformist pressures that Whyte reported, but those seemed minor nuisances, like the dirty streets of eighteenth-century London that Mandeville called "a necessary Evil inseparable from the Felicity of London" (Mandeville 1724, 4).

Bill Abernathy found much the same sense of community:

> I really felt I was a part of that company, that there was a relationship, an honest relationship between me, my fellow workers, my supervisors . . . that there was a camaraderie. . . . A community. . . . That we were more than a business. . .

In the course of time my own responsibilities increased and when I reached my mid-forties I found myself in the lower levels of top management, overseeing a large and rapidly growing division. About that time, somewhere in the early 1980s, my management contemporaries and I began to notice something about our younger colleagues. They were decent and hardworking people, no less so than any of us had been, but they seemed to have a very different idea of their relationship with the company. At the early stages of our career we were like Bill: believing that we would end our careers there. That put a definite stamp on behavior: you did what management wanted you to do, believing that what the company needed would benefit you in the long run. What we began to see among the younger people was a reversal of that perspective. They seemed to think that the job with our company was no more than a way station, so the best thing to do was to develop skills and to work on projects that outsiders would find significant. I was not unique in having taken many mundane and even treacherous assignments, just because management asked me to. We found now much less willingness to do things like that; their eye was on another ball. The philosopher Josiah Royce described loyalty in its highest form as "the willing and practical and thoroughgoing devotion of a person to a cause" (Royce 1908, 16). That is the type of company loyalty that seems familiar to many of a certain age. The younger people seemed more likely to hold to a lower standard of loyalty, what has been described as "minimal loyalty," merely the pledge not to betray (Fletcher 1993, 41).

Something had clearly changed over the years in people's sense of loyalty to the company. Now, it is, I believe, significant that I had noticed this waning of the old loyalty before layoffs became popular in American business. Like Bill Abernathy, I was with an organization which had never experienced a layoff. Bill talked about his start:

> . . . back in August 1977 and talking to people in Human Resources (about a job) and one of the selling points, they said, "You know, (this company), in 17 years has never laid off one person. . . . and we never will." Now that's kind of a stupid thing to say, but you know, I was 27 at the time, eager and, boy, it sounded great. You know it was a major selling point and for years I watched us grow . . . we kept growing . . . It seemed endless and you know, people at that time, we didn't worry about our futures.

Bill attributes his own loss of loyalty squarely to the actions of management, actions which awakened him from his illusions:

> We felt that our futures were secured and when things started to unravel, it was devastating. . . . It was frightening . . . to one day realize it wasn't true, that we were like that as long as times were good, but when times got bad, it was . . . "No, no, no, that's not really how it was" and . . . you want to say, "God, am I stupid for believing this? . . . or was I naive or . . . did the company really turn on us?" I mean, I don't know. . . . all I know is how I felt I was betrayed. Either someone lied to me or took advantage of me. And that hurts. If you find out your best friend . . . has been stealing from your bank account for the last 20 years, sure you're mad because you lost the money, but you're probably more hurt because it was your best friend and you trusted him and he basically violated that trust.

What we are hearing is perhaps a confirmation of Ambrose Bierce's sardonic definition of loyalty: "a virtue peculiar to those who are about to be betrayed" (Bierce 1958, 42). But Bill Abernathy would surely not find that amusing; he has a clear notion of the nature of loyalty, and the enormity of the moral failure when it is betrayed:

> It's real easy to be loyal in the good times. Where true loyalty is, is sticking it out through the bad times. . . . So many people

> worked so many countless extra hours without being asked to. Well, now, we were being asked to . . . give up a Saturday, "Can you come in Saturday, can you work through the next six months, Saturday mornings? . . . We need to get more for our money." And you know, so many people . . . just did it . . . But then when things really got bad some of those very same people came in one Monday morning and were led into their manager's office and were met then with a security guard and escorted out the door. . . . to us, from the workers' perspective, that was not loyalty. That, from the managers' perspective, that might have been good business, but that was not loyalty.

Bill Abernathy's story of betrayal is perhaps a common account of loyalty lost, but is it the only explanation? Is it just that companies started acting differently? Since I had seen the organizational bonds loosening well before layoffs began, I thought not. And that led me to this inquiry. Essentially I asked myself:

- Has employee loyalty to the company in fact declined in American business?
- Where did the widespread loyalty I experienced in my youth come from?
- Why does it seem to have diminished?
- What are the consequences of a general waning of corporate loyalty?

To answer these questions I conducted a survey of one organization (which I shall call "Softmatics" throughout), an information software and services firm. I was looking for correlations of loyalty with other attitudes and also with personal characteristics—particularly age, since my first hint that something had changed was my observation that younger people had a different outlook. I also interviewed some ninety-one people, including Bill Abernathy.

Softmatics offered some particular advantages for this research. The company is a strategic business unit (profit center) of a multi-billion-dollar information services company (here called "DRI"), which itself is a unit of a much larger diversified corporation (dubbed "ACC"). The employees are virtually all college graduates and professionals, and thus representatives of a key sector of the late-twentieth-century knowledge-industry workforce. Softmatics is equally divided in employee population between a Midwestern headquarters location, a California R&D site, and sales and service locations scattered throughout the United States. Thus, the attitudinal effects (if any) of regional location, headquarters location, and remote office location could be studied. Further, since the remote offices are comprised mostly of sales and sales support people, the differences (if any) in attitudes of sales-related people can be studied. (In the event, I found only minor differences in attitudes among the locations; rather, age cohort was the most reliable indicator of attitudes.)[2]

The firm had another advantage for my research: it is representative of many American companies in that Softmatics has experienced a prototypical round of mergers, acquisitions, and substantial reorganizations and "downsizings" in the recent past. Originally, Softmatics had grown to a substantial size as a unit of a large diversified company, a proponent of the paternalistic, "welfare corporatist" style of management described in chapter 8.[3] Most of my interlocutors had experienced this management style, and also its abrupt ending, when in 1988 a major layoff and restructuring occurred. This was followed by more layoffs and reorganizations through 1989 and 1990 and then by the most traumatic event of all: the unit was sold to DRI, a distinctively *non*-paternalistic company, operated in the modern manner with single-minded and hard-nosed attention to the bottom line. Softmatics went through another round of layoffs and restructurings under the new owners, and employees were exposed to new management policies and thinking. The layoffs continued sporadically almost up to the time of my survey and interviews, i.e., late 1994 and early 1995. And so, the experience of Softmatics employees can give us some insight into the effects of management practices on employee loyalty, particularly how welfare corporatism's passing is seen by employees.

There are, of course, disadvantages and limitations to my approach. First, the interviewees were rather obviously employed, so I gained no insight into the attitudes of workers who had lost their jobs. And the Softmatics employee population is hardly representative of the entire American workforce, both in its composition (highly educated professionals) and its prospects (as software professionals they presumably have better alternate employment than most). To the first issue, I should say that I was intentionally seeking a professional workforce to be able to compare my findings to recent studies, such as Bennett's *The Death of the Organization Man* (1990) and Heckscher's *White Collar Blues* (1995), and earlier work such as Whyte's *The Organization Man* (1956). To the second, I can only say that you will find that my interviewees in general did not express particular nonchalance about their long-term employment prospects.

This is the story of loyalty lost and we must acknowledge at the outset that the reasons are complex and difficult to untangle. Surely the American economy's difficulties in the last twenty-five years have pressed management to adopt new practices, which certainly affect employee attitudes. But I believe there are more fundamental causes afoot. This work argues that employee loyalty has indeed waned, partially as a result of different management practices, as Bill Abernathy proposes. But I believe the roots lie much more in a profound social change, tied to new attitudes held by new generations of employees and new generations of managers.[4] My argument is that American social character has changed markedly in the last thirty years, that the record of the public opinion polls shows a distinct shift away from older attitudes and values such as confidence in institutions, mutual trust, and a sense of connection to society. This is a matrix of attitudes that I have called "the old dispensation" in these pages, and I believe that employee loyalty, Royce's "devotion to a cause," is a component of that matrix, and has dissipated along with the other, older values.

In order to uncover the reality of this social change and its causes, I have taken an interdisciplinary approach. Psychology offers us some direction to explain the rather curious fact that people proffer loyalty to organizations in the first place. Sociology provides us both an enormous storehouse of data about attitudes, as well as theories of social change that can be quite useful to explain the phenomenon of shifts in employee loyalty. Economics, especially the "theory of the firm," gives us insights into changing management practices that have been, in part, responsible for both the creation, and the destruction, of employee loyalty. History as well is a source of useful material. I should say that this is not a work of history; I do not attempt any new revelations or new readings of the historical record. Rather, I use the events of history, such as the Depression and the Vietnam War, to suggest that historical events have presented new generations with different socialization experiences, and also that events served to confirm for many people the often rather vague changes in thinking which are in the air of the times.

Again, my argument is that a fundamental social change has occurred and this can be seen in the different attitudes of different generations of people. To test this hypothesis, along with my own research I have reviewed the record of public opinion polls. Now, these polls rarely ask about corporate loyalty, but they do attempt to measure attitudes that I believe are closely allied, such as job satisfaction, trust, anomie, and confidence in institutional leadership. Changes in these attitudes over time would indicate a transformation which I think can be associated with shifts in loyalty. It is important to note that I am reading the poll data on this matrix of attitudes in order to make a statement about the decline of loyalty and the possible causes of that decline, although the data report on other attitudes, such as trust and confidence in institutions.

Therefore it can be seen that two research techniques have been used. The survey and interviews I conducted provide a "snapshot" of attitudes that existed in late 1994 and early 1995 among employees of one firm. The public opinion data serve as a longitudinal data base, some with data reaching back over fifty years. I have tried to use both the point data from my own survey and interviews, along with the series data of the polls to determine both current attitudes on loyalty and how those attitudes have changed over time. There are serious limitations to this method. There is first the problem that the populations from the poll data and my own research are substantially different. My work involved professional workers in a high-technology industry, and the poll data relate to the general population. However, there is a strong congruence in the results of my survey and interviews with the poll data, indicating that the changes in attitude patterns are much more related to the respondents' age cohort than they are to their occupations and education.[5]

Secondly, there is the issue of age cohorts. My central finding is that loyalty attitudes have declined with each new generation, and often the poll data do not discriminate by age. However, I have located enough poll data that is differentiated by age such that I believe my central thesis—that loyalty and its decline are connected with pervasive social change led by new generations—can be substantiated.

Before going much further we should stop and lay some groundwork. First, has loyalty in fact diminished? Much of the evidence is anecdotal, but the fact that loyalty to employers has faded—if not disappeared—seems to be beyond dispute. It is not a new concern. As early as 1974, Sigband (1974) reported on a spate of corporate executive speeches, journal articles and business press notices, all decrying the lack of employee commitment. Mowday et al. (1982) state that the erosion of corporate loyalty is widely recognized, citing business press articles from 1979 and 1981, and noting that "the severity is startling." More recently, we see a constant drumfire of "loyalty" articles in the academic journals, the business press—even the popular press. *Business Week* devotes its 4 August 1986 cover article to "The End of Corporate Loyalty." *The Economist* matter-of-factly reports on the "Death of Corporate Loyalty" (*Economist* 1993). *Psychology Today* reviews "The Disappearing Company Man" (Marks 1988). We are told by *The New York Times* that we are in a "Time of the Disposable Worker" (Kilborn 1994) and *Time* speaks of an "Age of Insecurity" (Church 1993).

Nor does the press look far for the causes of loyalty lost: it agrees with Bill Abernathy that the reason lies with the tidal wave of downsizing that has engulfed Corporate America.

We read reports of Apple (Markoff 1993), IBM (Carroll 1993), and Kodak (Quint 1993) abandoning their traditional paternalism, their welfare corporatism, and we are told that, in turn, their employees view the old bonds with jaundiced eyes. The list of companies reducing managerial and professional staff is long and includes the most distinguished firms in American corporate life: AT&T, Bank of America, CBS, Dow Chemical, DuPont, Exxon, Ford, Merck, Polaroid, Time, etc. The Bureau of Labor Statistics reports that in the last five years, 1.5 million executives, managers, and professionals have lost their jobs—double the number laid off from 1981 to 1988 (Yates 1993).

Staff reductions have become fashionable. Layoffs to reduce costs in bad times are, of course, an old story, but we are now seeing healthy companies paring back with abandon. The motives are usually two: bringing cost structures in line with foreign competitors and eliminating bureaucracy (*Business Week* 1986). Both are, of course, aimed at maximizing return to shareholders. In nearly every case, Wall Street reacts positively to employment reductions. The pressures to reduce staff are overwhelming: Kodak fired its CEO (a 35-year veteran), for being too slow to reduce costs, although the company was profitable (Quint 1993).

The popular perceptions of loyalty lost are confirmed by some solid survey results. We shall have occasion to review survey data in detail in later chapters, but some samples will be instructive here. Harris and Associates conducted a survey among middle managers in 600 corporations in July 1986. The question was: "Compared with ten years ago, do you feel that salaried employees are more loyal, less loyal or about as loyal as they were back then?"

The results were as follows (*Business Week* 1986):

More loyal	5%
Less loyal	65%
About the same	29%
Not sure	1%

Another survey in 1993 showed that 63 percent of managers feel less loyalty to their companies than they did five years ago. On the other side of the relationship, 57 percent of American corporations feel less loyalty to their employees (Yates 1993). If anything, this picture is growing darker: A *New York Times* survey in 1996 found 75 percent of respondents believing that corporations were less loyal and 64 percent saying that workers were less loyal than ten years earlier. Supporting the notion that this loyalty lost is a part of a more general social change, 70 percent thought that employees today compete more one against the other than they did ten years ago (Kleinfield 1996, A-1).

And yet another straw in the wind: the Families and Work Institute surveyed a nationally representative sample of 3,400 employees across the United States in 1992. While 27 percent felt "extremely loyal" to their employers and 37 percent said they were "very loyal," the researchers concluded that "fewer workers answered positively in the extreme" (Galinsky et al 1993, 13). According to the Institute, conditions on the front line of the American workplace present a scene of turmoil: 42 percent of the respondents had been through downsizing and 28 percent had seen cutbacks in the number of managers. Forty-two percent felt "burned out"; almost one in five feared that they, too, would be fired. The researchers concluded that a different type of worker is emerging, one more committed to himself than his employer. On average, most believe they are devoting too much of their time and energy to their work, too little to themselves, their family and friends (Galinsky et al. 1993, 1–2 and 97).

Such findings are mirrored by a 1993 Roper study, which sought the springs of personal self-expression and feelings of worth (Crispell 1993). To the question "What about you conveys self-expression?," only 47 percent of the respondents listed "my job"—well behind the frequency of other things mentioned, such as: friends, music, hobbies, clothes. Even television shows watched, magazines read, vacations taken, and cars driven were rated more important than the respondents' work. To a slightly different question, "What says the most about you?," only 12 percent responded with "my job."

So, let us for now take as a given that loyalty has largely declined; we will have much to say about the ebb and flow of loyalty as we proceed. But in order to speak intelligently about loyalty and its life course, we must understand its nature. I believe that there is a widespread misconception of loyalty that is found now in both the popular press and more serious writers, and this misconception hampers our view of the reasons for loyalty's decline, and the effects of that decline. Effectively, many view loyalty as a species of contract between an individual and an organization. A 1994 newspaper article is typical of this view: "An employee gave the company loyalty and received a steady job, service pins, and a secure retirement" (Genasci 1994). A recent *Fortune* article mirrors this conception: "The job contract . . . the one that traded loyalty for job security" (B. O'Reilly 1994). More serious analysts fall into what I believe is this erroneous view. Amanda Bennett, in her *The Death of the Organization Man* (1990), describes loyalty as "A Faustian bargain . . . independence and autonomy for corporate loyalty" (Bennett 1990, 15). Even Charles Heckscher, in his fine study of corporate loyalty, *White Collar Blues* (1995), defines older management practices as "a relation in which an organization offers protection and security in exchange for undivided loyalty" (Heckscher 1995, 6).

The problem with this account of loyalty is that it presumes a conscious decision on the employee's part, a rational act to proffer loyalty in exchange for some benefit. This may be an adequate "rational choice" account of how minimal, utilitarian loyalty forms, the type of attachment denoted "instrumental commitment" in the literature of organizational commitment.[6] But as I argue further in chapter 5, the species of loyalty which is beneficial to both an individual and an organization is not formed in such a conscious manner and is more usefully thought of as an emotion rather than an act of will. And we can see how the confusion of the two types of loyalty leads to erroneous conclusions. If it were as simple as a consciously made contract, we would expect that the loyalty would disappear when the "contract" is broken by the company. In fact, that is precisely the conclusion that many commentators come to. For example, Grosman in *The Journal of Business Ethics* lightly assumes that "loss of loyalty flow[s] from downsizing and mass firings. . . ." (Grosman 1989). Beth Rubin's *Shifts in the Social Contract* (1996) claims that the "implicit social contracts underlying much of social life are breaking down as the explicit contracts shift" (Rubin 1996, 7), thus positing a causal arrow which I will attempt to demonstrate runs precisely in the opposite direction. The assertion that loyalty is lost due to draconian management action is, of course, the account that Bill Abernathy gave, but as I will argue throughout, that particular reason for loyalty lost is the historical experience of only one of the age cohorts, cohort 2, those between two worlds, those whose socialization period lay in the antiauthoritarian 1960s, but whose early work experience was colored by older notions of corporate benevolence. Simply put, the prevalent idea that loyalty—true loyalty or "normative commitment" in the nomenclature of the literature of organizational commitment—that true loyalty disappeared because a "contract" was broken is not supported by the historical nor the research record.[7] As we will see with cohort 1, the people of the "old dispensation" experienced the same dislocations as cohorts 2 and 3, but largely remained loyal. My own research is supported in this conclusion by the experiences of former IBM employees, as reported by Paul Carroll in his *Big Blues.* Carroll found that IBMers deplored the changes taking place at the company and scorned the management, but still retained a fierce loyalty to IBM—astonishingly, even when they had been forced out (Carroll 1993, 269 and 363). I found much the same thing in my study, but I found it with the cohort 1 people alone, who had been through the "fire," but retained their identification with the company. And, as I will discuss in later chapters, the youngest cohort (cohort 3) had never made much of a bond with the company and were mostly unconcerned when the layoffs began.

So, to summarize, the prevalent view that true loyalty results from a contract is, I believe, seriously in error. And the corollary—that employees lost their loyalty when the companies began to eschew paternalism—is flawed in that it appears to be true for an historically unique group—cohort 2—but is not true for their older or their younger colleagues.

There is another common reading of the historical record that I believe is mistaken. That is the idea, first popularized by William H. Whyte, Jr. in *The Organization Man* (1956) and David Riesman in *The Lonely Crowd* (1950), that a new American social character had appeared after the Second World War. Amanda Bennett, as just one example, asserts that corporate loyalty "could only have developed out of the kind of coddled stability (low unemployment, low inflation, mild and brief downturns) that America experienced for the 30 years after the war" (Bennett 1990, 21). In fact, Louis Galambos in his *The Public Image of Big Business in America* (1975) and Oliver Zunz, in his *Making America Corporate* (1990), both have demonstrated that corporate loyalty first began to form with the emergence of large corporations in the 1880s, and was a solid component of American social character well before World War II.[8] I take up this argument in chapter 12.

I have another disagreement with some writers on the effects of loyalty lost. Maccoby (1990 and 1988) asserts that the end of corporate loyalty is an unalloyed good, since it has freed people from dependence and allowed them to exercise their freedom. Heckscher (1995) as well, finds much to be praised in current attitudes. In this, they echo the view of William H. Whyte, Jr., whose *The Organization Man* (1956) raised the specter of Americans losing their precious tradition of freedom and individualism in the embrace of corporate conformity. As I argue in chapter 13, there are very serious negative consequences to loyalty lost, consequences for individuals, companies, and the economy. Briefly, people have an innate need for loyalty; companies need loyal employees to function efficiently; and the economy needs large corporations built on some type of loyalty. I believe that celebrating the passing of corporate loyalty fails to recognize the peril we face with its disappearance.

The remainder of this work is in four parts. In order to explore the causes of loyalty lost we turn in part one to the remnant of the old dispensation, the oldest group (called "cohort 1" in this work). Chapter 2 presents a description of the cohort 1 people, those born before 1941. It is this cohort which, in my view, is the last bearer of a set of values which had emerged in the 1880s and became dominant by the Second World War. We will hear from them of their work life experiences, both as young people and in the present time. Since people tend to hold onto a good portion of their earlier attitudes throughout life—a phenomenon called the "rigidity effect"—listening to these older people can give us a "fossil record" of a vanishing American social character.

We look then in chapters 3 and 4 to the historical experience of cohort 1's parents' generation and that of their own generation. We will touch upon the economy and the events of this time, which included the Great Depression, World War II and the immediate postwar era, positing that it was the experiences of those times which in part conditioned attitudes. Survey data from those years will be introduced to bolster the assertion of an association between historical events and attitudes.

In chapter 5 we move on to a discussion of the central concept: loyalty. There are philosophical and psychological literatures on loyalty which must be reviewed, but perhaps more to the point are definitions and descriptions of loyalty offered by my interview subjects themselves. In chapter 5 we will also explore the importance of loyalty, its importance not just to individual well-being, but to the economy as a whole. From our interviews, we can also note the cluster of values that the cohort 1 people have expressed, and the statistical correlations of values and attitudes garnered from the survey.

Part two is concerned with cohort 2—the middle cohort, the baby boomers, the people "between two worlds," born between 1941 and 1955. In chapter 6, we begin our exploration of the younger people and review how they differ in fundamental ways from cohort 1. As with their older colleagues, we review the historical experiences of these people and listen to their expressions of opinions and values. Many of these people's period of socialization lay in the turbulent 1960s, and that fact persuaded me to look closely at the "counterculture" and its impact on American attitudes. Also, a review of opinion poll data from the 1960s to the present shows the major shifts in attitudes and values that occurred in those years. The counterculture and the opinion data are found in chapter 7.

We return in chapter 8 to an exploration of Bill Abernathy's insight: that the practice of management is responsible for the loss of loyalty. As background for this, I present a sketch of the 1960s' economy, and the style of management called "welfare corporatism" which is a close fit to the world that Bill encountered as a young man. Here I introduce the notion of management ideology, and trace the changing ideologies of American managers over the last century and the impact that has had on how companies are managed.

Part three takes up the views and experiences of cohort 3, the youngest cohort, the new generation, born after 1955. Chapter 9 is devoted to their opinions and values and their experience is put in the context of the economic and social histories of the 1970s.

In chapter 10 we review the end of welfare corporatism and the social and economic effects of this development. We also explore the meaning of the "new employment contract" which has replaced welfare corporatist practices and the response of the different cohorts to that contract. Chapter 11 reviews the downtrend of mutual trust in America over the last thirty years, and the relationship of that decline to confidence in institutions and to "social capital," i.e., networks of trusting relationships. We will hear the views of the three cohorts on these matters.

Finally, in part four we arrive at conclusions and attempt some projections of current trends. In chapter 12, we look at the life course of the phenomenon of loyalty: when and why it first developed; how it persisted; and how and why it has faded. Briefly, the argument is made that the United States underwent a vast social change beginning in the 1870s and lasting through the end of World War I. This produced character types which were at home in large-scale bureaucracies. But I believe that beginning in the 1960s, we were undergoing another fundamental shift, a shift away from the large organization and its values. The three cohorts that I have selected give us a snapshot of this transformation. The oldest cohort, roughly people in their middle to late fifties, are in some way relics of the old bureaucratic culture of trust and loyalty. They have the highest degree of corporate loyalty, and are willing to give the company the benefit of the doubt as it abandons its old paternalistic practices. The middle cohort, people in their forties, are "wandering between two worlds," socialized in the turbulent and antiauthoritarian sixties, but encountering still the old values when they began their work lives. It is this group especially, epitomized by Bill Abernathy, that appears to have suffered most when the old dispensation passed. Their loyalty has dropped over the years, and while lower than the oldest cohort, it exceeds that of their juniors. The youngest cohort, those in their thirties and late twenties, are representative of the new values. They grew up in a time when antiauthoritarianism and distrust of institutions were the social norms; they have the lowest loyalty to the company, and a general *insouciance* about modern corporate practices, including layoffs.

The work concludes in chapter 13 with some speculations on the effects that the new values will have on society and the economy as the new generation in time inherits the earth. I look particularly at the pervasive cynicism of our times; the potential for *ressentiment*, i.e., destructive rancor, appearing in America; and, the possibility of a new "tragedy of the commons" as fewer care at all about the fate of American corporations. I conclude with the opinion—perhaps more accurately, the hope—that this tragedy can be averted if corporate management will give employees the means to forge new bonds of loyalty to the company's products, in lieu of loyalty to the company itself or its management.

As I have noted, the research included a survey and a series of interviews. The details on the methodologies and the statistical conclusions of the survey and interviews are presented in Appendixes A and B.

2
The Old Dispensation Speaks

[Generation memberships] endow the individuals sharing in them with a common location in the historical process and thereby limit them to a specific range of experience. . . . a tendency towards definite modes of behavior, feeling and thought.
—*Mannheim, Essays on the Sociology of Knowledge*

Birth and Fortune

First, let me explain what I mean by "cohort," and why I have sorted the survey and interview subjects into such categories. The term originally designated a Roman military unit, but in common usage it refers to companions or associates. In demographics, it is a technical term denoting people who have experienced the same significant life events, and therefore most usually it means those born at the same time (Glenn 1977, 9). The interest in accidents of birth date is sharpened by the assertion that different historical experiences, particularly in the formative years, will lead to differences in attitudes which can persist through life (M. K. Jennings 368).

Richard Easterlin has made much of this; his thesis is that different birth cohorts not only have different formative experiences, but those experiences are significantly shaped by the size of their birth cohort, in other words, different birth rates can account for different attitudes. I have therefore followed Easterlin and sorted the subjects by their birth years, according to the U.S. birthrate. This is shown in Table 2.1, from Easterlin (Easterlin 1987, Appendix Table 1.1).

TABLE 2-1
Definition of the Cohorts
United States Birth Rates, 1930 to 1966

Cohort	*Year of Birth*	*U.S. Birth Rate in Those Years (Per Thousands of Population)*
1	1930 to 1940	18.3
2	1941 to 1945	21.2
2	1946 to 1955	24.6
3	1956 to 1965	23.4
3	1966 and later	17.0

We can see here the significant changes in birthrates, and consequently the significant differences in cohort size that have occurred over the past sixty years. Our subjects in cohort 1 are members of the sparsest generation in American history up to that time. In order to appreciate how small the 1930–1940 birthrate actually was, note that the U.S. birthrate from 1870–1875 averaged 40.8 per thousand per year; as late as 1920–25 it was 25.0, more than 35 percent higher than when our cohort 1 people came into the world (Easterlin 1987, Appendix Table 1.1).

The Voices of Cohort 1

The people of cohort 1 are now in their mid-fifties to early sixties, a time of life when many have not yet had the fire die out, but all can now see past the last turning in the road and espy the end—the end, if not of life, at least of career. In the interviews they tended to be naturally more reflective than their younger colleagues; many were ready to essay a summing up of their lives and careers.

Their early lives are the mosaic of the American experience: some from small towns, some huge cities; some rooted in the place of their birth, some extensively traveled; some are the products of the best schools and some are self-educated. Here is Art Merrill[1] musing on his early days, and the casual, adventitious character of his decision to join a company he would serve for more than thirty years and in which he would rise to a senior management position. Note also the ease—

typical of this age group—with which he found employment, and his enduring satisfaction with his choice:

> I grew up in Mid City[2]. . . . My mother was one of seven children. We lived in a two-block area with more cousins, and aunts and uncles than you can ever imagine, so it was a very, very close-knit thing. I've always lived in Mid City. I went to school here. I planned to be a school teacher with my wife, my high school sweetheart. In terms of the career . . . I had signed a teaching contract in September and I graduated in March and wanted a job, I was going to be married in August so I . . . walked into RLX[3] Employment one day and said "I'm here to get a job." And they said, "What can you do?" I said "I can't do anything really." They said, "Great. Any computer skills?" "No" and I went through what they did at that time basically, aptitude tests and (they) offered me a job. From that (I) just got into a lot of very different things.

Or listen to George Francis tell about his decision to join RLX:

> Well, they made a good offer and I had math degrees and it just kind of fit. I kind of had an aspiration to go to RLX as I went through school and there were a number of people in the class . . . my instructor was also an RLX employee . . . so he kind of suggested I take my resumé down there and that's how it just kind of fell together straightforwardly so. When I got my master's degree I almost left, but they made me an offer to stay, so we were just about ready to move, we were going to . . . Georgia . . . but finally at the last minute we changed and stayed and I'm happy with that. So again, it's worked out great.

We must recall that all these people have been through very turbulent times in the last ten years: a series of layoffs, reorganizations, a change of ownership followed by more layoffs and restructurings. Their tone of satisfaction is quite striking in light of this. Ralph Simmons was particularly upbeat:

> Grew up in Mid City. Most of my friends are here. I went to school here and I enjoy the area. . . . When I graduated in 1960, with the B.S. in Engineering, I was offered five jobs and the highest job offer I got was from RLX. I did not take it. I took the lowest job offer which was for Bell Telephone Laboratories in New Jersey. So I went to work there for one year which was fantastic. Sometimes I wish I would have stayed there, but I didn't care for the East at that time and the weather . . . was just brutal in 1960 . . . and so I came here. A lot of my friends were still here, of course, family, and I'm kind of glad I came here because it was a

very good career for me . . . I happen to love management. I happen to be a guy that likes my job. I like the job challenge. I like to work with people. I have a lot of energy . . . all and all I've had a good life. Fortunately I have good health. I'm very thankful for that and I look forward to next week because of the challenges. I know at work today I had a miserable day today, but tomorrow's going to be better. . . . I think what keeps me here, first of all, is my family and that's important. But also the job challenge as I see it here. I really like my job right now. I like the people I work with. . . . I think the most important thing [about my job] is that I feel within myself that I'm making a contribution to the company to make the company successful. . . . So for me, it's the job challenge and the job accomplishment and getting the results. . . ."

We can see that Ralph stays on for the challenge and his love of his job. The others expressed similar feelings. Art Merrill said:

at this particular point I have no wants in life that I can't satisfy. I have a wonderful life, my family. My children are here in Mid City. My wife and I, we make enough money to live very comfortably. Our lifestyle wouldn't change with any job shift. . . . I'd have to be going to something that would give me more challenge than the job I have . . . since I have no wants . . . I guess it's more of I've got all of the challenges I can deal with. There's no lack of that. There's no lack of learning and I have a comfortable lifestyle. . . . my wife and I sometimes talk about it: I mean how could we have lived our life any differently? So it's a high level of contentment from that point of view.

They all seemed to have a good understanding of what is important to them, what their values are. We have seen it above in their comments on family and on the importance of a meaningful job. Some expressed other important values. Mike Jennings spoke explicitly of loyalty and the sense of contributing as the springs of his own motivation:

You know I keep saying over the years I thought . . . I'd eventually buy another company and go off and do something else, but I truly enjoy the people. You know I am so loyal to the product, it's unbelievable and to be honest with you, if (my superiors) told me to jump off a cliff, I'd probably jump off a cliff. I mean that's how much I think of them. . . . I think (my satisfaction comes from) being able to contribute to . . . my boss's goals, really. . . . When we make the number, I'm as thrilled as anybody in the world. . . .

> I'm as thrilled about (my boss) making his number as he and anybody else is. And that's my goal. . . . Make sure he makes his number every year, so I'm kind of driven by that.

Ralph Simmons has perhaps reflected more about his values as he talks about the things that are important:

> I am convinced of one thing, though. I am convinced that for somebody to get through life and to, say, work (here), you need within you some kind of a mean for your life. . . . Some kind of a code . . . that enables you to accept some of the bad things that happen. . . . You have to accept things like that (a friend's death) and depending on . . . the meaning of why you're here or where you're going, that's important. It allows you also to accept some of the vicissitudes of what happens around here. I had a horrible day today. I mean a miserable day. . . . Am I down? No, because that's going to get better, OK. . . . Each individual has their code of their life and what's important in their life and what's not. . . . You notice so far I haven't mentioned money about my job . . . My children right now, that's probably their measure of success and I keep telling them, "No, that's not important. You'll realize that as you get older." . . . I really think once you get above a certain level . . . does it make any difference whether you make seventy-five thousand a year or eighty-five thousand? No, not really. Then you're wondering about your moral values. . . . I've also noticed as you get older, above the age of fifty, you start thinking about what is your legacy in this life. Does anybody really give a damn whether you passed through the twentieth century or not? When they remember you, are they going to say "That lousy son of a bitch, nobody liked that bastard"? or are they going to say, which is important to me, "That guy was a nice guy. He had good values. He worked hard. He got results. He was easy on people. He made a contribution." . . . Because I'm thinking I'll be 56 next month. . . . What have I done with my life? And I think as you get older you think about that because your mortality is working on you. I'm going to die. Nothing I can do about that. . . . But in general I think I'm OK and I try to be nice to people and not cut anybody's throat and we have that in business . . .
>
> But I take it a day at a time and you look within yourself and you say, "Am I doing the right thing? And if I'm doing the wrong thing, do I have an informed conscience, OK." And that's important to me. . . . Something's telling you that that was not the right thing to do. Do better. Try to be on the ideal, even though you don't attain the ideal. That's my philosophy of life and that's important.

I asked these cohort 1 people, as I asked all my subjects, about their experiences of layoffs and the turbulent time of the acquisition. I was surprised at their relative equanimity in the face of a profoundly changed way of doing business, a far cry from the expectations about life and business they had formed as young people. Generally, they accepted the layoffs as a necessary corrective, but not without compassion for the people involved. It was as though the hurricane of changes had passed over, causing great damage and suffering, but in no way shaking the foundations of their beliefs. Again Ralph Simmons gives us a good perspective on this, as he talks about the layoffs:

> That was, in a sense, devastating and in another sense understandable . . . a lot of my friends . . . called me, people who were 49, 50 years old, or 47, with 25 years and out the door and your immediate reaction to yourself might be, "Well first of all, thank God it's not happening to me." . . . So number one, if you don't have humility, you should have humility at that point. You shouldn't be too prideful that, well, they laid them off so obviously they deserved it. . . . If anything, it should make you redouble your own efforts to say, "I got to be sure that I'm contributing because somebody may come for me with the piano wire, OK." You never know. But you can't help but be affected by that. I personally had to . . . get rid of people and that tore me up . . . But that is part of the business. I think some people realize that. . . . But I do understand the emotional anguish of people who go through it. It is devastating. . . . But do I actually get mad at the company? Totally, absolutely not. The companies do this corrective surgery to help those that are left and help the company. But there's a lot of emotion there.

Demography and Social Change

I have already made the observation that these older people seem to have different attitudes from their younger colleagues. This general sense from listening to them is borne out by the statistics from the survey; Cohort 1 displays statistically significantly different results from all the other cohorts on most of the attitudes measured. And, quite markedly, cohort 1 is essentially the only cohort which shows such differences: with a single exception, all other cohorts have similar attitudes. There is effectively no direct correlation with age, no monotonically increasing or decreasing attitude shifts with age; rather, the data show that there is clearly something different about these cohort 1 people. (As shown in detail in Appendix A, it is only when individuals are grouped into cohorts that the correlations are significant.) Their level of "organizational commitment," this study's empirical surrogate for loyalty, is significantly higher than all other cohorts.[4] Their job satisfaction is higher; their work values are different; they perceive greater autonomy in their jobs; and, they are more likely to believe they are fairly rewarded for their efforts.

To begin to explain these findings, we should look first at the effects that other researchers have noted about different birth cohorts. First, we have already noted the work of Richard Easterlin. He postulates that the size of one's generation has a great effect on one's formative experiences, simply from the fact that small generations experience less crowding in schools, less sibling rivalry, and more opportunities in the job market. As we have seen with cohort 1, they came to maturity at a time when jobs were plentiful; most had several job offers out of school and could pick and choose. Generally, Easterlin says that the fortunate small generation begins adult life with better chances, but also with a better, more self-confident outlook (Easterlin 1987, 15, 30, and 108). The world they enter as young people does not appear as "that dirty gray turmoil" quite so much as it does to the larger cohorts (F. S. Fitzgerald 1951, 304).

The entire idea that the period of birth can affect attitudes goes back to Karl Mannheim's essay, *On Generations*, which appeared in 1927. Mannheim was interested in "historical generation units," generations which seemed to have a definite, and new, outlook, and furthermore, had the cohesion to effect historical changes. I do not make that claim for cohort 1; in fact, as far as organizational loyalty and other attitudes, I am more inclined to the view that they in some way represent fossilized attitudes of a much earlier "historical generation unit," although their views are also colored by their own unique experiences.

For Mannheim, a generation unit is very like a social class: class or generation memberships locate people in history and provide a unique range of experience which gives them a tendency toward definite ways of thinking, feeling, and behaving (Mannheim 1959, 291). Now, the socialization that Mannheim describes is true of all individuals and of all generations.

A generational *unit* only forms, however, when the generation becomes widely conscious of itself as a unit—a phenomenon that did occur, I will argue later, for the generation which was young in the 1960s.

In a sense, Mannheim's "generational unit" is an extreme example of a birth cohort, extreme in that the cohort is very much self-conscious of its unity, and as a result can effect wide-scale social change. This has not been the historical fate of the great majority of cohorts. But Mannheim's analysis must still be taken into account. Each generation or birth cohort is different, since their formative experiences differed.

What makes Mannheim's idea important and compelling is its corollary: attitudes formed in youth tend to stay with people through life. This is the somewhat controversial "rigidity effect," which has been reported by some researchers. As but one example, M. K. Jennings's 1987 study of the 1960s "protest generation" found that "very strong continuities emerge from attitudes associated with the protesters' political baptism." The protest generation remained a distinct "unit" or "cohort" more than twenty years after its emergence (M. K. Jennings 1987, 367).

This is not to say that there are not life cycle effects, i.e., people change as they age and adopt lifestyles and have experiences (like having children) characteristic of their age. But the rigidity effect seems to be a real phenomenon. Glenn's study of political conservatism did show life-cycle effects, i.e., changes with age, but the changes were from a different base for different birth cohorts, indicating some degree of rigidity. I found much the same thing when I looked at confidence in business by birth cohorts, as illustrated in figure 2–1. The age groups used on the figure are not the same as those that I am using in this study, but the purpose of the figure is to illustrate the point on rigidity. All birth cohorts have shown substantial changes in opinions, but they start from different points and hold on to a good part of the attitudes formed in youth.

I have already noted that cohort 1 people have different attitudes and opinions from the other cohorts. I believe this is a manifestation of the rigidity effect, and that their attitudes are a reflection of those of an earlier time. Thus, they give us a window into much older attitudes, give us a picture of what was "the old dispensation."

FIGURE 2-1
Confidence in Business Leaders, by Age Group

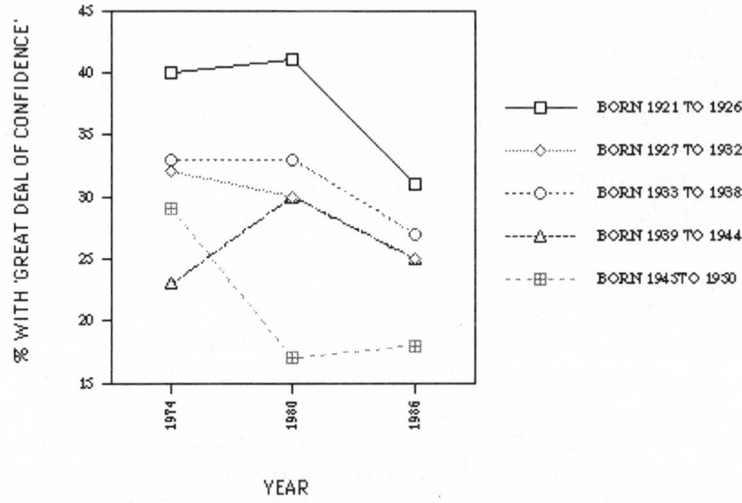

SOURCE: General Social Survey data; Wood 1990,646-8)

Social Character

We can conceive of the cohort 1 people as the remnant of an older view of work, an earlier day's notion of society, and thus a fossil record of the "old dispensation"; they cling to a "social character" they formed in their youth, but now confront a world of younger people who have quite different outlooks. To understand this better, we should look at how the elders view their juniors, but first let us define social character as I will use it in this study. We owe the concept to Erich Fromm who defined it as "that part of their character structure that is common to most members of the group." Its importance lies in Fromm's assertion that character "determines the thinking, feeling, and acting of individuals" (Fromm 1994, 275). Fromm is sometimes called the product of the marriage of Freud and Marx, the blend of individual psychology and social thought. He believed that social character is largely formed by social conditions, and that this character has an adaptive, even defensive nature:

> its function in the social process: by adapting himself to social conditions, man develops those traits that make him desire to

> act as he has to act. . . . The energies of the people are molded in ways that make them into productive forces that are indispensable for the functioning of the society. . . . The social character internalizes external necessities and thus harnesses human energy for the task of a given economic and social system. (Fromm 1994, 281–82)

Daniel Yankelovich describes the old social character, the old dispensation, as a cluster of values which fostered self-esteem, the essential need to make sense of others and one's self. These values were bolstered by clear goals and "a conviction that their private goals and behaviors were contributing to the well-being of others." Yankelovich claims that this value system was centered around some powerful symbols, and we have heard our cohort 1 interlocutors speak of these already: the nuclear family, "a haven from a rough world, major source of joy"; subordination of one's self to a complex network of obligations to others; sacrifice for the family; carrying out responsibilities to others (Yankelovich 1979, 6–8). As just one illustration of this "old" social character that I observed, here is Art Merrill's response when I asked him what was important about his job as a senior manager:

> Well I think at this particular point I've made so many promises to the people and to the customers. I ask myself the question often, "Why do we put up with this?" . . . because at times it's very difficult. But I think we want to see it work. I've made so many commitments, sincere commitments to customers to help them get their job done, we'd like to see the thing done.

That Art's "social character" is an exemplar of the old dispensation that is fading remains to be demonstrated in the remainder of this work. But that it is—or was—a definite American middle-class trait seems to be much less problematic. The views, the objectives, and the values that we can glimpse from our conversations with cohort 1 people are those most often described as "bureaucratic values," or more broadly, the "corporate culture," a set of values and beliefs once held by a majority of Americans.[5] We shall go into those notions in more detail below, but here it is important to understand that the "corporate culture" was a long time forming and is obviously still alive today, particularly with older people. William H. Whyte, Jr. and David Riesman popularized the notion that bureaucratic values sprang upon us full-grown after the Second World War. But, as Louis Galambos has shown, this corporate culture began to form at least as far back as the 1880s, precisely when large scale bureaucratic organizations were becoming common. Galambos assumes the same causation as Fromm, i.e., a supply-and-demand relationship: "Powerful bureaucracies demanded new types of followers, as well as leaders, and the United States eventually became the kind of society that could regularly provide the men and the values modern organizations needed" (Galambos 1975,14–15).

It is not as if everyone woke up one morning and decided to sign up to bureaucratic values and join the corporate culture. Galambos traces a long transition from older value systems, a transition from at least the 1880s to the end of the First World War (Galambos 1975, 117). The shift to bureaucratic values was solidified as the dominant American value set by the experiences of the Depression and World War II. As I explain in much more detail in chapter 12, this matrix of values, this "old dispensation," is unraveling all around us now, as American social character moves towards new values and new expectations.

I shall have a good deal more to say about this later, but for now it is enough to note that cohort 1 seems to be representative of this "old" value set, and that we shall see the younger cohorts departing from these older values: another major transition in social character is well underway. One way to see this, perhaps, is the reaction of the oldest cohort to the new generations. Now, age decrying the beliefs and behaviors of youth is the oldest story of mankind, but put that aside and judge the truth of what the older say. Listen to Joe Hirschfield, fifty-five, a former educator, and new to Softmatics. He is concerned that the values that nurtured him and his generation are being lost, and he is fearful of the consequences:

> Take a look at some of these attitudes that the people coming up have. It's getting scarier . . . they don't have any values and they're not tied to anything. As far as they're concerned, everything is transient and everything is questionable, and everything can be manipulated or pushed one way or another. Basically, it's what they've been shown and taught by the media and by the television . . . In many cases their own parents who came out of the 60s who have absolutely no sense of responsibility . . . I'm not sure how that's done, but if we don't teach . . . the people coming up in management, those attitudes are going to prevail

into business and that could affect where we're going to be in the year 2005. . . ."

Jeff Myers, at fifty-two just outside my cohort 1 definition, is a twenty-six-year veteran of Softmatics, and like Joe Hirschfield quite concerned about the direction of the new values he sees:

> I've seen this today where . . . young people that're in the work force seem not to have a relationship with the company. It's a place to work for X number of years until you can find another place to move on to. . . . I think that there should be an ownership or relationship in that respect . . . If it wasn't, I don't think I would be very happy with it.

Jeff raises the issue of corporate loyalty and I will have much to say about that aspect of the social character of cohort 1, for it is with loyalty, especially, that the oldest cohort's social character is distinguished from that of their juniors. But first, let us review in the next chapters the history which shaped the attitudes of cohort 1.

3

Social and Historical Conditioning: The Great Depression

It was the worst of times, a terrible, scarring experience that changed this country and its people forever.
—*Watkins, The Great Depression*

THE GREAT DEPRESSION

WE are all touched and formed by our own experiences, particularly the experiences of youth, when we make "fresh contact" with the world, as Mannheim puts it (Mannheim 1959, 293). We are also formed by the words we hear in childhood from our loved ones; you don't necessarily have to subscribe to Freud's theory of the superego to realize that the tales of our elders we heard as children have a peculiar and permanent resonance. So it is that those born in the 1930s have always with them personal memories of events and twice-told tales of heroic times from parents and grandparents, things which younger people have learned only in history books and secondhand accounts. The people of cohort 1 are closer to some of the most wrenching experiences in American history: the Great Depression, the Second World War, and more positively, the unprecedented affluence that came upon America in the 1950s and produced the world much as we know it today.

The world of the 1930s can be as remote and strange to younger people as the reign of Charlemagne. One of Studs Terkel's subjects, Tom Yoder, born in the 50s, told him:

> To realize that . . . about forty years ago, my mother's brothers. . . . were out with little rifles, hunting for food to live on. And if they didn't find it, there were truly some empty stomachs. I

mean, this is just too much. I don't think my generation can really comprehend what all this means. I've never gone to bed hungry. . . . I probably never will. (Terkel 1970, 87)

It may seem incomprehensible to Tom Yoder and people even younger, but anyone now in his fifties or sixties has a vivid picture of those days, though often through the eyes of their elders. My own family's story may be representative. (I was born in 1937.) I can now see clearly how the hard times affected the young of those days and how they somewhat differently marked the middle-aged. My maternal grandfather had been a relatively prosperous taxi-fleet operator in New York City; he found himself reduced to a precarious living as a cabdriver in the 1930s, an exhausting trade he plied until he was able to retire—well over seventy then—in the 1950s. My father, buoyed by the prosperity of the 20s, was the first in his line to attend college, but graduating in the grim year of 1933 at the top of his class, he alone of his classmates gained employment, and that as a "runner" on Wall Street, a job now mostly reserved for boys. I saw my uncles and aunts, young people then, postpone marriages and families, and get by on odd jobs and the scanty bounty of their strapped parents.

The Depression of the 1930s had a profound effect on American society: those who lived through it never saw the world in quite the same way again. The great American economy had, of course, never been immune to the business cycle. Bust followed boom, and a series of "panics" followed one another in a pattern that became expected, if not predictable: in 1837 and 1857, in 1873 and 1893, in 1907 and 1921. The financial Panic of 1873 led to a serious downturn in business activity, but it had relatively mild effects on people since, as classical economics would predict, falling prices made things easier for people, and in time demand came back to revive business. Prices declined, but not production, so employment was stabilized and in fact, real incomes rose (Wiebe 1967, 1–2). Again in 1893, a depression ensued from a "Panic," this time more serious and long-lasting and affecting employment. It was the longest depression in American history up to that time. But the nation pulled out of that by 1897 and the good times resumed (Galambos 1975, 83–84). Again in 1921–22, a short, sharp recession followed the decline in purchases ensuing from the end of wartime demand.

But nothing before could have prepared people for the Great Depression—its severity, its permanent effects on people. The effects were particularly pronounced, not just because of the depth of the economic downturn, but rather due to its inexplicable duration. Inured to periodic hard times as they were, no one expected them to last for ten years and more, and in time the fear grew that bad times might be their permanent lot.

To understand those bleak times, the stark statistics of the period bear recalling. Between 1929 and 1933, Gross National Product fell from $204 billion to $142 billion; 9,765 banks failed (over 4000 in 1933 alone); the value of NYSE-listed stocks declined to 11 percent of their 1929 value; and—the worst—nearly thirteen million people, one-quarter of the workforce, were out of work (Galambos and Pratt 1988, 100). Millions more had only part-time jobs. The automobile industry, the linchpin of the new consumer society, was especially hard hit: Ford Motor's employment fell from 128,000 in March 1929 to 37,000 in August 1931; General Motors from 233,000 in 1929 to 116,000 in 1932. Overall industrial production fell by more than half in the early years of the Depression (Bruchey 1988, 163). Nine million savings accounts were gone with the wind; 85,000 businesses failed, wages were reduced by 60 percent. The American standard of living fell back to a level last seen twenty years before (Heilbroner 1961, 217).

And it went on and on. The memories of earlier depressions had created a conventional wisdom: expectations that the business cycle was indeed a cycle; good times must return. Among the educated, this was an article of faith from classical economics. Recessions were even thought to be good things, correcting inefficiencies in the economy. The great economist Joseph Schumpeter was not alone in counseling a policy of benign neglect, so the self-regulating economic forces could work their corrective magic (Galbraith 1987, 195). But '33 turned into '34 and '35 and '36 and the depression wore on. Despite some gains in 1936 and 1937, the economy went south again in 1938: over 10 million people (19.1 percent) out of work; GNP still below that of 1929. It was not until 1941, driven by the war-production demand of World War II, that unemployment dropped below ten percent. The huge government deficits, far greater than the modest and much-decried deficits of the New Deal, finally confirmed Keynes's theory and pulled the United States out of the Great Depression.

The pervasive interconnectedness of a great market economy was laid bare by the Depression. How was it possible that just a decline in stock prices could so profoundly touch the lives of virtually everyone in a nation of 123 million people? One story among millions: Gordon Parks was sixteen years old in 1929, working his way through high school in St. Paul. He recalls the day, Thursday, 24 October when the evening papers broke the news of the crash.

> I couldn't imagine such financial disaster touching my small world; it surely concerned only the rich. But by the first of November I . . . knew differently; along with millions of others across the nation, I was without a job . . . I went to school and cleaned out my locker, knowing it was impossible to stay on. A piercing chill was in the air as I walked back to the rooming house. "The hawk had come." I could already feel his wings shadowing me. (Watkins 1993, 51)

And so it was for millions: for my parents and their generation, for my grandparents, for all the people who helped raise the people of cohort 1, "the hawk had come." We owe to John Steinbeck the definitive picture of the social effects of the Depression; we owe it to his novel *The Grapes of Wrath* of 1939 and the great John Ford film of 1940. The film images especially bring back that time, "images of farm homesteads buried in sand; Hoovervilles; men on park benches, eyes downcast; apple sellers (six thousand in New York City alone in 1930); uncomplaining ranks in breadlines; factory stacks empty of smoke; the clubs and guns of labor violence; the grim silent marches of the hungry" (Watkins 1993, 11).

Those fortunate to have jobs found their wages cut again and again. US Steel, prideful of its reputation as a caring employer, reduced wages ten percent in 1931; Henry Ford had ostentatiously heeded President Hoover's appeal to maintain wage rates, but he reneged on his pledge in 1931 (Brody 1993, 73). And all, the precariously employed as well as the out-of-work, all felt a terrible psychological burden. The journalist Marquis Childs observed at the time:

> What is surprising is the passive resignation with which the blow has been accepted, this awful pretense that seeks to conceal the mortal wound, to carry on as though it were still the best possible of all possible worlds. (quoted in Watkins 1993, 71)

Guilt gnawed at the unemployed and the underemployed. They had grown up with the American dream, the Protestant work ethic, the conviction that hard work, thrift, and honesty would be rewarded. And that ethic had manifestly failed them; but clinging to that faith, if followed that the fault must lie in themselves. Studs Terkel recalled those times: "The suddenly-idle hands blamed themselves, rather than society. . . . Millions experienced a private kind of shame when the pink slip came" (Terkel 1970, 5).

Management Practices

The Great Depression was indeed a "terrible, scarring experience" for virtually all Americans, changing their lives forever. But it was not only people that were changed: the Depression also had permanent effects on the practices of management, particularly those touching employee relations. Let us take a moment and review the practices of American corporate management, the proximate cause of loyalty lost that Bill Abernathy so readily posited, as we saw in chapter 1. My own view is that cultural change, economic changes, and management ideology changes are all intertwined, and together have resulted in the contemporary loss of corporate loyalty. But changes in management beliefs (ideology) and actions are surely part of the story and merit a closer look.

By the end of the 1930s management ideology was profoundly different from that of the 1880s and 1890s, when large corporations first formed; American management thinking had been revolutionized in this time span. In the early days, the dominant view was Social Darwinism, a doctrine that assumed that owners and managers were superior beings and the workers biologically unfit. Then, from about 1895 to 1915, the "New Thought" movement was in vogue. This approach emphasized the efficacy of willpower and positive thinking, Managers, of course, believed they had these qualities in abundance and the workers who failed to progress were simply lacking in them. (That at least was better than the racist tenets of Social Darwinism.) When the first wave of unionization came, management felt challenged in its complacency, but could justify itself with the belief—an essentially Calvinistic belief—that they were where they were because of superior virtue, and that their power was legitimized by their positions and success. The good workman complied with management, recognizing its superiority; the bad employee was a miscreant, insubordinate and unworthy.

Frederick Taylor introduced a new idea along with his new methods—his "Scientific Management." Managers were now seen to have unique skills, they knew the high road to labor efficiency. The worker was now viewed as a trainable *homo oeconomicus,* the good ones eager to learn so they could maximize their incomes.

Elton Mayo and the human relations school sparked a new ideology; the school posited that both managers and workers were disposed to cooperation. Human motivation went far beyond the simple maximizing of material wealth: people yearned for what Tönnies called *Gemeinschaft,* the warmth of a traditional, close-knit community. Mayo seemed to find this need just in the workers; managers were assumed to be rational and logical. But the workers wanted security, recognition, community. They failed only because managers had not handled them correctly, had not found the springs of motivation for them (Perrow 1979, 68).

The new ways of thinking culminated in practices termed "welfare capitalism," which had begun to develop around the turn of the century.[1] The objective was clear: find a way to create a sense of loyalty in workers, achieve a species of control over the workers that Etzioni calls "normative" control, persuasive or suggestive power—quite distinct from enforcing cooperation through coercion or remuneration (Etzioni 1961, 3–5).

Welfare capitalism sought to gain the workers' loyalty by showing how much the company cared for them as human beings. From this came a panoply of pensions, health care, savings plans, and recreational services (Edwards 1979, 90–91). But the effectiveness of welfare capitalism lies in the perceptions of the recipients. And there is some empirical evidence that the perception of a highly supportive organization does, in fact, lead to employee commitment (Shore and Wayne 1993). But it may not be perceived as support as all. Some suggest that the corporation was simply bribing the workers and oppression in the work place would still lead to alienation (Edwards 1979, 91).

That issue was brushed aside, and welfare capitalism was widely adopted and reached its heyday in the mid-1920s when over 80 percent of the largest firms had some form of welfare programs. But the system showed signs of strain. US Steel, an early adopter and a bastion of welfare capitalism, endured a prolonged strike, not over wages and benefits, but over arbitrary practices of the foremen. All the pensions and recreational activities did not seem to have changed the workers' attitude toward the company. This strike did not go unnoticed by other welfare capitalism firms, and by the late 1920s, many corporations saw that the costs of the system were not commensurate with the results (Edwards 1979, 95–97).

But before it waned, welfare capitalism had come a long way, with practices that the human relations school endorsed. The ideology of that school could be summarized by a simple assertion: large-scale, hierarchical, industrial organizations are good for people, or at least they are so potentially. If a manager believed that, he must also conclude that he should do something for the workers, and further, that the workers' poor performance must be due to management inactions or mistakes. That is a long and uncomfortable road to travel from the reassuring conclusions of Social Darwinism—that splendid idea that workers' problems resulted from their genetic deficiencies.

American managers to this day are peculiarly faddish in their taste for new approaches and welfare capitalism was no exception. The movement was vastly important for a time and was often successful, until it was swept away in the tempest of the Great Depression. But in its time it was embraced with great fervor and seemed the solution to many problems plaguing management. The early days of industrialization were marked by waves of strikes, often violent; this industrial conflict was enervating to management and seemed no nearer to solving the labor problem than ever. Taylor's (retrospectively) simplistic methods and theories were not providing much help, either. It began to dawn on management that the problem, as Elton Mayo contended, was a social, not an economic, issue. Very large firms, and hence firms very vulnerable to public opinion and government intervention, embraced welfare capitalism: Standard Oil of New Jersey, US Steel, and International Harvester all became leading exponents of welfare capitalism around the turn of the century.

What were the motives of the employers in this time? Some Marxists view the movement in starkly nefarious terms. Edwards asserts that the employers' motivation was purely one of maintaining capitalistic power. The scheme was simple:

the corporations provided services, which served to persuade the workers of its genuine concern; the services would also improve the workers' material condition, and thus dampen their militancy. And, most diabolically, the workers would become dependent on these services, and lose whatever bargaining power they ever had (Edwards 1979, 91). Welfare, by changing their material conditions, could perhaps change their consciousness, and establish the hegemony of a new and favorable superstructure of ideas. Or, we could say in the patois of game theory, that providing the men with benefits had not changed the game going on down on the shop floor; the cooperative equilibrium had not yet been achieved, the workers still found it beneficial to pursue a suboptimal strategy of shirking and resistance.

Welfare capitalism supporters often framed their beliefs in ethical and religious terms, and we have no reason to doubt their sincerity. At first there was not a direct functional tie between welfare and performance of the firm, perhaps just a vague sense that the men would return the favor with loyalty, certainly with contentment. But for many the moving impulse seemed to be simply duty. By the 1920s, the altruistic view was being supported by the pragmatic factor that better efficiency would result from greater worker contentment.

But the tide of history ran against welfare capitalism. If nothing else, welfarism was supposed to prevent strikes, but US Steel, a bastion of welfare capitalism, endured an ugly one in the 1920s as I have noted. For the discerning, the reasons for the strike were disturbing: not pay, nor benefits, but a reaction to long hours and arbitrary foremen. The conditions in the workplace might, in fact, be more important than the gifts showered on the employees. The employers were forced to think the unthinkable: Had the workers not embraced welfare capitalism? Did they still harbor resentments? This point has been argued back and forth by historians. Many, like Edwards, viewed the movement as a thinly disguised—and ultimately fruitless—attempt to mask true power relations in the workplace, to establish hegemony by convincing the workers that they had a stake in the industrial system. This view is supported by the evidence of the New Deal: when workers had a fair chance to organize after the Wagner Act's passage, they shunned welfare capitalism and joined unions.

Whatever the reasons, the growth of welfare capitalism had slackened by the late 1920s; few companies added new welfare programs between 1925 and 1930 and nearly as many dropped theirs. Some employers thought they should forego the expense because the workers were unappreciative. There were other causal factors, rooted in the changing American scene: cheap autos made company towns less compelling; cities now provided many essential services; new technologies called for lower skills, so turnover of skilled workers was less crucial a problem. And some employers feared that the psychological weapon would be turned against them: their benevolent image might attract organizers who would see them as pushovers. Indeed, the AFL targeted a textile company in 1930 because it had earned a reputation for fair labor practices (Brandes 1976, 141–42).

We can see in the ideology and the practices of welfare capitalism an attempt to use "conditioned power" to convince the men that they had a community of interest with their employers. But the basic conditions on the floor, as far as control of the work and employee participation, were unchanged, and the results were generally disappointing. The conditioned power, in the view of Edwards at least, was a more sophisticated form of compensatory power: the workers were being bribed in an attempt to obtain their loyalty.

The fundamental flaw of welfare capitalism is intimately connected with its central—and noble—principle: management has an obligation for the well-being of its employees. Welfarism was essentially an implicit promise to the American workingman that the company would look out for him. That promise was kept only because of the performance of the American economy in the booming 1920s (Brody 1993, 61). But in hard times, the promise simply could not be honored. Welfare capitalism, like so many other dreams and aspirations, was swept away by the fury of the Great Depression.

To their credit, the advocates of welfare capitalism from 1900 through the 1920s felt responsibility for the welfare of their employees. But their philosophy was a curious blend of paternalism and instrumentality. The employer knew better than the worker what the worker needed, and took up the duty to provide him security. At the same time, the employer believed that the workers' gratitude would increase productivity, output, and profits. Welfare capitalism collapsed in the cataclysm of the Great Depression, taking with it the sense of paternalistic concern when the men opted for unions rather than industrial charity.

The Depression ended it; welfare capitalism fell into a shambles. The veteran advocates could not even maintain the wage level, much less provide paternalistic services. Money still could be made by ruthless firms which could cut employment and wages to the bone, so the leaders like US Steel had to follow the ruthless to stay competitive, and Big Steel cut wages. Wage cuts became the order of the day as management faced the most difficult of business decisions: abandoning basic values in order to survive. All the good intentions of management were unavailing; the hard logic of depression-era economics could not be denied. The workers would have to seek other means to obtain their objectives.

Everywhere the American workers were desperate and resentful; where they had jobs at all they were victims of inhuman speedups, and ruthless wage and piecework rate cuts. If the employers had indeed achieved their goal of conditioning the workforce to its way of thinking in the 1920s, they were now reaping the whirlwind. The history of this period could be read as an example of Galbraith's assertion about conditioned power: when it is revealed as fundamentally false, when the employers could not keep the promise of security, the result would be indignation and the conviction that such power was illegitimate (Galbraith 1983, 13). Labor's embrace of New Deal labor policies is grounded in this resentment.

American industrial relations were fundamentally transformed by the New Deal. Formally, labor relations were now a legal matter, not determined solely by the power and/or goodwill of management, nor by the power and/or social conditioning of the workingmen. Organized labor had become a social force in the United States and its gains in the 1930s and wartime proved durable for two generations.

The Legacy of the Depression

We see, then, the transformative force of the Depression on management ideology and practices, as we have seen the effects on people's attitudes. Those attitudes were not as closely surveyed as they are in our day, but some data are available to us.

Not surprisingly, in the midst of the Depression some people turned against business, even against market capitalism. Although there was very little support for radical parties, a substantially greater number of those polled favored government ownership of industry in the 1930s and early 1940s than thereafter. In 1942, the Roper-Fortune poll estimated that 25 percent of the people believed that "some form of socialism would be a good thing." Still, 40 percent said it would be a bad thing. The Gallup poll for 1937 showed the public almost evenly divided on public ownership of banks (41 percent in favor and 42 percent opposed). The Roper-Fortune survey in 1939 found 34 percent in favor of nationalized railroads, 28 percent for public insurance companies, and even 22 percent for government ownership of "the factories producing the essentials of life, like clothes, food, etc." (Lipset and Schneider 1987, 283).

These anticapitalist numbers may seem high to you, but in light of the almost complete collapse of the American economy, they are a surprisingly mild reaction, especially when we note again that support for the socialist and communist parties remained minuscule. Why? Why was there not a much more severe reaction—even a move to overturn institutions? Louis Galambos, in his masterful content analysis of American middle-class journals, provides a compelling answer. Galambos posits that corporate values and pro-business sentiment made persistent, but uneven, progress through the American middle class from the 1880s on, and by the thirties these values were common, but not yet firmly anchored in all middle-class sectors. But still, there was enough residue of support such that the new value system cushioned resentment against business, far more so than it had in the 1890s after the Panic of 1893. In fact, looking at the written commentary of one middle-class sector, professional engineers, Galambos thought

> One could hardly conclude that an old order had been overturned or that the country had experienced the worst depression in its history. . . . The engineer remained aloof from the economic crisis. . . . Holding the engineer on a true course through the 1930s were the same . . . values and the same basic ideology that had guided his thoughts through the previous decade. (Galambos 1975, 242)

When he looks at all sectors of the middle class, Galambos concludes that the peak level of hostility vis-à-vis business in the 1930s was lower than earlier peaks. Indeed, each successive peak since the 1890s had been lower than its predecessors, lending force to his argument that bureaucratic values—the "corporate culture," was inexorably winning the allegiance of the American middle class (Galambos 1975, 246).

Galambos concludes that:

> a new set of values, part of an intricate corporate culture, had become the rule among middle-class Americans. . . . By the 1930s organizational values were dominant in the middle class as a whole, and this corporate culture survived the test of the Great Depression. The new bureaucratic norms muffled hostility . . . and on the eve of the Second World War they helped to ease Americans into an acceptance of big business. (Galambos 1975, 247)

That value system, that ultimate confidence in American economic institutions, explains a puzzle: the seemingly unaccountable optimism that people of the 1930s had for the future. A Roper survey in 1939 found that only 45 percent believed their opportunities, their future, would be better than that of their parents. But a full 64 percent thought their children would do better (Lipset and Schneider 1987, 151). This faith in the future was nowhere more apparent than at the New York World's Fair which opened that year. Millions (my parents, brother and sister, and I among them) went to see the General Motors Futurama exhibit which promised a new world of technological marvels and material comfort for ordinary people. People saw it, and they believed it. (And most of it, in fact, came true.)

This uncanny optimism in the midst of the death grip of the Depression (9.5 million still unemployed [over 17 percent of the work force in 1939]), could be ascribed to the old strain of American optimism, but none had ever seen such hard times before, a bleak decade of unremitting bad news. To believe that things would be better reveals a faith in the economic system which Galambos believes was well-entrenched by the 1930s. To look ahead for a moment, we should note that this stalwart optimism eventually gave out. In the 1970s, American confidence in the future was lower than any time since polling began in the 1930s, lower in fact than in 1939. The old faith that America would continue its enviable economic growth had faded by the 1970s (Ladd and Lipset 1980, 3). But that is another story, for another chapter. Let us look further at the legacy of the Depression years.

While a great deal of faith in the economic system survived the cataclysm of the Depression, not all economic institutions emerged unscathed. In particular, Americans seemed to nurture an abiding distrust of the "financial community." Their faith in the old Protestant virtue of thrift had been betrayed by its custodians, and it was not forgotten in later years. Business in general was viewed somewhat warily, leading to the restrictions and regulations now an integral part of our economy. The Great Depression spawned the regulatory state, a system still not one of government ownership, but nonetheless reflecting the belief that both business and the public must be protected from the former's excesses (Watkins 1993, 14).

As Galambos has noted, the 1930s—paradoxically perhaps—saw the consolidation of the "corporate culture," the bureaucratic values. The poet John Beecher recalls how his father, a former US Steel executive, underwent a conversion. The elder Beecher had lost everything in the crash of 1929:

> He had a hard time recovering from it psychologically. I remember how, after dinner, he'd just lie on the couch in utter despair, night after night, for hours. . . . But he did recover. He became a kind of coolly critical intelligence. He was ready for any kind of change in the system—perhaps this system was not eternal, perhaps there should be a more cooperative society. (Terkel 1970, 277)

Beecher's father's psychological struggle mirrors the old American struggle between individualism and community, between the "don't tread on me" impulse and the cooperative instinct. Individualism has marked the American character since well before its "discovery" by Tocqueville in the 1830s, and the era supreme of individualism was the 1920s. Individualistic geniuses like Edison and Ford were the cultural icons, along with the definitive individualistic achievement of Lindbergh, flying the Atlantic *alone*. But that very individualism seemed to have brought on the disaster of the Depression; after all, it was the speculators and greedy industrialists who were blamed for the debacle. By the end of the 1930s, the public no longer looked to solitary heroes, but rather to the ultimate organization men, J. Edgar Hoover and his G-men, the collectivist cops who foiled individualists like John Dillinger (Watkins 1993, 16).

Economically, the Depression had uncovered the weaknesses of the uncoordinated American economy. The unfettered market, Adam Smith's "invisible hand," no longer seemed capable of guiding a complex economy with sufficient stability. Government agencies and fiscal and monetary policies in time sought to control the business cycle, and to rein in private companies with regulations. Galambos sees these developments as evidence that a new culture was firmly in place, one in which "the individualistic orientation of an atomistic competitive society has given way to an emphasis on group or collective effort" (Galambos 1975, 14).

The emphasis on group effort clearly marked the labor movement, and the Depression insured an historic change in the relations between labor and its employers, as we have seen above. The Wagner Act of 1935 fundamentally changed the power relations between employers and workers. The act was heavily weighted on the side of labor, giving it the legal right to organize, and denying the employers their long-held expectations that the government, in a crisis, would side with them (Brody 1993, 105).

In general, on the eve of World War Two, the United States had laid the groundwork for the administrative state we see all around us today. The thirties saw the creation of the SEC, tight control over banking, Social Security and, perhaps most tellingly in the federal jobs programs, the new belief that the federal government had a direct responsibility for the economy, even to become the employer of last resort. The deeply held American distaste for intrusive government mellowed a good deal in these years. But even the economic collapse did not shake the faith in free enterprise and private property; those icons remained, albeit hemmed in by prudent regulation (Galambos and Pratt 1988, 100–105).

The great hurricane of the Depression altered American life forever. People who rode out the storm changed their views of the federal government's role; they became more skeptical of business, especially financial institutions, but they retained a faith in the value of free enterprise; and, they held on to a set of bureaucratic, cooperative values that had been forming since the 1880s. In fact, for some those values were strengthened by their belief that unrestrained individualism had brought on the tempest. And, an integral part of that "corporate culture,"—that old dispensation—was organizational loyalty: the sense of allegiance to some collective. I was talking to one of my interlocutors, Jerry Cialdi, who had been born in the thirties, talking about his expectations, how the company would treat him. He had the sense that the company would stick with him through a bad patch, just as he had done when business was shaky. I asked him what had given him that expectation, and he cited not his experiences with the company, but his parents' experiences:

> (For) almost everyone in . . . my parents and the generation before me, this was where they were coming from. There was a sense of longevity . . . You . . . went into a career or did something really for the duration. My father was a New York City policeman for twenty-five years. . . . My brother is a doctor. . . . He was in hospitals for that long. . . . They were in those types of positions where you would see . . . continuity: you know, you're there, you're doing your work and you're serving and you think that's the life so there's some sense of looking to that continuity. No one really was bouncing around that much. . . .

We shall hear a good deal more about loyalty from cohort 1, but first let us complete our review of these people's era of historical conditioning. We look now at the 1940s and 1950s.

4
Social and Historical Conditioning: The Forties and Fifties

Sheril Cunning: Immediately after the war was this rush: We're never gonna suffer again, we're gonna have everything bigger and better, and we're gonna build, build, build. . . .

—*Terkel, The Good War*

World War Two and the Late Forties

The enormous demands to clothe, feed, shelter, and arm millions of servicemen spurred the American economy as never before and lifted the nation out of the Great Depression. By the end of 1942 mobilization for war had dropped the unemployment rate to 4.9 percent and boosted the Gross National Product by 13 percent. The war created effective full employment for the first time since 1929 (Galambos 1983, 70).

But for businesses, it was not a matter of the rising tide lifting all boats; rather, the large manufacturing firms got bigger, and the small ones got smaller or just disappeared. At the war's outset, the large companies alone had the plant and equipment, the engineers and executives, to undertake the enormous and technologically complex wartime programs. More than half of the $175 billion in prime contracts awarded from June 1940 to September 1944 went to just thirty-three corporations; three quarters of the subcontracts went to big companies as well. The percentage of firms with fewer than 100 employees fell from 26 percent of the total in 1939 to 19 percent in 1944. Furthermore, the war proved fatal to many small businesses: 324,000 firms went out of business during the war, ten percent of the 1940 total (Bruchey 1988, 180–81).

But for the large firms, the war was an economic bonanza. Tight government controls could not prevent high profits from cost-plus contracts, and the enormous demands of the voracious war machine ensured high volumes and earnings. In essential industries like steel and aluminum, the government encouraged expansion, and capital was readily available for new plant and equipment. There were many advantages to wartime business for the big companies. The New Deal's antibusiness leanings were put aside and government actively cooperated with the corporations. Labor relations improved a great deal under the pervasive federal controls, as the unions directed their demands more to the government than to their employers (Galambos and Pratt 1988, 156).

Of course, the war also had a great effect on the people who lived through it. Clearly, their material conditions improved. Despite rationing and shortages, most lived much better than they had in the thirties. Good jobs at high wages were plentiful, and particularly so for middle-class professionals; the nation needed engineers, doctors, scientists, and teachers fully as much as it needed steel and explosives. The technical and scientific professions in particular were energized by the war, a factor that helped contribute to the great postwar boom (Galambos 1983, 81).

The experience of the war years, and that of the New Deal years, had an important effect on the American consciousness. Two phenomena characterized those years: the widespread experience of large bureaucracies, and the successful experience of sharing. Young Sheril Cunning talks about her family's experience of wartime:

> It was quite exciting . . . a spirit of camaraderie. . . . There was a large vacant lot and everybody got together and had a gigantic communal Victory garden. . . . They'd give things away to everybody. Nobody said, "This is mine." (Terkel 1984, 238)

The war can be remembered for lives cut short; the Depression seen through the lens of blighted lives and hopes. But there is another historical perspective: for the first time many experienced a successful application of sharing and collectivist bureaucracy. The Depression was only ended by the war, but it was clear to most people that it had been softened by the New Deal; and, the war had been successfully prosecuted by huge armies and fleets and provisioned by America's largest corporations. Over 12.5 million people served in the armed forces in World War II. They saw that bigness worked; the war was won. And many in the service saw as well that cooperation worked. Here is a World War II artilleryman remembering those times:

> You had fifteen guys who for the first time in their lives were not living in a competitive society. We were in a tribal sort of situation, where we could help each other without fear. I realized . . . that created the thing I loved about the army. (Terkel 1984, 5)

Louis Galambos believes that bureaucratic values, the "corporate culture," long in forming, came to full flower during the 1930s and the Second World War. A new generation became accustomed to the great hierarchies; they looked forward to bureaucratic—and secure—careers. They felt comfortable with bureaucracies,

> for a variety of reasons, including the excellent performance of the national economy after 1940, the "countervailing bigness" of labor unions and government, and the country's actual experience with bigness—an experience that put to rest fears about continued concentration, technological decline, and opportunities for individual advancement. (Galambos 1975, 17)

Implicit in Galambos's argument is a model of social change: people's values can change through prolonged exposure to institutions. The historian Thomas Haskell has proposed an example of this phenomenon. Haskell posits that antislavery sentiment grew from participation in a market economy: people began to see the causal connections between their private actions and the evil of slavery. Insensibly, consumers started to see that their ability to purchase, for example, cheap cotton goods was connected with the practice of slavery, and they began to feel as well that they were thereby tacitly assenting to the peculiar institution (Haskell 1992, 111). Long exposure to an institutional arrangement can, therefore, change minds and hearts. In like manner, Americans who had lived intimately with large bureaucracies in wartime came to appreciate their efficacy and, indeed, came to join their lives to theirs. The philosopher Ralph Barton Perry tried to assay the "American cast of mind" in a 1949 essay. Like Galambos, he found an American character substantially influenced by the growth of government and economic planning in the New Deal and the Second World War. Perry, like all before him, noted that Americans were characterized by the trait of individualism, but not the "cult of solitude"; Americans are gregarious and sociable.

> Their individualism is a *collective* individualism—not the isolation of one human being, but the intercourse and cooperation of many. . . . American self-reliance is a plural, collective self-reliance—not "I can," but "we can." But it is still individualistic—a togetherness of several and not the isolation of one, or the absorption of all into a higher unity. (Perry 1992, 39 and 42)

The performance of the American economy after the war seemed to confirm the faith in the federal government and in big business. After a sharp setback in 1947, Gross National Product went on a sustained upward path, through the late forties and fifties and on through the sixties. The healthy growth after the war was fueled by several developments. First, although investors and consumers were wary immediately after the war—Depression fears ran deep—pent-up demand for consumer goods and wartime savings (about $250 billion) had created an enormous consumer demand. Secondly, the wartime requirements for technologically complex products had brought a pooling of scientific and technical knowledge, resulting in the large-scale and systematic application of science to American industry. Petroleum, rubber, metals, food, and electronics companies turned their newfound technology to the production of new consumer goods. The exigencies of wartime mobilization had also improved managerial methods, and the large companies, particularly now, had management cadres capable of exploiting technology and managing growth (Chandler 1977, 476). Thirdly, with the European economies in ruins, the United States enjoyed a huge flow of purchasing power from abroad. Astonishingly, in the late 1940s the United States accounted for more than sixty percent of the world's manufactured output (Chirot 1986, 194).

Wartime had seen almost complete control of the economy by the federal government; the War Production Board was responsible for rationing, allocation of scarce materials, targeting public and private investment—and all of this was done with enthusiastic cooperation from business, labor, and consumers (Galambos and Pratt 1988, 131). But, government intervention did not survive the war. Although no one wanted further controls, there was a widespread fear of a return to Depression-era unemployment levels, inspiring the Employment Act of 1946 which called for "maximum employment, production and purchasing power." But the Act did not, as some had wished, give the federal government responsibility for full employment. Faith in government could only be taken so far; Americans held fast to their belief in private enterprise. For twenty-five years the performance of the economy had justified that faith. Americans had collectively fulfilled Sheril Cunning's dream, shown in our epigraph: "We're never gonna suffer again, we're gonna have everything bigger and better . . ."

The Fifties

The 1950s witnessed the onset of one of the greatest economic booms in American history, and a great uplift in standards of living as ordinary people shared in the good economic times. The average thirty-year-old man in 1949 would see a 63 percent increase in real annual income in the next ten years. (In contrast, the average thirty-year-old in 1973 would see a *decline* over ten years.) From the end of World War Two through the early 1970s, real incomes grew by 2.5 to 3 percent per year (Kamer 1988, 140). In the 1950s alone, per capita income rose 48 percent; real wages were up 30 percent; the average man could carry a home mortgage for 14 percent of his income. (By 1984, it took *44* percent.)

Thus, many families entered the middle class, embracing the corporate culture as they shared in the great bounty the corporations were producing. The universal optimism was made more heady by memories of the Great Depression, still a first-hand experience for most. But in the fifties, those hard times seemed as distant as the Flood. The optimistic mood was reflected in the people's trust and confidence in its institutions. Surveys indicated that over 40 percent had "great confidence" in Congress and the president; over sixty percent trusted the military. But the public reserved its greatest confidence for large corporations: 68 percent were "highly favorable" toward eight key industries and 69 percent were favorable toward a group of 22 major companies (Leinberger and Tucker 1991, 161). Later in this work, when we review surveys on confidence in institutions in later decades, these numbers from the fifties will astonish. But from the end of the Second World War and on until the early 1960s, the public opinion data show a steady increase in the perceived legitimacy of all institutions, business especially. Large corporations were viewed quite favorably as the provider of jobs, goods, and services (Lipset and Schneider 1987, 368). The corporate culture had definitely taken firm hold.

Let us take a closer look at the fifties, the time of youth for cohort 1. Perhaps we can capture the relative languor of the fifties when we remember what lay in the future for the young people of that time: the civil rights movement, the Pill, Vietnam, Roe vs. Wade, Watergate, the counterculture, the assassinations, stagflation, the oil crisis, and so on. The sixties and the seventies were a great divide, and the fifties appear as a calm and orderly world in comparison. These were conformist times; we can see it in memory (or in old photographs) in the dress styles: men in hats and suits, women in stockings and dresses, even children dressed like small adults. Surveys on parental attitudes from the time reveal the general climate of conformity: 57 percent of respondents from one 1954 survey agreed that children should conform, and 65 percent believed it was wrong for a child to talk back. To put that in perspective, in 1973 the comparable percentages were 27 and 41, respectively (Niemi et al. 1989, 267).

Conformity, but conformity in affluence. A great and unaccustomed affluence was the most important socioeconomic fact of the 1950s. These times were the full flowering of the advertising and consumer culture, the great proliferation of the media, especially television, and the access by ordinary people to unheard-of luxuries: detached houses in the suburbs; television sets and hi-fidelity systems; airline travel; even the two-car family. People, the young especially, began to focus their attentions on affluence, and most interests centered on material conditions. While the fifties were the time of McCarthyism and an alleged fear of communism, in fact, most people's concerns were narrowly focused on their material and physical well-being. When asked by pollsters in 1954 "What do you worry about most?," the overwhelming majority of respondents listed personal and family issues. Less than one percent were worried about civil liberties or communism. Another survey in 1959 showed the hold that prolonged affluence had on most people: 65 percent reported that their main goals in life were economically related (Hamilton and Wright 1986, 121 and 123).

This obsession with materialism and economic well-being was to have fateful consequences in later years. But at that time, the affluent society allowed many for the first time to take themselves seriously, to make a project of themselves, to shake loose from the old norms of self-denial (Clecak 1983, 25). The success of the postwar economy, and its ability to bring material well-being to ordinary people, ingrained the habit of defining one's life and that of others in terms of economic advance. It seemed only common sense, natural and right. In fact, in a 1956 poll, 56 percent asserted that *as a matter of right,* they were entitled to an ever-increasing standard of living (Yankelovich 1975, 762).

That ideal of middle-class prosperity became the moral center; and the institutions that fulfilled that ideal were accorded great respect and deference. In the managed economy of the 1950s, the expertise of the business and governmental managers was highly regarded (Bellah et al. 1991, 58–61). We saw above the great confidence that Americans lavished on their institutions and leaders. Let us look a little more closely at some of those confidence surveys. A University of Michigan 1958 poll found that 73 percent of the people trusted the federal government almost always or at least most of the time. In 1974, the figure was only 37 percent; in 1980 it was down to 25 percent (Sussman 1988, 54).

And as we saw above, business, especially big business, shared in this aura of confidence and trust: business was hailed as the prime provider of the material satisfactions that most people desired above all things. But people did not just want the goods they could buy from a paycheck: they also wanted to work. A survey in 1958 found enormous support for the old Protestant Ethic's moral code: 84 percent agreed that their moral code held their impulses in check; 62 percent thought one could not be too strict in matters of conscience; 91 percent supported the view that hardships make us better people. And it was not just the Calvinistic moral codes that won support, work itself was highly prized in the 1950s: more than three quarters of the respondents believed that laziness is a sin, hard work virtuous, that a person must respect his calling (McClosky and Zaller 1984, 104 and 108). The strength of these attitudes can also be measured by asking people if they would keep working should they become suddenly rich. This question has been asked in the annual General Social Survey since 1974, but was first systematically asked in 1955. Then, 80 percent said they would stay on the job, and significantly, the figure was 90 percent for those 21 to 34 years of age. Over the next twenty years, younger people displayed a major shift on this question: the proportion of 21–34 year olds who would quit work if rich rose by nearly 40 percent (Vecchio 1980, 362–66).

A 1955 Gallup poll showed similar attachment to work: people under thirty were asked if they enjoyed their work so much that they had trouble putting it aside at the end of the day. Forty-four percent said yes. (Twenty-five years later in 1980, Gallup asked the same question. This time, only 25 percent of the under-30 group agreed.) Veroff and his colleagues did large nationwide attitude surveys both in 1957 and 1976. They found the 1956 respondents much more in tune with bureaucratic values; more content with group sources of happiness; more integrated into the social structure; more accepting of social norms and authority. In contrast, Veroff et al. found their 1976 subjects much more articulate about their identities, more willing to talk about how they were unique. And they found the fifties people more at home with their work, getting more satisfaction from its intrinsic nature, more contentment from the climate of the workplace (Veroff et al. 1981, 13, 19, 155, and 326).

Yes, work was important in the fifties. And not just any work. This was definitively the age of the Organization Man: white-collar employment, mainly centered in large corporations, rose 61 percent between 1947 and 1956 (Leinberger and Tucker 1991, 125–28). The corporations themselves were larger and larger. Berle and Means, in 1932, had charted the concentration of American industry, finding then that the 200 largest firms had assets totaling one-half of all corporate wealth. They noted also that this concentration was proceeding apace: large companies were growing two to three times as fast as smaller firms, and in most key industries, a few gigantic firms dominated (Berle and Means 1932, 24–44). (As we have seen, government procurement policies during World War II accelerated this trend.) Whereas in 1905 forty percent of manufacturing output took place in 300 companies, by 1948 only 200 firms accounted for fifty percent of output (Bennett 1990, 79). These great companies were the lodestar for the young men seeking advancement and security, the rewards of life that had escaped their parents in the Great Depression. These were the "Organization Men" that William H. Whyte, Jr. dissected in his 1956 classic, *The Organization Man.* And with Whyte, David Riesman, and C. Wright Mills we begin to see already in the 1950s a critique of the bureaucratic society and the corporate culture which had been building for the past two generations.

Whyte defined his subjects as the mid-level professional and managerial class, but his definition speaks more to their attitude than their rank. They not only work for the organization but "belong to it as well—(they) have left home spiritually as well as physically, to take the vows of organizational life . . ." (Whyte 1956, 3). C. Wright Mills, writing in the same age, defined his "white collar" workers more functionally, as those who "do not live by making things; rather they live off the social machineries that organize and coordinate the people who do make things . . ." (Mills 1953, 65). With Mills we have much less of the notion of the organization man belonging to the corporation heart and soul; he writes of the fundamental conflict between man and organization. It is precisely the *absence* of such conflict that troubles Whyte; their embrace of the corporate culture disturbs him as it had not disturbed Ralph Barton Perry, whom we met above with his 1949 look at American social character. But we find in Tocqueville a close match with Whyte's formulation. Tocqueville depicts army officers in a democracy, and his description could well have been written by Whyte: "In democracies the man who becomes an officer breaks the ties attaching him to civilian life . . . His true fatherland is the army . . . that is where all his hopes are founded" (Tocqueville 1988, 652).

The issue that concerned Whyte and Mills was power, or a more-gentle word, "compliance"; Etzioni defines it as a "relationship consisting of the power employed by superiors to control subordinates and the orientation of the subordinates to this power." Etzioni posits three kinds of power, three distinct ways to ensure compliance: coercion, remuneration, and "normative power." The last relies on the manipulation of symbols; it is persuasive or suggestive power (Etzioni 1961, 3–5). At its best, normative power is exercised through the individual's identification with the organization and his internalization of its values—in other words, loyalty. Max Weber specified one essential means of effecting normative compliance through symbol manipulation. He grounded bureaucratic control in the legitimacy of management's authority, a legitimacy which is derived from the lawlike rules that the bureaucracy promulgates. Such rules, imposed by an accustomed procedure and impartially enforced, have a way of creating legitimacy for the hierarchy (M. Weber, 1966, 81–82). We could look at this in another light, as control rooted in Gramscian hegemony, a notion not far from successful "normative" control, which likewise has management in some way compelling the workers to internalize organizational values (Burawoy 1979, xii).

Whyte and Mills addressed a critical issue that we touched on earlier—Haskell's view of the effect that exposure to institutions has on social character. Whyte and Mills ask: what are the human effects of a bureaucratic environment? Tocqueville saw the issue clearly in his analysis of nascent American industrialization: an instrumental relationship develops between worker and manager. Unlike the aristocratic *ancien régime*, the industrialist feels no obligation to the employee and has no links to him born of custom or duty (Tocqueville 1988, 557–58). Even in a bureaucracy controlled by normative power, Tocqueville saw the danger ahead. He was forecasting a political despotism, but his projections serve as well for a business. Tocqueville posited the atomistic individual, "withdrawn into himself," and over him an "immense protective power . . . thoughtful of detail, orderly, provident, and gentle." This relationship is ultimately destructive to the individual, it "restricts the activity of (his) free will . . . and little by little robs each citizen of the proper use of his own faculties." In Whyte's fervor against the benign embrace of the organization, we find Tocqueville preceding him: "It does not break men's will, but softens, bends, and guides it" (Tocqueville 1988, 692).

Etzioni's and Weber's give us a dry analyses of "normative power." C. Wright Mills takes a more colorful tone. He too sees the manipulative nature of this control:

> The formal aim . . . is to have the men internalize what the managerial cadre would have them do, without their knowing their own motives . . . Many whips are inside men, who do not know how they got there, or indeed that they are there. . . . (Mills 1953, 106)

In Mills's *White Collar* it is not "The Organization" which takes center stage but, more ominously, the "managerial

Demiurge". Mills' Demiurge is not Plato's creator of a harmonious world, but is rather akin to Ialdabaoth, the Demiurge of Gnostic doctrine, the creator of a world subject to corruption, a world that is "the deformed copy of an abortive God" (Filoramo 1990, 81). For Mills, the Demiurge "takes on a motive of its own: to manipulate the world in order to make a profit." It controls the employees through "secret or impersonal exercise of power." And, it is none other than the Demiurge, the modern-day Ialdabaoth, who installs those "whips" within the consciousness of the workers (Mills 1953, 106).

Mills' figure is well chosen for his purpose, since he—like the Gnostics before him—sees if not an evil world, certainly one corrupt and imperfect, far from the harmony preceding it. For Mills that harmony lay in the time of craft labor before the managerial Demiurge sent all to perdition (Mills 1953, 220–24).

Whyte believed that he had uncovered a new type in America, a new social character typified by his Organization Man. He thought that these were the people whose values will "set the American temper" (Whyte 1956, 3) and he worried that their attitudes were seriously at variance with traditional American values. In particular, the Organization Man seemed to have turned his back on the Protestant Ethic, the old catchword for traditional American values, the virtues of hard work, thrift, independence, and competitive spirit. In its place, Whyte asserted that a new social ethic had evolved. Now, we have just seen above from poll data that Whyte's concern over the Protestant Ethic was misplaced in the 1950s. And, as I have repeatedly said, the formation of Whyte's New Man preceded the fifties by several generations. In fact, his New Man could be found working for Standard Oil in the 1880s; Galambos asserts that by this early date, the professional engineer in the large corporations of the time "was already devoted to modern corporate values—he stressed the role of group activity, the need to control emotions and remain neutral, the necessity of universal standards and highly specific definitions of responsibility" (Galambos 1975, 76). Zunz as well found the "Organization Man" with his bureaucratic values at work in the railroad hierarchy in the 1870s (Zunz 1990, 40).

Whyte's New Man puts no special value on independence and self-reliance, since he sees it as natural—even desirable—to work for someone else (Whyte 1956, 5). It is more than risk aversion that keeps him from entrepreneurship: he abhors greed and acquisitiveness, he finds a moral failing in the entrepreneur's motives (Whyte 1956, 690). In these things the Protestant Ethic is rejected, but more importantly for Whyte, the Organization Man has given up the virtue of independence and personal responsibility. The group is the source of creativity and harmony. Belonging to the group is the individual's ultimate need (Whyte 1956, 7). And, indeed, he does want to belong to the organization: Whyte says that every older executive has reservations about company fealty, but the young Organization Man "cherishes the idea that his relationship with The Organization is for keeps" (Whyte 1956, 131).

So we have Whyte's New Man—without avarice, content to work for others, driven to belong heart and soul to The Organization. What can we make of this picture? First, it is a picture not substantially different from that painted by David Riesman in 1950. Rather than the Protestant Ethic and the social ethic, Riesman contrasts the inner-directed and the other-directed as character types. The inner-directed individual has internalized his elders' precepts and this "psychological gyroscope" directs him through life. His character is formed early and guides him through all subsequent experience (Riesman 1950, 26). For the nineteenth-century American, the gyroscope was calibrated for the Protestant Ethic virtues, since the principal problem was building a new country, struggling against nature more than society or his fellows. But in this century, the increasing urbanization and bureaucratization of society turns the focus elsewhere: the problem becomes dealing with other people. And so, the other-directed character type emerges. The other-directed look to their contemporaries for direction—their acquaintances and the peers they see in the media. They tend toward a narrow conformity "through an exceptional sensitivity to the actions and wishes of others" (Riesman 1950, 38). Within the psyche of the other-directed Riesman finds not a gyroscope, but a sort of radar, constantly scanning the others for cues to his appropriate attitudes and behaviors. The highly individualized character of the inner-directed disappears; within the corporation, the "white collar people . . . sell not only their time and energy but their personalities as well" (Mills 1953, xvii).

This brings us back to the issue of conformity, so characteristic of the fifties. It is an issue on which Tocqueville preceded Whyte, Riesman, and Mills in his concern. Tocqueville observed that American individualism, this new phenomenon for him, was strangely compatible with conformity. The individual, left to his own powers, finds his opinions in those of the majority (Tocqueville 1988, 435). And that majority can become a tyranny, just as Whyte and the others feared.

Whyte saw his Organization Man falling victim to a new and subtle form of despotism, no less a despotism for being, in Tocqueville's words, "provident, gentle." Whyte feared that the American ideals of freedom and democracy were fading as the Organization Man accepted the corporate collective in the 1950s. Perhaps it was easier to resist when the collective's power and purposes were raw and obvious. Earlier corporate forms, the monopolies and trusts of the turn of the century, were "passionately resisted . . . it was believed that they threatened the very foundations of our society, based as it was on the consent of free and equal citizens" (Bellah et al. 1991, 84). But in Whyte's day, the corporation put on a more benign face; the old fears of "economic royalism," fears that Americans had voiced from the late nineteenth century up to the New Deal, had abated in the 1950s (Bellah et al. 1991, 99). Whyte thought it critically important that these fears be revived. But Whyte, Riesman, and Mills seemed to have little effect on the pervasive optimism and complacency of the fifties.

Theodore Roszak looked back on the fifties in 1969, after the counterculture had crested. He was unremitting in his attack on that bland era of conformity and complacency, the "pathological passivity" of the "parental generation whose god was Allen Ginsberg's Molloch . . . trapped as they have been in the frozen posture of befuddled docility. . . ." And Roszak thought he knew the reason for the complacency and the materialism:

> The memory of the thirties, the War, the pathetic search for security and relaxation afterwards, the dazzle of the new prosperity, defensive numbness before the idea of atomic war, the protracted emergency of the 40s and 50s, the barbarism of the McCarthy years. And, the momentum of the technocracy, coming out of the

> war with heavy wartime industrial investments, centralized decision making, and the reverence for science. (Roszak 1969, 22–24)

As I said, Roszak wrote his rather extreme analysis with the benefit of hindsight, however myopic. There were other contemporary critiques of the conformity and affluence of the fifties, not by the mainstream intellectuals of the time, but mostly under the surface and ignored by the majority. The "Beats" were a handful of discontented intellectuals, virtually invisible to the popular consciousness in the 1950s, but fated to assume a critical influence in the 1960s. The Beats were everything the dominant culture was not: they opposed workaday routine, material acquisition; they embraced principled poverty, sexual liberation, self-actualization (Gitlin 1989, 28).

The youth culture began to show surface signs of rebellion and disaffection, though contentedly ignored by most adults. Rock 'n' roll music first appeared in the 1950s, a raw and raucous sound, discordant to adults raised on the saccharine popular music of the past. The new media heroes for the young were also nothing like the ballplayers and movie stars who had captivated the world of the 1930s and 1940s. Instead, they were Marlon Brando and James Dean: antiauthoritarians, antimaterialists.

But adults were largely oblivious to these seeds of change, discounting them, as the elder always do, as the fleeting follies of youth. There was one event, though, that practically everyone followed, and many began to interpret as the worm in the apple of their confidence in the system. This was the quiz-show scandal that broke in 1959.

The first such show, an update of an old radio program, was CBS's "$64,000 Question," airing first in June 1955 and becoming an immediate hit. The producers strove to add drama to the program by emphasizing the integrity of the process: questions locked all week in a bank vault, delivered by the bank's executive at show time; the isolation booth for the contestant to ensure no outside coaching. The other networks followed CBS and the airwaves were soon awash with quiz shows. The producers of these shows were not trying to provide an object lesson in American meritocracy, throwing the shows open to talent and letting the best-informed win. That was not their intent at all: their mission was to provide entertainment. Dan Enright, the producer of "Twenty-one" saw it clearly in retrospect, after the Fall: "The shows had never been about intelligence or integrity . . . they were about drama and entertainment" (Halberstam 1993, 649). And to entertain, one must attend to casting.

The producers learned quickly that their ratings were determined by the personalities of their contestants, and there inexorably followed the manipulation to have the popular guests win. The sponsors told the producers whom they wanted to win, and any remnant of impartiality vanished: the "good" contestants were coached, the "bad" told when to lose. "Twenty-one" became a completely crooked entertainment: Enright, the producer, cast it like a drama, with not just winners and losers, but heroes and villains. He "cast" Herb Stempel—the prototypical unattractive know-it-all—against Charles Van Doren, the scion of a distinguished intellectual family—handsome, modest, everyone's ideal son-in-law. And Van Doren proved a good actor as well, stumbling over answers he well knew, stuttering, perspiring as he racked his brains for a fact he had actually learned that morning.

It all came a cropper in 1959 when Stempel, who had been told to take a fall on an answer he knew as well as his own name, took his bruised ego and his knowledge of the shenanigans to the authorities. The public reaction—outrage and contempt—astonished the producers and the sponsors—astonished because they believed that the public, too, thought of the shows as mere entertainment. Did anyone believe Laurence Olivier was really the Prince of Denmark, that Gary Cooper was Lou Gehrig? Did anyone really believe that Charles Van Doren really knew all those arcane facts? Apparently they did. Van Doren had come to be a cultural icon, the incarnation of the best in American society. The newspapers treated his chicanery not as minor scandal in the fantasy world of entertainment, but as an event emblematic of the decline of something precious in America, as the loss of innocence, the disintegration of some moral certainty (Halberstam 1993, 645–64).

Confidence in institutions is a fragile thing, and has been found to be correlated with the perception of those institutions' moral and ethical standards. It is noteworthy that two of the institutions involved in the scandal suffered a sharp fall from grace: by 1975, corporation executives and advertising executives were rated as having good ethical practices by only 33 and 30 percent of the public (Lipset and Schneider 1987,

77–79). The public heretofore had believed what they read in the papers, and had come to trust what they saw on television. No more.

This loss of innocence can be viewed in terms of power relations. Galbraith's theory of power centers on what he calls "conditioned" power, power which is exercised, without the awareness of its object. This is the form of power, says Galbraith, which is central to the smooth functioning of a modern society (Galbraith 1983, 6). Conditioned power is usually hidden; it operates through advertising, through education, and through socialization. Socialization is the most hidden and the most effective means to exercise power: it is concealed in the cultural norms that we absorb as children. Once socialization has become effective, submitting to the will and the desires of others is not thought of as submission at all, but rather the exercise of one's own will in accordance with one's own moral sense, the feeling that it is the "right" thing to do (Galbraith 1983, 34–35).

In Galbraith's view this quite ordinary and universal phenomenon of social conditioning involves a serious risk to the society, the corporation, and the individual. The great strength of conditioned power is that it is hidden, it is not seen as power at all but as an integral part of the self of each person, Riesman's "gyroscope." Foucault emphasizes this point, claiming, in fact, that "power is tolerable only on condition that it mask itself. Its success is proportional to its ability to hide its own mechanisms" (Foucault 1990, 86).

A crisis can occur if this conditioning is revealed as contrafactual, when, e.g., the patriotic person is confronted with the misdeeds of his own government, or, more to the point, when Charles Van Doren is exposed as a liar and a fraud. Then, when the masks are torn aside, one is thrust into the bald realization that the world does not work the way one has been conditioned that it does. There is first indignation, and then the deep feeling that power so long concealed must be fundamentally illegitimate (Galbraith 1983, 13). The resulting bitterness and cynicism are phenomena that should not be surprising when we encounter them in the sixties and seventies.

And so we have traced some of the factors that shaped the young cohort 1: the experience of affluence and conformity, the culture of bureaucracy sketched in Whyte's *The Organization Man*, the bare stirrings of cultural revolt and the beginnings of disillusionment epitomized by the quiz show scandals. It is time now to return to our cohort 1 people and learn their views on our main topic: loyalty. We will do that in the next chapter, along with some discussion of the nature of loyalty.

5

The Heart of All the Virtues: Loyalty

In loyalty . . . is the fulfillment of the whole moral law. . . . Justice, charity, industry, wisdom, spirituality, are all definable in terms of enlightened loyalty
—Royce, The Philosophy of Loyalty

The Nature of Loyalty

What *is* loyalty, after all? How can we define it? What does it mean to say you are loyal to someone or to something? I asked just that question of my interview subjects. The question caught most of them off guard; the cohort 1 subjects by and large struggled a bit with what seemed such a pervasive part of their existence: it was as though I had asked them "What is life?" Let us hear first from Dennis Madison; he is fifty-five and receives a pension from RLX, the former parent of Softmatics. He had actually chosen to retire after the acquisition but stayed on at Softmatics when Art Merrill asked him to lend a hand. Listen to him work his way through the idea of loyalty:

> Gee, I don't know. I mean, that to me—I don't know. It's kind of general. I mean loyal to this place? I'm loyal to guys like Merrill . . . to people that I work with and to people that work for me and so forth. Like see, I go through this situation when I agreed to stay. Art and I had a long talk about it: "If you are going to stay . . . you're going to have a real responsible job. . . . I need you here for a few years. . . ." So even though now I'm doing it and probably . . . I get up in the morning and feel like I wish I wasn't doing this, I couldn't leave, because I couldn't come in and tell (him and the others) that I was leaving. I mean they couldn't do anything to me. What would they do to me? I mean I'm getting my retirement . . . But it's more of—I'm committed to do this and

if they fire me I wouldn't care. . . . but if I'm here, I'm doing a good job and then to leave them—Now, I can walk away from this thing and I can go and tell Art in three months I'm going to leave. I couldn't even think of it. . . . I mean what would I tell them? I can't tell them. I mean he's not going to—and he probably wouldn't care, you know. He'd probably say: "Great, if that's what you want to do. You know, if that's what you want to do, fine." So now I'm kind of to the point I wouldn't do it unless my wife was sick and she needed me . . . but just to say I'm tired of it now, I won't do it—and that's a strange thing because I'm just kind of committed to, and it's not Merrill and it's not (the other people). It's just kind of—I committed to do this thing and I'm going to do it and I'm either going to do it until I fail or I'm going to do it until I do enough of it so I can put somebody else in there and then they won't need me anymore, so that's what it (loyalty) is . . .

I want you to note several things about Dennis's rambling answer. First the fact that it rambles, as he thinks out loud about something he values but has never given much thought to. And note that he first makes a personal attribution: the objects of his loyalty are Art Merrill and others. But he changes his mind on that, concluding "a strange thing because I'm just kind of committed (not to Merrill) . . . to do this thing . . ." So we have a man with his material needs satisfied, a man who has found himself compelled to work at a demanding job from some attachment to "do this thing." The philosopher Josiah Royce, the Apostle of Loyalty, called "this thing" a "cause" and defined loyalty in those terms:

(Loyalty is) the willing and practical and thoroughgoing devotion of a person to a cause. A man is loyal when, first, he has some cause to which he is loyal; when secondly, he willingly and thoroughly devotes himself to this cause; and when, thirdly, he expresses his devotion in some sustained and practical way, by acting steadily in the service of his cause. (Royce 1908, 16)

These are words and concepts that probably would seem foreign to Dennis Madison, but they do seem to explain his behavior and fit his inchoate sense of why he does what he does. Somehow, the job he is doing has transcended simple attachments to other people, and transcended even the inherent satisfaction of doing it ("I get up in the morning and feel like I wish I wasn't doing this."). It has become a "cause." And Royce's idea that the loyal person "expresses his devotion in some sustained and practical way, by acting steadily in the service of his cause," is exemplified by this response from Jerry Cialdi, whom we met earlier:

> (Loyalty is) a matter of, just . . . sticking with them, you know. I think you're going to be there through the thick and thin. I think that loyalty to this organization, to this product . . . those people . . . people who are loyal to the company, to the direction, to the sense that you're going to have . . . positive and negative cycles and you're going to stick with that organization or you're going to stick with that person through the good times and the bad . . .

Art Merrill as well seems to grasp that attachment to a cause, and the behavioral implications—not just persistence, as Jerry articulates, but the added element of sacrifice:

> I guess loyalty would be in the case because of that relationship I might do something that I wouldn't normally do for the sake of the relationship . . . So if I were loyal to RLX, I'd do something that intellectually, my personality, would normally make me reject. (It's) the relationship I'm trying to maintain.

This "cause" in Royce's terms is something larger than the loyal person's private self, but it is also an object which unites the person to others—a social tie of some sort is fashioned by loyalty, as we have glimpsed in the words of our cohort 1 interlocutors.

Let us look a bit further at Josiah Royce, whose 1908 classic *The Philosophy of Loyalty* first systematically explored this peculiar human quality. Now, if Spinoza was the "God-intoxicated man," Royce surely was the "loyalty-intoxicated." As our epigraph shows, he saw all of morality and virtue springing from loyalty; it is "the heart of all the virtues, the central duty amongst all duties" (Royce 1908, vii). The key to Royce's concept of loyalty is that it is a *virtue*, and the entire thrust of his argument is to exhort his reader to embrace this virtue, to *choose* loyalty. For Royce believes choose we can and must: "The loyal man's cause is his cause by virtue of the assent of his own will. His devotion is his own. He chooses it . . ." (Royce 1908, 16). But does one really choose to be loyal? Recall Dennis Madison's account: it is rather clear that most days he would rather be enjoying retirement, and if he had actually chosen to be loyal, it is a choice he would seem to regret.

The scholar George Fletcher, I believe, can move us closer to an account of loyalty's sources. He asserts that one's "historical self," the product of personal history, inclines one toward loyal commitments (Fletcher 1993, 153). As we have seen above, our personal history is in fact the creation of an historical self, a self that has been formed by our experiences as they have been filtered through our early conditioning. In our interview, Joe Hirschfield elucidated this idea of the "historical self" for me:

> When you talk about loyalty to something . . . What it means is that there is something solid there that carries a mutual belief from what you've grown up with to what you understand as right and wrong and standards, if you will, of what's expected . . .

But let us return to this notion of choice, essential to Royce's conception. It seems to miss the mark; it implies something of entering into a contract, weighing the benefits of a commitment and then opting for or against. The idea of "choice" perhaps gives too much credence to the idea that we have complete control of our lives, that we have the personal power and autonomy to make choices in matters of intense emotions like loyalty—or love (Fletcher 1993, 57). But today's conventional wisdom assumes that people make such choices. *The Economist* speaks of the "security of long term employment in exchange for dogged loyalty" (*Economist* 1993, 63). And a brief summary of any recent article on loyalty would run: "In the past a bargain was made; people gave companies loyalty in exchange for security. When security was withdrawn, loyalty was withdrawn." The fallacy in this—for I do think it is fallacious—is the assumption that loyalty is a commodity, an item of exchange, when in fact it is an emotion.[1] Most likely, to explain loyalty we would do better to look to psychology than to moral philosophy, and we will in fact move on to psychology shortly.

But look again at the "bargain" model of loyalty and substitute "love" for "loyalty." Can you see the absurdity of a person falling in love as an act of will, in order to gain security or any other useful thing? In fact, the causal arrow runs the other way: We become loyal in a manner similar to making friends, a slowly growing emotional attachment is formed. The loyalty thus formed then affects our views—our own goals and values gradually become those of the organization (Ewin 1992). Of course, we then believe that our cause is just, our organization's values meritorious; it is impossible to commit oneself to something believed "to be trivial or totally bad" (Trigg 1973).

Dennis Madison talked further about loyalty in our interview, and his explanation began to converge on more emotionally laden objects: family and friends. Listen:

> You know there's a certain loyalty you have to certain people and other people are just kind of equal and I know them, but I'm not loyal to them I don't think. So, but . . . I got this group of family at work and friends that I think that's what loyalty is to me, to do anything that they want done. It's just to me whatever they want done. You know, if somebody says, if that group says "Would you do me a favor?," I'd say: "Sure, anything. I don't care what it is. You don't even have to tell me. I'm not going to blink about it."

Dennis Madison is raising an issue that Royce seems to underplay: loyalty by its very nature is particular; we favor the rights and needs of one party over those of another. This may only be human nature, but it is in direct opposition to Kantian ethics, which obligates us to treat all our fellow creatures equally. Alasdair MacIntyre describes this neutrality as a "moral fiction," an objective and impersonal criterion that is impossible in real human lives (MacIntyre 1981, 70). But, this partiality raises the issue of a "constant moral danger," in MacIntyre's phrase. We are at risk of failing in our duty of justice to others, in preference to the demands of our cause (Fletcher 1993, 6). This is the "Paradox of Loyalty," the "disposition to prefer, not anyone who satisfies universal conditions, but this or that . . . given person . . ." (Petit 1988). This partiality toward the object of one's loyalty can result in some bad judgments, in fact you could say that suspending good judgment is part and parcel of loyalty: remember Dennis Madison's predicament. But, which is the more important to humanity, the Kantian, impersonal categorical imperative, or the demands of simple—but particularist—loyalty? I think we can agree with Oldenquist (1982): "Loyalties ground more of the principled, self-sacrificing, and other kinds of nonselfish behavior in which people engage than do moral principles and ideals . . ."

But there are loyalties and then there are loyalties; Fletcher has given us a very useful distinction, that between minimum and maximum loyalty. Minimum loyalty, or instrumental commitment, is merely the desire to maintain the relationship, which of course requires rejecting alternatives. We saw that with Art Merrill, who framed loyalty in those terms when he said: "(It's) the relationship I'm trying to maintain." Well, "minimum" it may be, but as Fletcher notes, some of the most odious epithets in the language are reserved for those who cannot meet this "threshold of loyalty": adulterer, traitor, betrayer (Fletcher 1993, 15).

In Fletcher's maximum loyalty we find true loyalty, a quality akin to Royce's virtue, the notion of thoroughgoing devotion, Christ's stern admonition: "He that is not with me is against me" (Matthew 12:30 and Luke 11:23). Maximum loyalty demands an emotional, even an irrational, attachment to its object. Fletcher describes maximum loyalty very like love:

> There comes a point when logic runs dry and one must plant one's loyalty in the simple fact that it is *my* friend, *my* club . . . In loyalty, as in love, there is not even an illusion of scientific neutrality and intellectual impartiality. . . . (Fletcher 1993, 61)

I believe it is precisely in emotions like love, compassion, and sympathy that loyalty is born. Our human need for sociability is at the very core of loyalty, and since it is such a deep need, loyalties are not just fine things, they are a requisite for a proper life. This is one of Royce's strongest conclusions, and his insight fits well with what we know of the psychology of loyalty. For Royce, loyalty solves the paradox of existence by finding, outside of ourselves, a reason for service and striving, for "unless you can find some sort of loyalty, you cannot find unity and peace in your active living" (Royce 1908, 46). Loyalty is a human need, ingrained in our makeup, bred in the bone. To elucidate this point, let us look closer at the psychology underlying the quality of loyalty.

Upon a moment's reflection, loyalty must seem a most peculiar phenomenon, this bond to others, even to abstract organizations, this bond which is capable of calling forth the most extraordinary selflessness and sacrifice. In the rational calculus of orthodox economics, which enshrines self-interest as its basic tenet, loyalty is literally *non*sense. Yet we all know from everyday observation that people are capable of a loyalty that can at times approach the heroic. How can we account for it? The springs of human motivation are deep, perhaps impossible to plumb. As we consider an exploration of the psychology of loyalty, we should heed D. H. Thomas's caution,

"The heart of man is a far country, that cannot be approached or explored" (Thomas 1981, 295).

From Sigmund Freud, the greatest explorer of that "far country," we learn the essential point: the tie that binds an individual to a group is an *emotional* tie, reflecting unconscious motivations far beyond the reach of rational calculation. For Freud, the mutual tie between group members is one of identification, rooted in the need for a father (Freud 1922, 62 and 66). Of course, this is not a conscious thought; Freud's great paradox—a paradox now the stuff of conventional wisdom—is that we have many purposes we pursue without any conscious knowledge of them. Freud mapped these purposes for us, but left unexplained why we should have such motivations at all—conscious or not. Below, we will review the speculations of evolutionary psychology, which provide some rationale for the existence of our characteristic emotions—loyalty included.

It is a Freudian axiom that it is desire, not thought as Descartes would have it, which is the basic essence of man (N. O. Brown, 1959, 7). But man's desires are infantile, says Freud, they are in conflict with reality; so, they are repressed, and importantly, they are sublimated. If Freud is right, the sublimation of sexual energy has produced all of human culture, including the basic cultural activity of work. The emotional ties binding people together also result from that sublimation. (N. O. Brown, 1959, 135).

Freud is well-known for his pessimism, and that pessimism does not exclude the world of work. Men sublimate desires and accept the reality principle; they engage in useful toil, but it is toil without pleasure, painful. Freud finds no room for an original instinct of workmanship, or for the joy of productive labor (Marcuse 1955, 82). Hence, man is in a cruel trap: his basic desires are repressed; he is forced to work by the reality principle and those sublimated desires; and, he is tricked into loyalty by a false identification with the father.

But perhaps things are not that bleak. For a more positive view of work and loyalty, we now look to Erich Fromm's revision of Freudian theory. With Fromm we find, in a sense, the marriage of Marx and Freud, the reconciliation of man's social nature with his individual psychology. Fromm took issue with Freud's assumption of the fundamental split between man and society, Freud's idea of that irreconcilable conflict bedeviling us all. Freud certainly viewed the individual in relation to others, but it was a relationship more competitive than cooperative. The theory of sublimation of desires portrays individuals in an "object" relationship with others; one's fellows are always a means to one's ends.

Fromm saw it differently. For him the key problem of psychology was not the satisfaction or frustration of desires; rather, the problems were how a person can relate to the world, and importantly, how the historically determined structure of society can determine that relationship (Fromm 1994, 10). Fromm rejected Freud's view that the individual is in perpetual war with society, a society which tries to domesticate him by permitting him some satisfaction of his biological drives. Rather, Fromm viewed society more positively, as a potentially creative force in shaping individual development. We all have a basic need for society, and it is the need to avoid aloneness, moral isolation, the sense of insignificance. That need—and that fear of isolation—stem from our earliest experiences. As infants, we enjoy "primary ties" with our parents but we soon reach a stage of individuation, the knowledge that we are separate beings, separate from our parents. This is perfectly natural and does provide us the opportunity to develop our own strength, our own capacities. However, the separation from the parents also creates a moral aloneness; just as Freud reads human life as the fruitless quest for infantile pleasure, Fromm reads it as the search for a replacement for the primary ties (Fromm 1994, 24–31). But, unlike Freud, Fromm maintains that the quest need not be fruitless, provided we are fortunate enough to be born into the right type of society. The Middle Ages were for Fromm that type of society, providing people with the bonds of solidarity and mutual obligations that readily substituted for the primary parental ties (Fromm 1994, 41–43). Modern man's course is much more problematic since the market economy is much more insecure: human relations are more instrumental; each must prove his own worth.

Unless a person is fortunate enough to achieve an acceptable substitute for the primary ties in love and/or productive work, anxiety is the common outcome. Fromm asserts that one must find a means to escape this anxiety, and people find that escape in one of three ways: conforming in an automatonlike manner, i.e., mass behavior; resorting to sadism, i.e., reducing the feared "other" to nothingness; or, surrendering freedom in the hope of reciprocated security (Fromm 1994,

140, 155–56 and 184). It is this last mechanism, the surrender of one's freedom, which bears directly on the subject of corporate loyalty. A person who is unconsciously trying to replace the primary ties by submitting to another person or an organization is under the spell of what Fromm calls "the magic helper."

> They expect protection from "him," wish to be taken care of by "him," make "him" responsible for whatever may be the outcome of their actions. . . . Frequently . . . the "magic helper" is personified: he is conceived of as God, as a principle, or as real persons such as one's. . . . superior. (Fromm 1994, 172–73)

Who of us has not longed, more than once in life, for the magic helper? And how much of our feelings and actions have been a quest for that magic help, whether we were conscious of it or not? Tellingly, I encountered the magic helper in my interview subjects; usually the reference was to an idea they once—naively—had about the company. For example one said he thought once that "the company . . . had a plan for you, that there was some sort of, you know, God-like presence that was defining everyone's particular career path."

I think Fromm's theory here rings true. It is difficult to conceive of a better explanation for the psychology of organizational loyalty; Fromm's "magic helper" seems to capture the feeling of the contented employee in a paternalistic corporation. And, it captures the essential universality of the need for attachment: we all need to replace the primary ties; we all want and need the magic helper; we all wish, as Randall Jarrell puts it, to "Come back to that calm country / Through which the stream of my life first meandered" (*Thinking of the Lost World*, Jarrell 1985, 67).

Whatever we think of the details of Fromm's theory, he makes a very strong case for an essential point: people *need* to be attached to others and to groups in meaningful ways. The nature of the life course assures us we will never again enjoy the primary ties with our parents; we must replace those ties with something: better the healthy choices of love, meaningful work, or unconscious submission, loyalty if you will, to something greater than ourselves—better, that is, than the alternatives: sadism, automatonism, slavery.

There is another way to explain the impulse toward loyalties, and that is from evolutionary psychology. The claim of this field is a logical extension of Darwinism: that our mental and emotional constitution is every bit a product of evolutionary pressures as our physical bodies. And it is that emotional makeup which ensures the social bonds holding society together, our instincts for moral virtues like duty, truth-telling, sympathy, justice—and loyalty (Wilson 1993, 23). All of us experience a wide variety of emotions: gratitude, shame, remorse, pride, honor, love. Their existence is unquestionable; the question is why such things exist in us, if we believe in evolution, what "fitness" purpose could these emotions possibly serve?

The Darwinian answer is that our feelings are "logic executors," urging us to behave in ways that fulfill the logic of evolution, i.e., individual survival and reproduction (Wright 1994, 190). Evolutionary psychology also notes that our minds and emotional structure were not necessarily "designed" to maximize our fitness today, to insure our genetic legacy; rather, our minds were formed to maximize fitness in the "ancestral environment." Since evolution works so slowly, the bodies and minds we have now are essentially identical to that of Cro-Magnon man and have remained unchanged for at least 100,000 years. The "ancestral environment" is thus that of a hunter-gatherer society, and differs radically from the twentieth century—even from the Neolithic, when agriculture was introduced and high density populations ensued (Wright 1994, 37–38).

Darwin himself noted that people seem to be unusually sensitive to what we would now call "public opinion"; he thus asserted that adherence to moral laws had an innate basis, that humans had a set of "social instincts." Chief among these instincts, Darwin counted sympathy for one's fellows (Wright 1994, 184). But what evolutionary purpose could be served by this sympathy, this altruism? Rather simply, a person who has many friendships will have an evolutionary advantage, he has a network of helping friends available in times of stress (Williams 1966, 94).

Reciprocal altruism can be conceived of as a strategy—importantly, an unconscious strategy—in a "game." If viewed in the context of game theory, the arena of human interaction can be a 'non-zero-sum' game, i.e., the rewards of a cooperative strategy can exceed those of an exploitative one. But this system of reciprocal altruism itself requires "logic executors," genetically determined emotions to regulate the system, and of these we can count such feelings as friendship, dislike, gratitude, trust, sympathy, suspicion, trustworthiness, and guilt (Wright 1994, 190).

One-on-one reciprocal altruism can be extended to larger groups and hence encompass the virtue (or strategy) of loyalty. It is conceivable that the capacity to think of others as parts of a unified team has a genetic basis, that an individual may develop a more diffuse altruism and be capable of sacrificing for the group as a whole. Presumably, such practices could have developed in the hunting environment, which demands individual risks for group success. A hunter would not expect direct repayment for his risk-taking, but be content with others taking similar risks for the benefit of the group. In this way, an instinct for loyalty could be developed, a set of emotions which are satisfied if, all in all, others are willing to do their part as you have done (Wright 1994, 207). And so, we can find some evolutionary basis for loyalty, confirming Josiah Royce's insight that everyone has a *need* to find something to be loyal to (Royce 1908, 21), and confirming as well Fromm's view that we are driven toward attachments larger than ourselves or our immediate families.

The "logic executors," the suite of universal emotions, signal us that our behavior is deviating from the norms of evolutionary logic. We heard Dennis Madison struggling between his rational intelligence and his emotions as he tries to explain why he stays on past retirement age. He knows intellectually that it doesn't matter to the company, but:

> I couldn't come in and tell [him and the others] that I was leaving. I mean they couldn't do anything to me. What would they do to me? I mean I'm getting my retirement . . . Now, I can walk away from this thing and I can go and tell Art in three months I'm going to leave. I couldn't even think of it. . . . I mean what would I tell them? I can't tell them. I mean he's not going to—and he probably wouldn't care . . .

"What would I tell them? I can't tell them." What Art fears is not any material consequences—he fears being shamed, shamed by betraying a loyalty he has unwittingly formed. That "logic executor" keeps him at his task, preserves the bond of loyalty, overrides his intellectual assessment of the situation. Here is another example of the logic executor we know as "guilt," which steers us toward loyalty: this from a younger person:

> I think I have always been a fairly loyal person. . . . I would feel guilty if I was in an organization and I didn't participate properly or I didn't live up to my commitments . . .

The logic executors work for us all: that is why betrayal of loyalty is so universally despised; remember Dante reserved a special place in Hell for those who had betrayed a trust. So I think we can conclude that the need for loyalty is deep within us, it lies in our basic psychology, it is implanted in our genes and shows itself in the emotions we feel when we are disloyal. It is very far from being a consciously willed "contract"; it is an emotional state, derived from feelings that are at the very basis of our being.

Fromm and evolutionary psychology show us that loyalty is a natural, instinctive part of our makeup. We still, however, must consider how loyalty to organizations actually forms. I think the essential psychological concept that is important here is that of *identification.* In his research on organizational commitment, Sheldon defined the term as "an attitude or orientation toward the organization which links or attaches the identity of the person to the organization" (Stevens et al. 1978, 381). I think this is essentially correct, but it leaves open two vital questions: how does the identification form? and, why do we need to identify in the first place?

The psychological model of Ajzen and Fishbein, as extended by Wiener, seems an adequate answer to the first question. The theory begins with Fletcher's notion of an "historical self," formed by our socialization and our attention to the effects of our behavior. From this we develop beliefs, which become attitudes and internalized norms; these norms then determine our subsequent behavior (Ajzen and Fishbein 1977, 91). Wiener carries this a step further in regard to the workplace. He posits that we bring to our employer norms developed in our earlier experience and conditioning, but those norms can be changed, expanded by the right conditions. If the workplace satisfies our needs for meaning, for society, for material rewards—if we find that, then we begin to change our norms by internalizing the goals and values of the organization (Wiener 1982, 418–22). Their way becomes our way; we become loyal.

I believe that the above is a satisfactory account of the psychology of loyalty, but since many authors[2] have used the theory of cognitive dissonance to frame organizational commitment, let us take a moment and review that theory. It has been called "one of the most controversial [theories] in social psychology," but "an extraordinarily useful tool for the study of attitude and cognitive change" (Kiesler et al. 1969, 191 and 237). Festinger, the father of the theory, lists its basic hypothesis as follows:

> 1. The existence of dissonance, being psychologically uncomfortable, will motivate the person to try to reduce it and achieve consonance.
>
> 2. When dissonance is present, in addition to trying to reduce it, a person will actively avoid situations and information which would likely increase the dissonance. (Festinger 1957, 3)

Dissonance reduction is closely related to behavior, so when we experience dissonance our tendency is to change the behavior (or deny or distort its meaning) or change our opinions or attitudes vis-à-vis the behavior. Our attitudes are altered by our actions and decisions so we can justify the decisions to ourselves. Once having chosen one thing over another, we have the tendency to distort the attractiveness of the two and thereby reduce cognitive dissonance (Kiesler 1971, 16). The connection with loyalty is simple: having invested time and energy in an organization, we reduce cognitive dissonance by assuming a positive attitude towards that organization.

Cognitive dissonance is one of those theories whose self-referential nature makes it virtually impossible to disprove. (Freudianism and Marxism come to mind in the same vein.) No matter what the outcome, the theory has a ready answer in all cases: the actor is reducing cognitive dissonance. Just as an opponent of Freud can be accused—within the Freudian system—of repressed hostility, and a critic of Marx labeled with "false consciousness," it is possible that one who does not believe in cognitive dissonance is reducing his dissonance by his disbelief.

The Psychological Contract

There is a good deal of talk today about the "psychological contract" that purportedly existed between employers and companies. I believe the term "contract" is poorly chosen, since the condition that is described is in reality an emotional state. Nonetheless, let us take a brief look at it, because it as well can explain some facets of corporate loyalty. The idea is that the employee may perceive that the organization is committed to him, and in turn feels an obligation to the company. It is a contract of some sort, in the sense that it is certainly a relationship, but how did it arise? The theory is that the following sequence of events took place:

- Expectations are held. (E.g., hard work will assure tenure)
- Consistent patterns emerge. (The company retains hard working people)
- Trust develops. (Confidence in management's commitment to the employee)
- A "psychological contract" is in place. (The employee believes he will be retained). (Rousseau 1989, 121–39)

In a nutshell, the perspective of the employee is something like the following:

> You work hard, contributing your time, your energy and your creativity to help your company grow. You make sacrifices, many of them personally painful ones at the expense of your family. In return, your grateful company rewards you with promotions and a fair wage for the next 30 or 40 years. (Yates 1993, 16)

Of course this "contract" is one-sided; it is the employee's beliefs that are at issue here, not the company's. A true "contract" would be an "implicit" contract, a *mutual* obligation. Implicit contracts can exist when each party can unerringly predict what the other will do. The psychological contract sketched above could be an implicit one as well if the company had an inviolate rule of not laying off in bad times—it must be something more than an employee's personal observation that this was not done. But, for many, the contract was real and enduring. Recall Bill Abernathy whom we met in the first chapter, and his shock and dismay when the perceived contract was abrogated:

> I really honestly believed that . . . I could put in my 35 or 40 years, I could grow as an individual . . . We felt that our futures were secured and when things started to unravel, it was devastating. . . . it was frightening . . . to one day realize it wasn't true, that

> we were like that as long as times were good, but when times got bad, it was . . . "No, no, no, that's not really how it was" and . . . you want to say, "God, am I stupid for believing this? . . . Or was I naive or . . . did the company really turn on us?"

Bill is describing a psychological contract, one that had great saliency for him, as his emotions betray. He has learned, though, that the contract can be one-sided, illusory, what Matthew Arnold sang of in his lament, *To Marguerite:* "The heart can bind itself alone / And faith may oft be unreturn'd" (Arnold 1986, 60).

But the effects of psychological contracts—enforceable or not, real or imaginary—are powerful. Dore notes in his comparison of British and Japanese companies that an English Electric foundryman, if asked what he does, would be likely to reply that he is a foundryman, then to name his plant location, and only last that he works for English Electric. An Hitachi man would naturally and invariably identify himself as first a member of Hitachi, then from his plant locale, and last as a foundryman. Corporate identity is first; occupation last. The psychological contract is firmly in place (Dore 1973, 115).

The Value of Loyalty

That loyalty is valuable to individuals can be seen, then, as a matter of fulfilling a basic human need; from the deepest parts of our being, we have a need to find an object for loyalty. That an organization is an appropriate object for that loyalty is more problematical. Perhaps it reflects the passing of the old dispensation which began in the sixties, but in 1963 Kurt Vonnegut made light of organizational loyalty in his best-seller, *Cat's Cradle.* Vonnegut invents a religion, Bokononism, and some playful neologisms to go along with it. The Bokononist credo: "We . . . believe that humanity is organized into teams, teams that do God's Will without ever discovering what they are doing. Such a team is called a *karass* . . ." (Vonnegut 1963, 11). But most people find themselves enmeshed in a false *karrass,* an entity that Vonnegut labels a *grandfaloon,* a collection of people that seems to be meaningful, but in reality has nothing to do with God's—or anyone else's—plans.

> examples of *grandfaloons* are the Communist party, the Daughters of the American Revolution, the General Electric Company,

the International Order of Odd Fellows—and any nation, anytime, anywhere" (Vonnegut 1963, 67–68)

Well, Bill Abernathy and many others today may rue the day they pledged their fidelity to a *grandfaloon*, but let us look at the other side of the matter, the value of loyalty to the corporation. The conventional wisdom for a very long time averred that employee loyalty is vital, that fidelity is of unalloyed benefit to the corporation. Chester Barnard, an icon of American business thought, was unequivocal: "The most important single contribution required of the executive, certainly the most universal qualification, is loyalty . . ." (Barnard 1950, 220). Now, it is unlikely that Norman Mailer ever read Barnard, but he presents an object lesson of loyalty's value in *The Naked and the Dead*. His Sgt. Martinez believes he is loyal to his superior, but when the crisis comes he abandons him to save the unit, because he remembers that he is a sergeant in the United States Army, and there his loyalty must lie (Mailer 1948, 538). And long before Barnard, Machiavelli advises his *Prince* on loyalty's value: "How to deserve loyalty, how to win it, buy it, inculcate it, cultivate it . . ." (Jacobs 1992, 68).

For many years business thinkers as well have been universal in their esteem for loyalty, and have asserted its pragmatic value, its utility in making employees more cooperative, dedicated, and productive (Lee 1968). As late as 1990, one writer still could claim that loyalty benefited the organization, that the loyal had better attendance and turnover records, that they exerted more effort and were more apt to act in the organization's interests (Romzek 1990, 377). It is this purported linkage of loyalty and performance, an article of faith for many observers, which we must explore. For if it is true, then loyalty lost is a business problem, an issue whose roots and consequences demand our attention.

Intuitively, most believe that committed people perform better; they must work harder and with greater devotion to their employers. However, the news on this score from the front lines of social science research is ambiguous. As early as 1955, researchers had begun to conclude that there is little evidence of a simple relationship between attitudes and performance (Vroom 1964, 181). Subsequent research has not contradicted this view. There is at best a weak relationship between a supervisor's ratings of performance and measurements of an employee's commitment (Mathieu and Zajac 1990).

Of course, there are contrary findings, significantly when it is *normative* commitment, the measurable attitude closest to loyalty, which is studied. One study found that normative commitment *was* positively correlated with rated performance, but instrumental commitment was not. It is this latter form of commitment—simply a desire to stay and be paid—which appears to be of little use to the corporation, and in many cases does more harm than good. It does the company no good to have low turnover if some employees are there only for instrumental reasons, and it harms the company if they are motivated to perform only at the minimum level required to keep their jobs. (Meyer et al. 1989). So, organizational psychology does not give us an unequivocal answer; there is no certain evidence that higher commitment results in higher performance, at least within the limits of measurement of those rather vague terms, "commitment" and "performance."

We can also look at the question of loyalty's value from an economics standpoint. But what does loyalty have to do with economics? It is not a commodity, subject to the price system; there is no formal market for loyalty. But Kenneth Arrow insists that values such as trust, truth-telling, and loyalty are critically important "lubricants" for an economy:

> They have real, practical, economic value; they increase the efficiency of the system, enable you to produce more goods or more of whatever values you hold in high esteem. (Arrow 1974, 23)

But how do trust and loyalty actually "lubricate" an economy, as Arrow proposes? The work of Douglass North can illuminate this for us. North believes that institutions are central to economic performance, but we must be careful to note his definition of "institution": for North, they are "humanly devised constraints on human interaction." These include formal rules, but also "informal constraints (norms of behavior, conventions, and self-imposed rules of conduct) . . . they are the structure that human beings impose on their dealings with others" (North 1993, 3–4). The great value of institutions is that they reduce uncertainty in our everyday life; they structure our behavior such that much of what we do is guided by an institutional framework that requires little thought (North 1990, 6). If you are loyal, a great deal of your interactive behavior in the organization is, in a way, predetermined by that loyalty. Herbert Simon makes much the same point. Organizational loyalty for Simon is a key simplifying device. The loyal administrator need not consult the entire range of human values in making a decision; his task is made easier by loyalty, since he need only act in the interests of the organization (Simon 1961, 12–13).

In short, what North, Simon, and Arrow are saying is that loyalty reduces "transaction costs," and therefore makes for a more efficient system, whether it be the economy *in toto*, or an organization. Now the theory of the firm claims that the very existence of the corporation can be justified only as a means to economize on transaction costs (Williamson 1975, ix). But low transaction costs in a hierarchy posit some modicum of trust and loyalty, some means to minimize the costs of motivating and monitoring potentially recalcitrant employees. Loyalty, in this perspective, can be seen to have substantial economic value.

Yet today there is growing evidence that companies have simply given up on the attempt to instill loyalty, and are reverting to the market system which is always a viable alternative, as transaction costs economics suggests. "Outsourcing" to independent contractors is a growing trend, which seems to suit both the contractors and the companies. More and more, corporate managements seek only an instrumental relationship with their employees, and outsourcing is the logical endpoint to this attitude, offering management both true variable costs for labor and "guiltless" firings. The costs to management are the costs of specifying, coordinating, and monitoring the work of contractors. If these costs are less than those of fringe benefits, morale-boosting, and monitoring the work of distrustful and disaffected employees, the correct business decision is to opt for the market over the hierarchy.

That trend of ignoring loyalty is a tacit statement that companies no longer see a value to employee loyalty, or at least fail to see that the costs of fostering loyalty are worth any benefits which might accrue. However, they may be missing a more subtle benefit of loyalty, what Albert Hirschman calls "voice."

Before we explore Hirschman's theory, here is an example of "voice" from my interviews, this from Jerry Cialdi:

> I think that loyalty to this organization . . . (is) the sense that you're going to have . . . positive and negative cycles and you're

going to stick with that organization . . . through the good times and the bad and you're going to counsel when you can counsel and you're going to be a friend . . ."

Or listen to Harry Dobbs from cohort 3:

> you want things to change and you—I guess I'm the kind of person that maybe I bitch a lot, but I'm not bitching to bitch. I'm bitching, hoping that someone's going to listen and will change something, I guess.

Or this response, when I asked Andy Freese, another from cohort 3, what loyalty meant to him:

> Well, I'm not so sure it means you agree with them all the time. I think I have a great deal of loyalty to past and present management here. I mean that's not to say that we haven't had a number of arguments about it. I guess loyalty is that you're able to voice your opinion, get your two cents in, when the decision's made, then you . . . I think there's an attitude issue too. I mean just going through the motions is not loyalty either. . . . It does not include agreeing with somebody all the time.

Let's examine what we have just heard: "counsel"; not "bitching to be bitching"; loyalty as "able to voice your opinion . . . getting your two cents worth in." This is the value of loyalty that Hirschman sees; he presents his analysis in a work aptly titled *Exit, Voice, and Loyalty.* Hirschman starts from the premise that any organization is inevitably subject to departures from efficiency or rationality. It can be saved from those lapses, though, if management gets the proper signals, gets the feedback that something is wrong. The feedback is not likely to come from employees or customers who quit or stop buying, they have "exited." Only if the exit reaches tidal proportions will management get the message, and it then may be too late. But the loyal stay, and, more than stay, they complain. They complain, they choose "voice" over exit, because they *are* loyal; they value the organization and want to see changes. Their loyalty prevents them from taking the easy way out—exit—so they voice their disaffection, and that helps management see what is wrong. Hirschman sums up the value of loyalty thus:

> As a result of loyalty, those potentially most influential customers and members will stay on longer than they would ordinarily, in

> the hope or, rather, reasoned expectation, that improvement or reform can be achieved "from within." Thus loyalty, far from being irrational, can serve the socially useful purpose of preventing deterioration from becoming cumulative, as it so often does when there is no barrier to exit. (Hirschman 1970, 79)

And so we can conclude, first, that loyalty is of great—perhaps vital—importance to individuals. Royce said that loyalty "furnishes . . . a personal solution of the hardest of human practical problems, the problem: 'For what do I live? Why am I here? For what am I good? Why am I needed?'" (Royce 1908, 57). And loyalty is important to the organization as well: perhaps not in the simpleminded notion that the loyal work harder and produce more output, but that they can be counted on in ambiguous situations to look out for the organization's interests, and when they see things going awry, they will voice their dissatisfaction.

The Old Dispensation: Cohort 1 Values

I asked all of my subjects about the trend in their loyalty, whether it had waxed or waned or stayed the same. I found that their responses correlated significantly with the measurement of organizational commitment obtained from the survey.[3] Those with high organizational commitment were more likely to express an increase over time in their sense of loyalty to the company. Now, the survey showed that cohort 1's organizational commitment was significantly higher than all the other cohorts, but in general their loyalty trend was flat. Like all the other cohorts, they expressed different views on their loyalty trend, but most were matter-of-fact about their company loyalty: they had been and apparently always would be, loyal. George Francis, who had been in upper-middle management and then, after the reorganizations and downsizings, found himself in a staff job, could not shake the "habit" of loyalty.

> Well, obviously since I went up to management . . . through a managerial department head and then a Director, yeah, I was very loyal, very conscientious. You're there and you go home at seven at night and you have dinner and then you open the brief case again and go at it . . . Although strangely enough I find I'm doing that now.

Generally I found with these "loyalists" what Charles Heckscher found in his recent study, *White Collar Blues:* they stayed loyal even after substantial downsizing and brutal layoffs, and they believed the layoffs were necessary for the healthy survival of their "cause," the company (Heckscher 1995, 11 and 55). Ted Fletcher, one of the old cohort, put it his way:

> I think that there's been justification for the downsizing. I mean, let's face it. . . . All of U.S. industries at large are downsizing because of the cost issues and so we aren't any different than anybody else. . . . . I don't think it affected my attitude at all because . . . I think that I understand the business side of it, that you have to control costs. . . . It could have affected me just as well and I would have looked at it no different. I would have said, "that's it." And even at my age which would not have been something I would have wanted, obviously, but I certainly think I can look at it as a professional and say, "Well that's just part of the business decision."

We have talked a good deal about loyalty and cohort 1; let us look at my survey results as they apply to this older group.[4] Loyalty—by any of the definitions we have seen—is a difficult thing to measure. The closest that social science has come to it is the construct called "normative commitment," which is defined in the literature in various ways; perhaps the best is derived from Etzioni's work and states that normative commitment is "an intense orientation toward the organization based on internalization of the organization's goals, values and norms; the individual identifies with authority" (Mowday et al. 1982, 21).

The notion of loyalty has thus been "operationalized" in that manner, and tools—survey questions—developed to measure this surrogate for loyalty. My own survey of Softmatics was consistent with the literature in important ways, which I can summarize as follows:

1. Organizational commitment, or loyalty if you will, is correlated with work values and work rewards, i.e., the needs for society, meaning and material remuneration and the perceived company fulfillment of those needs. This is a substantiation of the psychological model of Ajzen and Fisher we saw above.

2. Organizational commitment is positively correlated with three other attitudes: the Protestant Ethic, Expressive Individualism and Job Satisfaction.

3. Commitment is correlated with tenure, but not with gender.[5]

The above are all consistent with the literature. But my survey of Softmatics found something else, something I believe quite significant: commitment is not correlated with age, but rather with cohort. And it is not related to cohort in a monotonic way, i.e., increasing commitment with cohort. Rather, cohort 1 has statistically significantly higher commitment than all other cohorts, but cohorts 2 and 3 are not significantly different one from the other. This finding on cohort 1's uniqueness also applies to other attitudes and values. Not just organizational commitment, but a number of the work values and rewards, as well as expressive individualism, show that same, asymmetric pattern: cohort 1 people have a different set of attitudes and values than their younger colleagues. It is from this finding, as well as the interviews, that led me to conclude that cohort 1 represented a remnant of the old dispensation which is rapidly passing away.

Before we move on to the younger cohorts, let us conclude this chapter, and this exploration of cohort 1, with some other views and values that my cohort 1 subjects expressed. I am asserting that cohort 1 is more representative of bureaucratic values, the corporate culture, the culture of collective effort, and, of course, loyalty. The survey statistics we have just very briefly reviewed confirm the point on loyalty, but what about other facets of the bureaucratic culture? Here is Art Merrill, talking about making difficult decisions (actually layoff decisions), and he shows how he values the group process, the very thing that dismayed William H. Whyte, Jr.:

> the easiest part of such a decision is getting together in a group, especially all the people involved who know they are going to stay. It becomes sort of a group thing, right. It's sort of everybody is trying to reinforce each other in terms of this is the right thing to do.

I asked Joe Hirschfield what he thought was the most important thing about his job, and his answer had less to do with autonomy or pay, and more to do with the social values of the job:

> it's helping other people grow and . . . think outside of the box. That's what I've wanted. I'd like to see myself more as a mentor than a manager. I've got a lot of years of experience that can do a lot of the younger people a lot of good. . . . My primary purpose here is develop as many really prime, prize people as we possibly can and if there's going to be a legacy of any kind, it's a fact that you are a change agent that helps and moves things along . . . That's really what I get out of the job.

I found one of my interlocutors, Mike Jennings, to be ambivalent about his allegiance, vacillating between the old corporate culture of cooperation and the new, more atomistically individualistic stance. It was as though he knew that what his heart was telling him just did not fit with today's conventional view that cooperation and sacrifice for others were folly. Mike's job is to support the sales director to "make his numbers," and he is unusually committed to the company; his commitment rating is greater than one standard deviation above the company mean. Listen to his musings on values, and note the contradiction; I asked him first, as I had asked Joe, what the most important thing he got from his job, and we saw some of that answer earlier:

> I think being able to contribute to, you know, my boss's goals, really. I think that . . . when we make the number, I'm as thrilled as anybody in the world. . . . I'm as thrilled about (him) making his number as he and anybody else is. And that's my goal. I mean, make sure he makes his number every year, so I'm kind of driven by that.

But then I asked him if the company should owe anything to its employees, and the "other culture" emerged in his answer:

> Absolutely not. And I've pounded that into my kids' heads for years . . . A company pays you everything they owe you when you collect your paycheck. . . . let's face it, you know, life is competition and you might be the best or you might be somewhere near the bottom.

We see Mike's split feelings: from his own heartfelt endorsement of the value of cooperation and helping, to advising his children that company loyalty is folly, that it is a dog-eat-dog world. He holds on to the old world of values and the satisfaction it brings him, but realizes the old world is fast passing. Well the old world—the old dispensation—is not quite dead: it lives on with this aging generation of cohort 1. But the new world is much more apparent in the next generations; it is a strong strain in the younger cohorts, whom we meet next in Part Two.

Part Two

Between Two Worlds: The Middle Cohort

6

The Baby Boomers: Cohort 2

Thinking of his own Gods, a Greek
In pity and mournful awe might stand
Before some fallen Runic stone—
For both were faiths, and both are gone.

Wandering between two worlds, one dead,
The other powerless to be born,
With nowhere yet to rest my head,
Like these, on earth I wait forlorn.
—Arnold, *Stanzas from the Grand Chartreuse*

The Baby Boom

In the next three chapters we explore the world of cohort 2, a group often characterized as the "baby boomers." My cohort 2 includes both the war babies, born in 1941 through 1945, and the postwar baby boomers, born 1946–55. Taking 1948 as the middle date for their birth years, we can place these people in historical perspective. They had no memories of the Great Depression or World War II; they were eight years old when Presley's "Hound Dog" hit the top of the charts and Eisenhower was reelected; they were twelve when the civil rights sit-ins began and Chubby Checker introduced "The Twist"; fifteen when JFK was killed; seventeen when Johnson began the escalation in Vietnam and Bob Dylan's "Mr. Tambourine Man" was the big hit; they turned twenty in the "plague year" of 1968; twenty-six when Nixon resigned in disgrace; and thirty when stagflation was at its worst in 1978. Seldom has any generation lived through such a tumultuous period, such a time of fundamental changes in the economy, in popular culture and mores, and in politics.

In this chapter we will look at their views and some of the commentary that has been made over the years on this generation. We will also review some of the public-opinion-poll results for the critical youthful period for these people—the 1960s. We move on in chapter 7 to a review of the social history of the sixties, and in chapter 8 to a study of the 1960s economy and the management practices of that day, in particular the form of corporate governance called "welfare corporatism." Let us look first at the times when these people came into the world.

In addition to the widespread affluence, the American postwar world was characterized by a substantial demographic change. Between 1950 and 1986, the population grew by 77 million people; more than half that increase, 42 million, had come between 1950 and 1965 in the postwar "baby boom" (Bruchey 1988, 199). American birth rates had fallen steadily with the onset of industrialization in the 1870s, and then declined sharply in the Depression years, the birth years of cohort 1. The war years saw a recovery of birthrates to the level of the 1920s, about a 16 percent increase over the 1930s rate. But then the return of the servicemen and the glowing prospects for prosperity led to a great surge in births: an increase by 19 percent from 1945 to 1946, then another 12 percent the next year. More babies were born in the period 1948–52 than in the previous thirty years (Gitlin 1989, 13). The cohort 2 birth years, 1946–55, saw birth rates almost 35 percent higher than in the 1930s.

Now, there had been large generations in the past: as we have seen earlier, the fertility rates in the nineteenth century were nearly double that of even the peak baby-boom years.[1] But the conjunction of affluence and a large generation had a unique impact: children for the first time, in the aggregate, were a major market and attracted a range of cultural and other products that catered to them. And their parents' relative affluence had another effect: this cohort grew up as the "first standardized generation." They grew up in much the same surroundings, the kitchens and houses specified by the building codes of the 1940s. They were taught the standardized curricula that came with educational reform in the 1950s (Light 1988, 10–11). And perhaps most significantly, they watched the same television programs and the same commercials, and were bombarded by relentless exhortations to own things, the things that everyone else owned. For this was the first generation which took television for granted, as something that had always been there, a part of the natural order of things.

It is this unusually large generation as well that experienced the crowding that Richard Easterlin wrote of, the increased competition always and everywhere. One student of the baby boom notes that they "packed the maternity wards as infants, the classrooms as children, and the campuses, employment lines, and mortgage markets as young adults" (Light 1988, 9). As I have noted, this large and affluent generation attracted entrepreneurs of all stripes, particularly popular-culture marketeers. The movies and pop music had traditionally targeted young adults and the middle-aged: they had the disposable income. But once children had the spending money, the focus of entertainment shifted to them, with messages and forms they might find congenial. One of the oldest dramas of mankind revolves around disaffected youth, so it is not surprising that the appealing messages were in conflict with the existing order, the adult world of the 1950s and its staid conformity. The personas of Brando and James Dean challenged adult authority; *Mad* magazine mocked the adult world; rock 'n' roll shouted out unbridled sensuality.

And all these factors had the effect cf creating an unusual unity among the young of this generation. The standardized upbringings, the homogenized culture of television, the anti-adult messages of pop culture, and of course, their very numbers and their awareness of that—all these factors gave this generation a sense of unity and identity, stamped them with a different social character, gave them a shared *zeitgeist,* the knowledge that they were special, that they were a "generational unit" in the sense that Mannheim uses the term. For Mannheim, a generation unit is very like a social class: class or generation memberships

> endow the individuals sharing in them with a common location in the historical process and thereby limit them to a specific range of experience. . . . a tendency towards definite modes of behavior, feeling and thought. (Mannheim 1959, 291)

Membership in a generational unit gives one a privileged view of society; the information "given" to you is different from that "given" to other generations. As with a social class, a generation has a unique and limited view of the world, a view conditioned by their different absorption of the culture they find themselves in. In this process of absorption, some cultural elements are forgotten, and some are interpreted anew.

Being born at the same time does not necessarily create similar social location. What locates a generation is their shared experience of events, and their sharing of them at a time of formation of a worldview. Since older people have already passed through their formative periods, events will not have the same effect on them. All youth experiences the world anew, and in a way shaped by their experiences. Older people, living through the identical experiences, do not incorporate the experiences in the same way as the young.

> One is old insofar as he comes to live within a specific, individually acquired framework of usable past experience, so that every new experience has its form and its place largely marked out for it in advance. . . . Early impressions tend to coalesce into a *natural* view of the world. All later experiences then tend to receive their meaning from this original set . . . (Mannheim 1959, 296–98)

Potentially then, each new birth cohort in a particular place can form a generation unit from the fact of their unique experiences and early conditioning. But generation units which play a decisive role in social change rarely form in actuality. They come to actuality, as it were, when a concrete bond is created among them, when they are exposed together to the symptoms of a destabilized society. (Mannheim offers the example of German youth during the Napoleonic wars.)

Generation units form when people of the same age find themselves responding to society and events in a similar fashion. At first, it is necessary that a group be in contact with each other to discover their similar leanings. In time, as their new view solidifies and becomes spread more widely, others of the same age will see the resonance of the new perspective with their own experiences and be incorporated into an actual generation unit (Mannheim 1959, 290–316).

The generational sense can be formed in times of rapid social change, in conditions of great physical and social mobility, and when youth experiences major economic, technological, or military events (Yinger 1982, 56). As we will discuss in the next chapter, these of course were the conditions facing this age cohort in the 1960s.

And so, we should not be surprised that the baby boomers have quite different outlooks and values, a quite different social character, from the older cohort 1. And they do.

Cohort 2: Views and Values

We saw above that cohort 1 measured differently from cohort 2 on attitudes. Specifically, cohort 1 has higher organizational commitment than this middle cohort; cohort 1 has higher job satisfaction, and perceives the company as being fairer in its material rewards. There are also cohort differences in the interview variables that I analyzed through content analysis.[2] The loyalty trend mean for cohort 1 subjects was flat—neither up nor down. For cohort 2 the trend was downward, and the size of the difference between the means for cohorts 1 and 3 is significant within 6.8 percent confidence interval, i.e., the odds that the difference is due to chance are about one in fifteen. So we have some statistical evidence that the cohorts are different; there is also anecdotal evidence from the interviews, which we shall see shortly, and there is a body of commentary on the baby boomers themselves.

Much has been written about the baby boomers and their mentality; generally observers have noted a marked difference from older generations in their social and political attitudes: everything from the government's role in the economy, war and peace, marriage, sexual liberty, and drugs. They are said to be more tolerant of social diversity and varied lifestyles than their parents, and these attitudes are reflected in their own lives: the baby boomers are much more likely to have smaller families, to have two breadwinners, to divorce when their children are still young. As a result, the American "family"—the 1950s ideal of three kids, Mom the homemaker and Dad the breadwinner—that dominant social organization is as dead as feudalism (Light 1988, 28–31). And, most tellingly, the baby boomers have quite different attitudes toward institutions and their trust in and loyalty to them. We shall have a great deal more to say about this as we proceed, but for now let us be content with one observation. *Business Week*, in a 1986 article, asserted that "Younger managers don't subscribe to a code of loyalty . . . Neither do they demand it from their employees." John Francisco, one of my subjects born in

1941, articulated this cohort's ambivalence toward company loyalty:

> this whole concept of company and employee loyalty ; that might have been an implied myth. A long time ago it may have been actual.

The world changed a great deal as this generation matured; indeed, they helped change it. The culture, the politics, the economy, and corporate governance changed almost beyond recognition. The world of their adulthood was nothing like the one they expected to find. One observer, writing in 1969, traced the corrupting influence of affluence on this generation, how the middle class could afford to prolong the "ease and drift of childhood"; how the young, unlike their parents, did not have to sell themselves to get the consumer goods so remorselessly advertised. The result was a generation "infantized . . . nurturing childish fantasies," in every way ill-prepared for the real world (Roszak 1969, 31–32). Their economic status in particular was hardly what they expected in their early youth. Having been raised in an affluent era, the conditions of their maturity must seem baffling, even a betrayal of some promise. Above we found John Francisco musing about corporate loyalty as a "myth"; he represents a generation which began in great promise but saw their real incomes decline, their rate of housing purchases lag their parents', their prospects for promotion evaporate, and the prospects for their children look even worse than theirs. Economically, they are everywhere besieged: whereas incomes increased by 150 percent between 1972 and 1987, housing cost nearly tripled and social security and state taxes soared (Light 1988, 46). A few polls found this sense of economic malaise. A 1986 CBS/New York Times poll of 30- to 39-year-olds found that a third thought they had accomplished less than they had anticipated when they were in high school; Harris's 1984 poll confirmed Easterlin's insight: almost three quarters of the baby boomers thought their generation faced more competition from their contemporaries for jobs and promotions; Roper's 1986 poll found half the baby boomers agreeing that the American dream was harder to reach now than a generation ago (Light 1988, 72–73).

The attitude you might expect from the historical experiences of these people is disillusionment—even cynicism—and

I found a good deal of that in my conversations with these people. We saw it in the first chapter with Bill Abernathy, born in 1950. Recall how he thought he had been part of a corporate community until he experienced a round of brutally executed layoffs; the pain of disillusionment comes through in his remarks as he talks about his realization that "That's not really how it was and . . . you want to say, 'God, am I stupid for believing this . . . was I naive or . . . did the company really take an about face, did they turn on us?'"

He is representative of his generation and his times, a man caught between two worlds, struggling with older ideas of loyalty and new realities, of early promise and present day, harsher realities:

> I had no problem defending RLX. I call that loyalty, but, I don't know, the whole thing seems to just dissolve around you to where, if you did all those things, that was no longer any guarantee that you were going to be here next Monday. That did not save you from the ax. Now, talking a little about DRI, . . . my salary is almost stagnant. You know, what I'm making today, if I stay with DRI, over the next 10 years, with their new salary structure . . . my salary is not going to be increasing. It's going to be relatively stagnant and I'm now faced with that specter . . . considering (that) the next ten years, will be the greatest financial burden of my life and that's a scary proposition. So, you know, it's very, very hard to say that . . . I owe this company anything . . .

Not all were as bitter as Bill, but I found a surprising amount of disillusionment and cynicism in cohort 2, attitudes virtually absent from my cohort 1 subjects. Listen to Ed Jurgen, a generally cheerful and optimistic sales manager, a veteran and professedly loyal employee talking about the time just before the acquisition. I asked him if the acquisition changed his opinion of the company:

> Yeah, I think it did. I really think it did because and that was somewhat of a gradual shift because, on the one hand, as a manager you understand what the point of view of somebody in the shoes of (RLX's CEO) is, you know. You don't show your cards to everybody you're playing poker with, but at the same time, I mean he made these . . . fairly clear statements of . . . no intention of selling off any more divisions and I think we heard that every time they sold off another . . . By that point no one really felt surprised and no one really believed him that there was any doubt that they would sell us off if they needed to.

Such attitudes are clearly destructive of loyalty, as we can see with our next interlocutor, Jane Light, who talks of experiences of disillusionment as well. First note her evocation of something very like Erich Fromm's "magic helper":

> I think when I was younger I expected like a lot of young people do, I think—and especially used to—that my employer would be more of like a good parent for me. Would take care of me. I don't expect that anymore.

A number of these subjects talked about the magic helper, always in terms of a naive illusion they once had. One put it very succinctly, saying he once believed that "the company . . . had a plan for you, that there was some sort of, you know, God-like presence that was defining everyone's particular career path."

I asked Jane Light why she felt disillusioned and she gave her reasons for loyalty lost:

> Well I think for me it's several things, one of which is experience. I mean . . . I have watched myself and other people get booted out the door so many times that after a while you say, "Well OK, I got to look out for number one . . . They're not looking out for me, so I got to look out for myself." But part of it I think is almost a societal thing. Sort of everybody for themselves kind of attitude and I think companies used to be more loyal to their employees. Especially in the last few years I think it's gotten even worse in the last several years with this whole American business, "lean and mean" attitude and "produce or you're out the door" and you know that kind of thing. . . . I've seen a lot of incidents . . . of people who are older that have lost their jobs and you know they can't prove it, but it's like they know that their employers can pay someone 28 years old . . . to do the same thing that they do for half as much and you know that undermines your trust in them you know and I've seen a lot of that. . . . I'm 48 years old and I worry, you know, ten years from now, fifteen years from now am I still going to have a job. . . . Am I going to be able to retire and have any kind of comfortable standard of living? . . .

Jane was twenty years old in 1966, still good economic times and the heyday of welfare corporatism, that paternalistic system we shall review in chapter 8. I asked her if she thought things would turn out this way when she was twenty:

> No. . . . When I was twenty I expected to get married and have some man take care of me for the rest of my life, like a lot of

stupid young women do. I mean I didn't act that way . . . I worked most of the time. . . . always saw myself as a working person, but it's like in the back of my mind and a lot of women's minds . . . it's like there's this safety net. . . .

The cohort 2 folk, between two worlds, expressed different conceptions of loyalty, really not loyalty at all as we have defined it in chapter 5: it is articulated much more as a bargain, a commercial transaction, than the emotion of a lasting attachment that we saw so clearly with Dennis Madison, who kept working beyond retirement and the need for the income. In fact, my survey showed that cohort 2 has a statistically significantly lower level of organizational commitment than cohort 1.[3] Let us listen a little more to the baby boomers' attitudes on loyalty. I have just asked Tim Wright to tell me of his reaction to the acquisition; note his feeling that loyalty is a type of bargain or contract:

it wouldn't surprise me that they wouldn't sell (it) or that they wouldn't do some layoffs, restructuring, and so on. None of that surprised me. All along, for a long, long, long time I've felt like it's only worth so much loyalty and so much dedication to a company because, you only have so much (coming) back to you too. You know what I'm saying? As long as it's good for you, it seems you should work hard and do the best you can because that's kind of how they're going to view you as an employee, as long as it works for them, they pay you well, they treat you well and if push ever comes to shove and they need to lay off some people, I mean you could just be laid off. . . .

Al Preston has a similar sense of the "new" idea of loyalty. Note also that he, too, evokes the "magic helper" in a disillusioned way. He is telling me about the company's use of the new reengineering management practice and how it affected his attitudes.

It showed me that your job is never secure. If they want to come in and they want to change it, they think they can do with less people, a new different way of doing business that they could get rid of you anytime . . . So you have to—you don't get the feeling that you're going to be here long-term with the company. Like with RLX I felt . . . if I stayed there long enough I could retire early and that didn't happen. I mean when they sold us to DRI, that sort of woke me up . . . to think . . . the fact that I had planned to retire early, that the company can do something like

> that and you don't have any control over it . . . So, you just have to . . . do the best you can. Plan more on yourself than let the company plan for you.

Al said his loyalty had changed with his "wake-up call"; he no longer believes in the "magic helper" and sees his "loyalty" only in instrumental terms: effort for pay:

> I'm loyal in a different way. In other words, I'm not going to believe now the company is going to take care of me when I retire. I believe now that I have to take care of myself, but I will give my best effort for the company while they're paying me to complete the job or to do a job or to pay me to exceed that job if I have to. But I'm not going to think that the company's going to nowadays . . . take care of you like they did in the past. . . . It's a whole new environment that we're in. . . . When I first started at RLX I got the feeling that the company was there to take care of me and I should work hard and help take care of the company. . . . Really now the new environment is . . . if they're not making money, then they'll . . . do whatever it takes to make a profit and that includes cutting back on employees or benefits . . . So you don't get the same warm and fuzzy feeling that you did years ago . . . But at the same time you realize that getting paid for a job, then you have to do the job and so you've got a different type of loyalty to the company.

Here from Jerry Austin is more on the baby boomers' definition of loyalty:

> I think that the word takes on different meanings, depending on what the topic is. If we're talking about family, that's a whole set of values that I have. Family's first, you know. After my faith in God comes family and the rest—everything else—goes to hell.

Jerry describes how it used to be for him at work:

> I think I was much more "anything to help out." Anything, always, always going the extra mile. I don't want this to sound that I'm not dedicated or hard-working because I think I am. I'm here enough Saturdays and Sundays . . . but I've seen too many instances of individuals who have been with the company a number of years, they're three years from retirement . . . and like fire you and hire two college students . . . and still have a net savings . . . Bye. Or . . . an article in the paper today about (a company). . . . they laid off eighty-nine people this week, you know. Three weeks before Christmas . . . That's not company loyalty to employees..

I've seen so much of that in the corporate world . . . A perfect example: Sealey Mattress Company. . . . the union contract said if you do not work the day before a holiday, you do not get paid for the holiday. So the plant manager laid everybody off before the day before so that he wouldn't have to pay them for the holiday. Now what's that? . . . Should those people be loyal? . . ."

The examples abound—examples of a sense of trust betrayed, of their loyalty exposed as folly and naïveté by the actions of callous company managers. One of my interlocutors could speak for all when he said: "You get up to some point above you in the chain of command and basically the people down there are numbers."

The baby boomers are different from cohort 1; we have seen it in their measured attitudes and in the subjective sense we get from their words. They are different in that they had a quite different response to the layoffs and restructurings. Cohort 1 folk, with a strong foundation of loyal attitudes, survived these events with loyalty largely intact, but those of cohort 2, socialized in a different time, lost their faith under the pressures of these events. And, as we shall see further on, cohort 3 people reacted differently again: they were relatively indifferent to the events which shattered cohort 2's world view, and took it for granted that companies would act solely in their economic interests.

Our cohort 2 friends are different as well in their satisfaction with their jobs. Job satisfaction is not the same as commitment or loyalty, it is not the sense of identification with the company's goals and values, but simply satisfaction with the employment situation. People can be satisfied with their work—or dissatisfied—for many, many reasons: pay, benefits, a friendly environment, a job which is not taxing, etc. Job satisfaction was highly correlated with organizational commitment in my survey, an unsurprising finding, since those who are loyal would be expected to be satisfied as well, although the equation does not work in reverse: many are satisfied with the pay and ease of the job, without any sense of loyalty.

Cohort 2 was found to have lower job satisfaction than Cohort 1—significantly lower.[4] There is a substantial literature on job satisfaction, much of it controversial, stemming from assertions made in the 1973 report, *Work In America: Report of a Special Task Force to the Secretary of Health, Educa-*

tion, and Welfare (O'Toole et al. 1973). Those authors used opinion data that seemed to show that American workers were mostly dissatisfied with their jobs. Other polls seemed to contradict this: Gallup has surveyed work attitudes for over forty years with the simple question: "On the whole, how satisfied are you with the work you do?" The surveys indicate a very stable (and high: near 80%) level of job satisfaction since the early sixties (Flanagan et al. 1974). And Veroff et al.'s massive longitudinal survey (2460 workers in 1957 and 2267 in 1976) concluded, "By and large, people in 1957 and 1976 give very comparable responses on how satisfied or dissatisfied they are with their work" (Veroff et al. 1981, 542). Job satisfaction is, as I said, not loyalty nor commitment, not even an indicator of performance and effort. In fact, it has been suggested that the stability of high levels of job satisfaction is merely attributable to reasonably benign conditions: adequate pay, undemanding tasks and leisurely pace (Lincoln and Kalleberg 1990, 25).

But nonetheless, there have been signs of a general decline in satisfaction, signaled by fewer people responding "very satisfied" and more simply saying "satisfied." In the 1990 Gallup poll 89 percent expressed some degree of satisfaction, but only 28 percent were completely satisfied (Kalb and Hugick 1990, 21). In my survey, 72 percent were "very" or "somewhat" satisfied, but fewer than 19 percent were "very" satisfied. Other researchers have also noted what I found: job satisfaction rates are related to birth cohort: Glenn and Weaver report "very persuasive, although not absolutely conclusive evidence for important cohort effects, whereby each birth cohort . . . has been less inclined to be satisfied with work than the one before it" (Glenn and Weaver 1985, 89). There are a variety of possible explanations: older people are more stoical, and thus less likely to express dissatisfaction; or, being dissatisfied with one's work would be an unbearable psychological burden for those raised to value work—in other words, the theory of cognitive dissonance could account for this. Or, younger people may have been more influenced by pop psychology and self-help literature which exhorts them to express their "true" feelings (Glenn and Weaver 1985, 91). This last possibility assumes, of course, that everyone is dissatisfied, but the younger are just more willing to articulate it. But there is another explanation, one that seems to fit the data that I have assembled: the people of cohort 1, those of the old dispensation, are more satisfied because they are more loyal; they gain satisfaction from working for a firm which has inspired their loyalty. If nothing else, the very high correlation between commitment (loyalty) and job satisfaction would buttress this explanation. Let us look further at poll results, but rather than the present day, let us look at results from the 1960s to try to gauge what the mood was when our cohort 2 subjects were coming to maturity.

Some Survey Results from the Sixties

In the 1960s, Americans experienced a sharp mood swing: the dominant attitudes changed abruptly in the middle to late 60s, moving toward critical, even cynical views of society and its most important institutions. Daniel Yankelovich called it "an explosive increase in public mistrust, resentment, and cynicism, an erosion of confidence in national institutions, and an upsurge in feelings of powerlessness" (Yankelovich 1975, 761). In a dramatic turnaround from the 1950s, by the mid-1970s the majority of Americans were expressing opinions very like those of the radical college youth and civil rights protesters of the 1960s.

The shifts in opinion occurred across the board: everything from alienation (the sense of powerlessness) to trust in others. But nowhere is the shift more dramatic and apparently enduring than in confidence in American institutions, institutions of all varieties. The best way to see this is to look at figure 6–1. It presents the average confidence in institutional leadership for all important American institutions: government, business, medicine, science, education, media, etc.

There is a reasonably good fit of this data (R-squared = .494) to an exponential model, indicating a "half-life" of 26 to 27 years, i.e., every twenty-five years or so confidence in institutions dropped by half. If we just look at the critical period—1966 to 1977—the half life is only fifteen years. (And the fit is better: R-squared = .756). In fifteen years, confidence was halved.

The fate of confidence in the institution of business has been even worse than these composite figures we have seen. A Yankelovich survey asked for agreement to the statement: "Business tries to strike a fair balance between profits and the interests of the public." In 1968, 70 percent surveyed

FIGURE 6-1
Confidence in Institutional Leaders, 1966–1986

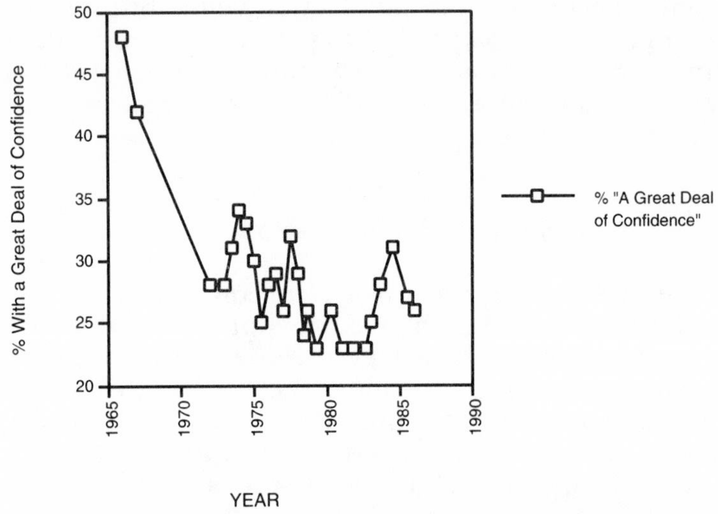

SOURCE: Lipset and Schneider 1987, 50

agreed. In 1969, it was 58 percent and in 1970 it was only 33 percent—less than half the number of only two years earlier (Lipset and Schneider 1987, 183). Charles Pearson, one of my cohort 2 subjects, born in 1951, addressed this point on profits in saying:

> I think a lot of companies have lost the trust of their people or the people lost trust in the company they worked for. I think Corporate America . . . has changed because . . . the bottom line anymore, it's profit. . . . I think we put too much emphasis on the almighty dollar—greed.

Charles is a ten-year veteran of Softmatics, but says his loyalty has waned over the years, and in fact his measured value of commitment was 2.7. (3.0 is "neutral"; 2.0 is "somewhat uncommitted.") He might be an exemplar for the American loss of faith in institutional leadership, the sense that authority has feet of clay. Listen:

> A lot of changes in the last 25 or 30 years I've seen and I know my parents have said things were different when they were grow-

ing up and maybe it's just the way things progress with time, but it seems like to me that people that are in high positions, they make rules that their . . . subordinates should govern themselves by [but] that in their minds . . . shouldn't be applied to them . . . I've seen a lot of that.

Somewhere and somehow, many Americans have "seen a lot of that." The roots of this disaffection are complex, especially when we realize that confidence, trust, and social cohesion *all* plummeted in the 1960s. A popular explanation, the effects of singular events such as Vietnam and Watergate, does not really suffice. For example, mistrust of the federal government began to grow in the early 1960s, well before the Vietnam buildup and Nixon. In 1958 only 12 percent distrusted the government; this more than doubled to 27 percent by 1968 and doubled again in five years to 51 percent in 1971. And it is difficult to ascribe the climate of distrust and loss of confidence solely to events when we realize that it was not just government, but business, the courts, the professions, the military, and the educational establishment—-all saw a great fall from grace beginning in the early to middle 1960s. By 1975, nine out of ten expressed a generalized mistrust of "those in power" (Yankelovich 1975, 761).

Along with this loss of confidence in institutions, there went a rise in feelings of alienation. In the mid-1960s about one third of the people felt that way, but by 1975 a Harris poll found a majority feeling "neglected, impotent, manipulated . . . and convinced that 'what they think does not really count'" (Yankelovich 1975, 762).

It was not always so. Poll data from the 1930s through the early 1960s show a steady, upward trend in approval of American society and government. There was a low point in the 1930s, but America weathered that confidence storm and steadily raised its approval of institutions up to the high-water mark in the early 1960s, when a large majority expressed approval and confidence. Trust in government was almost 80 percent in the late 1950s; it fell to 33 percent in 1976. Confidence in business was at 70 percent, as we saw; in the late 1980s it was 15 percent. Lipset and Schneider, who did a very detailed analysis of polls on confidence, concluded:

The change is simply massive. Within a ten to fifteen year period, trust in institutions has plunged down and down, from an almost

FIGURE 6-2
Percentage Favorable to 22 Large Companies, 1959–1977

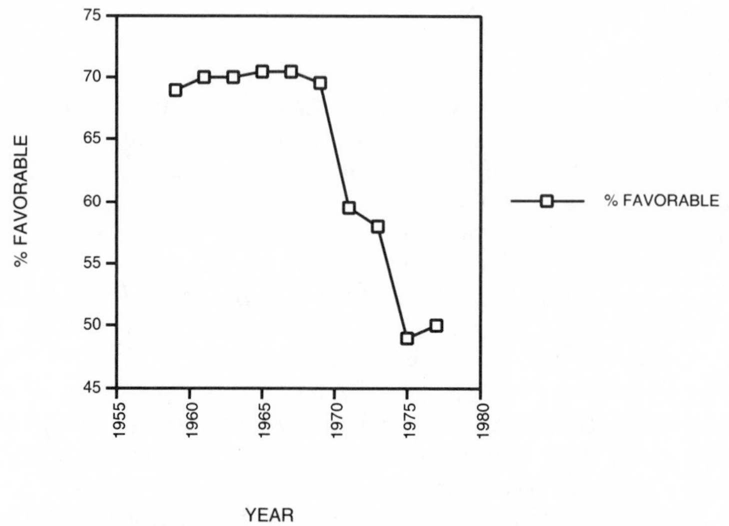

SOURCE: Opinion Research Corporation, Lipset and Schneider 1987, 35-6

consensual majority, two-thirds or more, to minority segments of the American public. (Lipset and Schneider 1987, 15).

It took ten or fifteen years for confidence to erode, for trust to evaporate and for alienation to grow to majority proportions. But there was clearly a distinct turning point, an "inflection point" in the curve, and that was somewhere between about 1965 and 1975, when the average cohort 2 person was between seventeen and twenty-seven. Just leaf through the figures on the following pages and see how trust in government and business, trust in other people, alienation—how they all turned sour in the middle to late 1960s. Figure 6–2 is representative, showing the sharp break in the public mood toward just one institution: large companies. But the story is the same for other institutions, and for levels of mistrust and feelings of alienation, as shown in the other figures which conclude this chapter.

For more than twenty-five years, from the trough in the Depression, Americans had increased their faith in the system and its bureaucratic values. That system and those values

FIGURE 6-3
Mean Confidence in Ten Institutions, 1966–1973

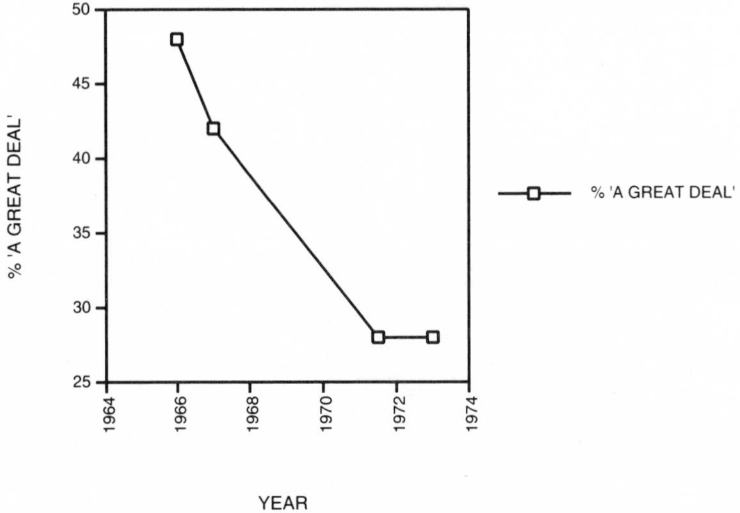

SOURCE: Harris and NORC Surveys. (Lipset and Schneider 1987, 50

carried them through the Depression, won them the war, and brought them great prosperity well into the 1960s. Then, the faith was lost. Why? What happened? We shall look for some answers to that question in the next two chapters.

FIGURE 6-4
Percentage Agreeing 'Cannot Trust the Government' 1957–1974

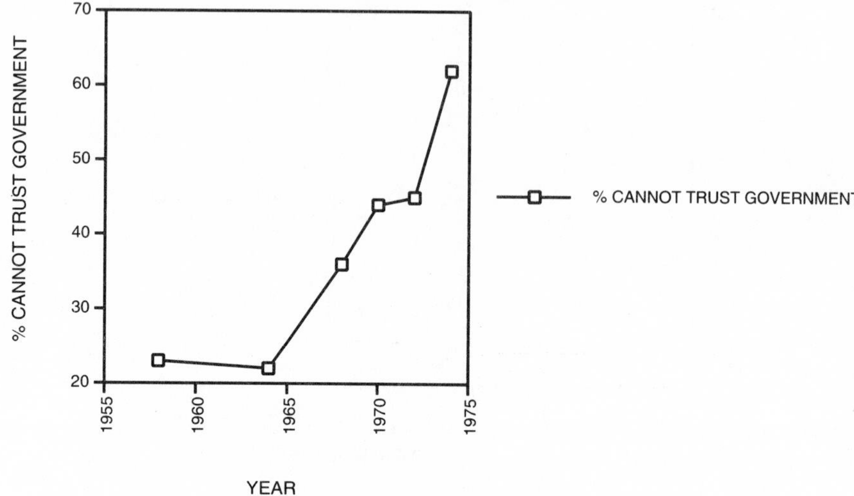

SOURCE: Lipset & Schneider 1987, 17

FIGURE 6-5
Social Trust, 1960–1978

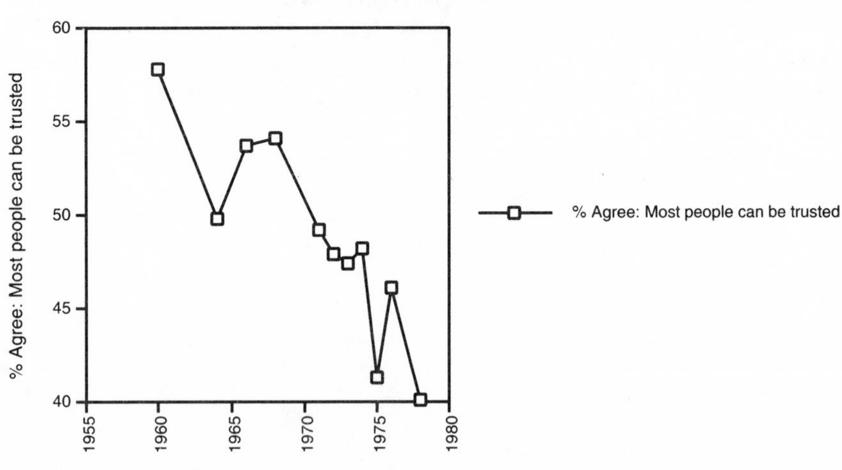

SOURCE: Uslaner 1993, 79

FIGURE 6-6
Social Alienation, 1966–1976

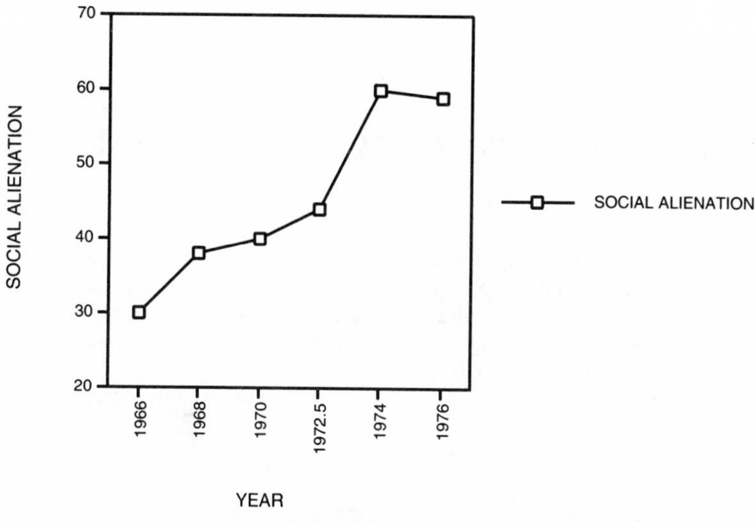

SOURCE: Putnam 1994

7

"The Long Unraveling, The Fresh Start"

> *One can see the late Sixties as a long unraveling, a fresh start, a tragicomic Kulturkampf, the overdue demolition of a fraudulent consensus, a failed upheaval, an unkept promise, a valiant effort at reforms camouflaged as revolution—and it was all of these.*
>
> —*Gitlin, The Sixties*

The Sixties

HISTORICAL epochs seldom follow our arbitrary calendar; for example, some say the "twentieth century" began with the outbreak of World War I. And when we speak of the "Sixties," most often we mean a period of social, political, and cultural change which began roughly with John Kennedy's death in November 1963 and ended with Nixon's resignation in August 1974. In that brief period, American society changed profoundly, lending to the 1950s, in nostalgic memory, an aura of placid assurance and confidence. Back in that time before the "Fire," most Americans were proud of their country, sure of its future, enjoying unprecedented affluence and mass consumption, and commanding the high ground in the world—politically, militarily, and, it seemed, morally. In the space of ten to twelve years, that complacency came tumbling down. Many place-names now have a portentous ring for Americans who lived through those years: My Lai, Selma, Watts, Detroit, Kent State, Berkeley, Chicago, Woodstock, Haight-Ashbury. And this was the era of sit-ins, teach-ins, demonstrations, riots, bombs. It was the era, too, of movements of all descriptions: civil rights, black power, native Americans, the new left, women's lib, the antiwar movement. Every conceivable aspect of American society and its institutions came under attack, every flaw in the system was raucously exposed. Bad news came from every quarter: cities decaying, public schools no longer functioning, the economy in stagflation, unemployment, drug abuse. Solutions of every variety abounded, the more bizarre the more hearkened to: the charismatic religious movement, est, astrology, Zen, mind-expanding drugs (Gerlach and Hine 1973, 4–5).

The sixties are remembered often for the counterculture and some of its naive and gentle messages, but there was a good deal more to these times than Woodstock and the Haight. It was an exceptionally violent time, with conspiracy trials, political violence on both the left and right, the Weathermen, the hard hats beating hippies and war protesters, riots and burnings in Watts and Detroit, political assassinations: John Kennedy, Robert Kennedy, Martin Luther King, Jr., and protests, incessant protests (Light 1988, 184).

What were they protesting against? At times it seemed like everything: the war in Vietnam, the university system, minority oppression. Perhaps they were just opposing the adult world, because, in one sense, it was a protest against the kind of society that had developed in America, the society of which so many adults were proud of and grateful for in the 1950s. Louis Galambos asserts that it was a protest against nothing less than that bureaucratic society and its values, the corporate culture which had been forming since the 1880s. Galambos argues:

> Central to the New Left movement and its opposition to big business were the close ties . . . between . . . foreign policy and the large corporation. . . . Woven into this new critique were other, more subtle charges. Students rejected the bureaucratic lifestyle, and tie-dyed jeans expressed the contempt many felt. . . . The counterculture was braced against bureaucracy. In music, dress, and political action, young Americans fought a highly organized, impersonal system that seemed to control their future without regard to their feelings, goals, or even their lives. (Galambos 1975, 267)

And nowhere was that impersonal system so threatening to the young than in the Vietnam war. Kennedy had begun the U.S. involvement in the war, but it was left to Lyndon Johnson to "escalate" the American presence and bring on the storm of protest. As early as 17 April 1965, twenty-five thousand students marched in protest on Washington—at a time when there were only 25,000 troops in Vietnam. But by the end of 1965 there were 184,000, and then the relentless buildup took off: 385,000 by the end of 1966; 486,000 by the end of 1967. The American armed forces mercilessly pummeled a small and backward country; by the end of 1967, nearly two million acres of land had been defoliated; a million and a half tons of bombs had rained down on North and South Vietnam.

Fifteen thousand young American servicemen had been killed by the end of 1967 and the protests became larger, more shrill, and more violent. In April 1967, Martin Luther King, Jr. denounced the war to a New York City rally estimated at 400,000 people. Color images of the war's horror and brutality opened every evening television news. Draft cards were burned, young men fled to Canada and Sweden, the Pentagon was besieged by thousands of protesters (Gitlin 1989, 242).

The war in Vietnam certainly mobilized protest, but more than that, it crystallized for many a once-vague sense that something was wrong with society, a sense that had been developing long before the war seemed to confirm it. But for every antiwar protester there were scores of young people who seemed interested only in personal fulfillment, living out their hopes and fantasies of a more abundant life, a life of free expression of their personalities, a revival of individualism aimed at realizing their potential (Clecak 1983, 9–10). Vietnam helped shake confidence in American political institutions, but it was the counterculture of the 1960s which has cast the longer shadow on American attitudes. Perhaps St. Paul was right: "God hath chosen the foolish things of the world to confound the wise" (I Corinthians, 1: 27). Let us turn now to that "foolish" enterprise, the counterculture of the Sixties.

The Counterculture

When I refer to the "counterculture" of the 1960s, I intend that eruption of new lifestyles and rejection of old norms, rather than the antiwar movement and New Left, which shared the same historical stage, and indeed overlapped a good deal in membership with the counterculture folk. My thesis is that it was the values and beliefs held by a relatively small number of these young Americans in the 1960s that became dominant beliefs in a later time, and those new attitudes were to sweep away the bureaucratic values and corporate culture that had slowly come to prominence by the end of the Second World War.

Countercultures are an historically rare but not unknown phenomena; the social and cultural change of the 1960s was not unique when we consider what is meant by the term. Ideologically, a counterculture is the rejection of a society's dominant value system and the proffer of an alternative set. This may be, and often is, accompanied by behavior which is radically nonconformist (Yinger 1982, 9). The Christians of the second century displayed both this ideological and behavioral deviation from the dominant Roman society, and did so in so public and disturbing a manner that many were martyred for it.

In the 1960s, an observer from afar might have concluded that the "hippies" had made a close study of the American middle class and determined to behave and think in diametrically opposite ways. Our observer would have seen a "carnival of youthful rebellion that embraced every conceivable negation of the dominant values and mores of the WASP culture of the 1950s. . ." (Clecak 1983, 51). One analyst, writing in 1971, saw this *Alice in Wonderland* quality in all the counterculture beliefs:

> Immediacy *contra* past preoccupation and future concern; the natural . . . *contra* the artificial . . . the colorful and baroque *contra* the classical . . . the direct *contra* the mediated . . . the spontaneous *contra* the structured; the primitive *contra* the sophisticated; the mystical *contra* the scientific; the egalitarian *contra* the hierarchical. . . (F. Davis, cited in Yinger 1982, 10)

And it could be viewed in those purely negative terms: the negation of intellectualism and rationality, of the ethic of labor and responsibility, of the norms of family obligations and sexual behavior (Yinger 1982, 21). Or, it could be seen by some, even in the older generation, as a long-overdue end to the dead hand of repression.

I have touched a bit on the ideology of the counterculture, and I will return to that, but for now let us look a bit more closely about the behavioral side, the lifestyle aspect, the young free at last to shape their own lives, no matter how bizarre. The dress, tastes, and lifestyles of the young had been changing in ways largely unnoticed by the adult world for some time, but the counterculture first became "news" in early 1967. On 14 January of that year, the "Human Be-In" was staged in San Francisco's Golden Gate Park. It was billed as "The Gathering of the Tribes," an invitation to the discontented of any persuasion. The politically minded students from Berkeley mingled with Haight-Ashbury dropouts, Hare Krishnas and local teenagers. Apocalyptic and ecstatic messages were the order of the day, and the theme was the unity of all opposed to the dominant culture: Hell's Angels and Free Speech advocates, Allen Ginsberg and Timothy Leary, Jerry Rubin from the New Left, the Jefferson Airplane and the Grateful Dead. Leary, dressed in white with flowers in his hair, exhorted all to "turn on, tune in, drop out." Ginsberg chanted a Buddhist mantra and told the crowd that "We are primitives of an unknown culture." But the crowd itself was the real show: free food, tinkling bells, balloons, incense, harmonicas, flutes, and guitars. *Newsweek* set the tone for the national media, reporting that it was "a love feast, a psychedelic picnic, a hippie happening" (Roszak 1969, 275–76).

Much had happened already before the national news awoke to the counterculture. Ken Kesey and his Merry Pranksters had helped set the styles in the early 1960s, then joined with the Grateful Dead in a series of concerts, "The Acid Test." The objective was to form a new consciousness, opening the mind to new ways of thinking through LSD, music, and visual experiences. Light shows, the participants' very costumes, the drugs and music, all violently assaulted the senses and purportedly induced new states of consciousness. The clothing styles were lurid; Day-Glo paint adorned everything. Free LSD—still legal in California—was distributed at the concerts. In January 1965, Kesey and the Pranksters mounted the "Trips Festival" at Longshoreman's Hall in San Francisco, and drew 20,000 celebrants in wild costumes. For more than a year, teenage dropouts had been drifting into the old working class Haight-Ashbury district, and with Kesey's festival they discovered their numbers and built a community of sorts on drugs, music, libertinism, and bizarre clothing. By the summer of 1967, the Haight was big news nationally. *Time* magazine did a feature article and the adult world everywhere psychoanalyzed, ridiculed, and condemned the movement, or looked on with bemused detachment (Matusow 1984, 202 and 301). 1967 was in a way the high-water mark: the Be-In, San Francisco's Summer of Love, the first edition of *Rolling Stone*, the Beatles' "Sergeant Pepper," Dustin Hoffman in *The Graduate,* turning off to the bureaucratic culture and seeking some other meaning for his life.

But as the media trumpeted the new Haight culture, it was already disintegrating. The San Francisco police, concerned about the runaways, rousted the "freaks" unmercifully; the New Left used the kids as cannon fodder in increasingly violent demonstrations. As Haight-Ashbury fell to violence and exploitation, across the country another event revived the movement: Woodstock. In August 1969, 400,000 gathered for three days for a peaceful and loving celebration of sex, drugs, and rock 'n' roll. But just four months later at the Altamont racetrack in California, the dark side of the counterculture showed its face. The Rolling Stones put on a free concert to climax their American tour and drew 300,000 young people. The scene was chaotic: an inadequate sound system irked the crowd, sanitary facilities were poor, a great deal of bad drugs circulated. The Hell's Angels, ostensibly the security force, clubbed people indiscriminately, and stabbed a young man to death only a few feet from Mick Jagger's performance of "Sympathy for the Devil." All of this was captured on film and made into a popular documentary, exposing the dark side of the counterculture's rejection of all norms (Matusow 1984, 302–4).

Haight-Ashbury died, and Altamont horrified the adult world, but the counterculture did not disappear. In the late 1960s and early 1970s, the message of sex, drugs, and rock 'n' roll seduced ever more of the young. When the counterculture generation looks back, the things they remember most were, of course, the music, drugs, and the radical politics, but also the sense of unity with other young people and the feeling of "cutting loose" from the old culture and its values (Weiner and Stillman 1979, 31).

Where had the counterculture come from; how did the placid fifties turn into the raucous sixties? The sources of the counterculture are complex, and not reducible to any one thing, surely not just the availability of cheap drugs and amplified music. Theorists of social change dispute among themselves on the influence of a variety of factors: the spread of ideas, demographics, education, charismatic figures, precipitating events, educational levels, and exposure to certain institutions. I believe that each of these mechanisms played a part in the emergence of the counterculture.

We have already covered one of the proximate causes of change in chapter 6, i.e., the affluence of the postwar era coupled with an exceptionally large birth cohort that gave rise to a generation that saw itself as unique, a "generational" unit in Mannheim's terms. And the counterculture folk were overwhelmingly from the middle class, able to postpone the need to make a living and indulge their quest for self-expression (Weiner and Stillman 1979, 4). The counterculture can also be read as a widespread cognitive shift, what Weber and Comte suggested as the root cause of social change. Bernice Martin has taken up this line of analysis and asserts that the counterculture is the culmination of a long tradition of thought whose principles were formed in the Romantic era, at the beginnings of the modern age. The counterculture, in this view, was nothing more than the acceptance of values long held by intellectuals and culture-makers, the ideals of the primacy of the self, expressiveness and radical individualism. With rising educational levels, these once elite ideas became the common coin of mass consciousness (Martin 1981, 1–2). The prophecy of Joseph Schumpeter seemed to be working itself out:

> capitalism creates a critical frame of mind which, having destroyed the moral authority of so many other institutions in the end turns against its own; the bourgeois finds to his amazement that the rationalist attitude does not stop at the credentials of kings and popes but goes on to attack . . . (the) whole scheme of bourgeois values. (Schumpeter 1950, 143)

Max Weber placed great weight on the influence of charismatic figures as agents of social change. (Weber, 1947, 43). We can see such an influence first in those harbingers of the counterculture, the Beats. The reason they had influence and the reason we know of this small and marginal group at all is simply because they had the good fortune to include a number of talented writers: Kerouac, Burroughs, Ginsberg. Their group formed in the early 1950s around Columbia University, young and disaffected men rebelling against the bland and purposeless culture of mass consumption and repression of instincts. They explored the limits of consciousness in music and drugs, inspired by the earlier black hipster culture of the 1940s: cool jazz devotees, without sexual inhibitions, "into" drugs, and into alienation. Ginsburg especially became the hippie saint, his *Howl* their anthem and rallying cry against "Moloch," the technological and bureaucratic society. With Ginsberg, Jack Kerouac came to San Francisco and found other like-minded people, and long before the Human Be-In, a hippie culture was developing in the Bay Area, with the Beats as the charismatic exemplars (Matusow 1984, 280–84).

The counterculture is always described as revolt and rebellion, but we must return to an earlier question: what were they rebelling against? The Brando motorcycle-punk character in the 1953 film *The Wild One* was asked just that question, and he replied: "Whatta ya got?" Well, with the appearance of Ginsberg's *Howl* in 1955, the question was answered definitively. It was "Moloch! Nightmare of Moloch! Moloch the loveless!" (Gitlin 1989, 46). Moloch was an acute symbol, since that Phoenician god received the sacrifice of children burned alive. Moloch was for Ginsberg the symbol of modern industrial society, which made burnt offerings of its children on the altar of economic efficiency and materialism. Robert Wiebe in his *The Search for Order* has described the long process by which American society had bureaucratized itself as it sought to deal with the increased complexities of industrial production and the attendant urbanization. But with those bureaucratic solutions, a great divide formed, between the impersonal, rational bureaucratic values of the office, and the expressive values of private life. The counterculture revolted against this dichotomy, and sought to bring expressive values into all spheres of human life (Tipton 1982, 20). In particular, it revolted against the "technocracy," and it was the ever-present, insistent contact with the institutions of a technological and bureaucratic world that fed their resentment. Reason and order were eschewed, the young followed the advice of Norman O. Brown to give in to "the life instinct, or sexual instinct," to approach the world in the spirit of play, uniting oneself with the world "based not on anxiety and aggression, but on narcissism and erotic exuberance" (N. O. Brown 1959, 307).

Brown's prescription is a far cry from the spirit of the technocracy, whose *raison d'etre* has always been efficiency. Bureaucracy itself is a form of technology, a set of techniques for the efficient control of people's work. In the modern world, technology has provided many other techniques to control and manipulate people, everything from psychologically researched advertisements, to the distortion of information in the news media, to psychotherapy. This is Ginsberg's Moloch writ large: the subjective evaluation of persons is lost; the objective rules and procedures reduce the person to an abstraction, an object of the technique, sacrificing him to the need for efficiency (Stivers 1994, 10 and 73). As early as 1962 the young articulated their fear of and disdain for the technocracy in SDS's Port Huron statement:

> We regard men as infinitely precious and possessed of unfulfilled capacities for reason, freedom and love . . . We oppose the depersonalization that reduces human beings to the status of things. (Roszak 1969, 58)

That technologically based efficiency represents a danger has been the main concern of Jacques Ellul. Ellul notes that it is pointless and childish to be opposed to *la technique*, it is ineluctable, like cancer or an avalanche. Like Smith's Invisible Hand and Gramsci's hegemony, there is no conspiracy—just a natural development within the order of things. But nonetheless, the spread of technique is a serious danger to human morality and freedom, and if we cannot master it, it will master us (Ellul 1990, xiii–xiv).

Ellul is optimistic that men will be intelligent enough and courageous enough to rein in technology and use it to better society. But in the counterculture, many just turned their backs on the modern industrial world. The Diggers of Haight-Ashbury employed street theater to ram home their antimodern message, proclaiming "The Death of Money and the Birth of Free," burning dollar bills and distributing flutes, flowers, and food to all comers. They lived out Proudhon's dictum, *la propriété, c'ést le vol*, and stole it back, ladling out stolen beef stew every day in Golden Gate Park and operating a "Free Store" with "liberated" goods. It was all theater, a deliberate attempt to instruct the young on the fallacies and dangers of the technocratic world of property, money, and oppression (Gitlin 1989, 222–24).

But the influence of the Beats, the spread of new ideas, and the increasingly close contact with the reality of the technocracy would not in themselves have sparked the solidarity of the counterculture and its long reach down to our own day. For that, external events were needed to hold up the old views to a new reality. Social change most often occurs in a societal crisis, when the old norms are thrown into new relief and become problematical. It is then that the long-dormant conflicts in idea systems come to the surface. But the cause of this surfacing is often not something immanent in the society, but is rather due to some extraordinary, external events. It is under the pressure of such events and their effects on lives that the old assumptions often are questioned, the old ideology held up more to scrutiny (Nisbet 1972, 32–34). The event was, of course, the Vietnam war, which focused youthful—and then adult—attention on the shortcomings of American society, exemplifying what was perceived to be wrong with all American institutions.

And so, many of the young of America in the sixties had heard the messages of discontent and liberation, had seen the threat of service in a foreign war and had come to reject a future in a technocratic society they had come to loathe. In Durkheim's term, they were experiencing "anomie," or normlessness. Anomie is the sense that the cultural goals and values of your society are not your goals and values, that the dominant value system is bankrupt. Merton suggests that an individual then can take one of three paths: ritualism, or going through the motions of society's forms, without believing in them; "retreatism," or dropping out; and rebellion (Merton 1968, 140–55 and 217). In rebellion, one does not just reject the dominant value system, one seeks to transform it. That is what much of the sixties was all about for many young people: anomie and rebellion.

But if that is so, what was the new value system that the young proposed to replace the bureaucratic values of their elders? As you would expect in a movement as anarchic as the counterculture, there was a great disparity in values expressed by the counterculture folk. The career of Bob Dylan, the shifting themes of his songs through the 1960s, gives us some insight into countercultural views. Bob Zimmerman from up-country Minnesota, more than anyone else, was admired and heeded by the young of those times. He began in the early 1960s as a folk singer in the Woody Guthrie tradition, singing of social injustices in that singular voice, alerting the young to the plight of the unfortunate in "Blowin' in the Wind," and making them agents of historical change in "The Times They are A-Changin." He mocked Cold War ideology "With God on our Side" and stirred the fears of nuclear war in "Hard Rains Gonna Fall," written during the Cuban missile crisis. But the political and social messages soon gave way to the surrealistic and psychedelic, when Dylan went electronic and spread his messages through the medium of rock 'n' roll. In the spring of 1965, Dylan popularized the message of Norman O. Brown, the call to pure sensuality in his romantic visions of "Mr. Tambourine Man." When "Like a Rolling Stone" was released, Dylan became the Pied Piper for this generation. With sarcasm and bitter words, Dylan mocked the "straight" world, and exalted the counterculture world of kids on the street, rejecting the materialism of the adult world and the selling of souls which paid the price for it.[1] "If you ain't got nothin', you got nothin' to lose." Dylan's influence was enormous; in later years some three-quarters of countercultural folk remembered Dylan most especially as the one they admired and followed (Weiner and Stillman 1979, 79). With his peculiar genius, he could combine the antitechnocratic/bureaucratic message of the Beats with the hedonistic and ecstatic urgings of Norman O. Brown.

Let us look more closely at the counterculture's messages. One survey found five sets of values that seemed to cover the spectrum and were held by most participants; this survey was confirmed by a comparative content analysis of counterculture and mainstream publications.

First there is the "fun ethic" that surely characterized many of the participants, particularly those on the margins who found the new culture a year-round costume party and bacchanal. But beyond fun, there was also the value found in uninhibited relationships and opposition to all constraints. The second set of values revolved around the rejection of the technocracy, the desire for a simple and natural life, exemplified by handicraft production. Third, we have those unmistakable marks of counterculture lifestyle: pop art and music, mysticism, communal living and child-rearing. Fourth are the concerns that Ellul voiced, the worries about runaway technology, pollution, depersonalization by the technocracy. Last was the prototypical countercultural stance: "non-deferential, anarchist, reformist, activist." Here we have the attitudes that are antiauthoritarian and anti-institutional, opposing rules and law enforcement, rejecting the work ethic and the power structure of all American institutions: economic, political, even the family (Yinger 1982, 44–45).

What are we to make of this potpourri of counterculture values? A number of them have rather clear roots in the American tradition. If you admit an admixture of romanticism, the fierce independence and "don't tread on me" stance can be traced to the old strain of American individualism, the supreme value of the individual and his freedom of choices for his life, no matter how odd. The other values, or desires, however, represent a romantic rejection of the modern world: wishing for a simple, nontechnological existence in a communal setting with like-minded people. But this, too, can be seen as an attempt to return to much older American values, those before the bureaucratic culture had become dominant. The desire for community can be expressive of bureaucratic values, but its rejection of technological civilization is really the antithesis of the corporate culture. And the call to communal living had its roots in an old American tradition, the nineteenth-century Utopian communities that sprang up from the inspiration of Robert Owen and Charles Fourier. At one time there were over forty Fourierist *phalasteries* in the United States, and if Owenite and religious communities are counted, there were about 180 Utopian, communal sites. The North American Phalanx thrived between 1843 and 1855 and lingered on until the 1930s; Alexander Wolcott was born there. Nathaniel Hawthorne lived at the Fourierist Brook Farm outside Boston for a short time in 1841. None of these communities ever fulfilled the expectations of their founders to transform American society, but they expressed an impulse for communal living which surfaced again in the 1960s (Heilbroner 1961, 103).

Radical individualism, oddly coupled with a desire for communal living; tolerance of sexual and lifestyle deviancy; antitechnocracy and antiauthority—these antibureaucratic values and beliefs marked the counterculture folk. As we shall see, some of these stood the test of time, and leached into the general consciousness; others became historical oddities. Let us look now at what the counterculture left in its wake.

The Watershed of the Sixties

Did the sixties have any lasting effect, other than a general loosening of moral strictures? It is not uncommon to dismiss the counterculture as having done little but that. After all, the counterculture folk did grow up and go to work, the communes largely disappeared and most people got on with rather ordinary lives.

Did anything change, was this just a Saturnalia, an interlude? Some dismiss it as such. But it was a lot more than that; in fact, it was a general cultural transformation that had effects reaching into our own day. Because in a very large sense, the dominant culture in time came to absorb the counterculture. The quest for a new social reality led America on a voyage through some strange times and we had to hearken to some odd figures.

A great deal changed on that voyage: some superficial things, like gutter language acceptable in "polite" society; some more profound, like tolerance for promiscuity and divorce. "Recreational" drugs became acceptable to many and sexual "perversions" were no longer thought of as such (Matusow 1984, 306).

At least as late as 1979, a Harris survey revealed strong support for counterculture themes: 89 percent said they wanted experiences that made them feel "peaceful inside"; 81 percent wanted to be involved in activities "where people cooperate rather than compete"; 91 percent wanted "ample opportunities to use their creative talents"; 72 percent preferred "breaking up big things and getting back to more humanized living" (Yinger 1982, 46). And beyond this self-focus, the counterculture and various liberation movements of the 1960s left permanent changes in other attitudes, important changes in attitudes toward women, minorities, homosexuals (Ladd and Lipset 1980, 2).

But perhaps the most important legacy of the sixties was the seemingly permanent effect that the antiauthoritarian stance has had on American attitudes. "A loose antiauthoritarianism was normalized" (Gitlin 1989, 431). Many at the time dismissed the 1960s assault on virtually all American institutions as the rantings of social deviants who wanted to indulge themselves and avoid responsibility. But the critiques of the government and other authorities, once thought bizarre, began to resonate with many ordinary Americans as the Vietnam war and Watergate unfolded. We have seen the high marks that Americans had given government, business, and other institutions through the 1950s. Americans had become accustomed to trusting and valuing their institutional leadership, had become socialized for just that. The countercultural antiauthoritarian critique seemed mindless and destructive to those brought up in an older way of thinking. But events, amazingly, seemed to confirm the "folly" of the freaks.

FIGURE 7-1
Mean Confidence in Institutional Leaders
1966–1974

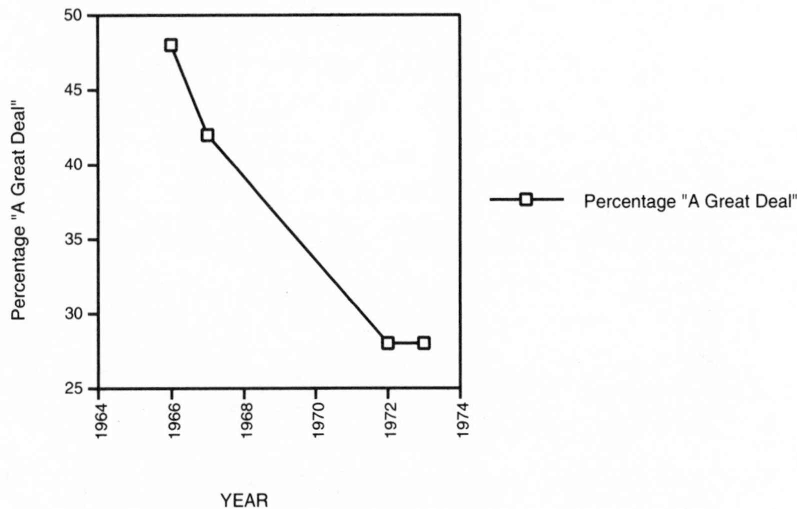

SOURCE: Lipset and Schneider 1987, 50

God *had* seemed to have "chosen the foolish things of the world to confound the wise." Then, when the masks were torn aside, many were thrust into the bald realization that the world does not work the way they had been conditioned that it did. As we have seen, Galbraith asserts that in such cases there is first, indignation and then the deep feeling that power so long concealed must be fundamentally illegitimate (Galbraith 1983, 13).

It is an open question whether Americans seriously question the *legitimacy* of their institutions, as Galbraith predicted, but it is an irrefutable fact that confidence in institutional leadership abruptly declined in the 1960s and has never recovered. The antiauthoritarian strain of the counterculture has cast a very long shadow: look at Figure 7-1.

Figure 7-1 is derived from Harris surveys and National Opinion Research Corporation data (Lipset and Schneider 1987, 50). The sharp decline in confidence in institutional leadership could be explained by the events of that period, but as we saw in Figure 6-1, the low level of confidence has been sustained well into the 1980s. And this melancholy state of affairs is still with us, as seen in Table 7-1, compiled from the latest NORC GSS surveys (Davis and Smith 1994).

TABLE 7-1

Percentage with Great Confidence in Thirteen Institutions[2], 1989–1994.

Year	*% with Great Confidence in Institutional Leaders*
1989	24.9
1990	24.7
1991	37.1
1992	37.1
1993	21.5
1994	22.1

Confidence in leadership ebbs and flows with events, the ups and downs of the economy, new national administrations; but the level oscillates around the lows first experienced in the early 1970s. The decline that began in the 1960s seems to be a permanent condition. Business in particular has suffered from the low esteem of the populace; from a high of around 70 percent in the late 1950s, confidence in business leadership has settled around a 25 percent level. The old bureaucratic values of trust in hierarchical business establishments, the value of cooperative effort—in short, loyalty to the firm—has eroded along with so many other features of the old dispensation. New attitudes toward work have resulted; we have seen the erosion of formerly high levels of job satisfaction.

The Opinion Research Corporation has been surveying employees since the 1950s, and by 1979 could report that workers were discontented and expecting more from their jobs. It seems that the corporation, which we will look at more closely in the next chapter, was the last holdout for the old attitudes and practices. The 1960s were generally characterized by increasing demands for self-expression and self-fulfillment, and many found such goals blocked in the large companies (Cooper et al. 1979, 117–24). These aspirations can be attributed to the counterculture's self-discovery theme, making bureaucratic work somehow opposed to the life-enhancing experience sought by the young of that day. You could say that there were two possible countercultural strategies vis-à-vis the workplace. The first strategy, rejection of the work ethic entirely and a studied avoidance of work, did not permanently attract a large following, save in a vague sense of the pointlessness of the job, evidenced by the decline in job satisfaction rates. But the second product of countercultural project appears to have taken hold more generally. This stance shares with the first the view that jobs are meaningless, but goes further and criticizes the economic organization of large corporations and their effects on society (Yinger 1982, 215–17). We shall see some of these viewpoints expressed in our interviews in later chapters. Such attitudes can be seen in the concern for the environment, but also most significantly in a generalized loss of confidence in large corporations.

The world of the large corporations was preeminently the world of loyalty, the old dispensation, and in the next chapter we will look at that world in some detail. But here, it is important to note that the loss of confidence in business which began in the 1960s was characteristically aimed at *big* business. Small businesses did not share that fate. What is it about large companies that sparked such disdain? The Opinion Research Corporation's surveys for 1975, 1977, 1979, and 1981 provided some answers to that. People were asked to judge a number of institutional leaders on two scales: integrity and efficacy. Corporate executives were rated high on the ability to get things done, but woefully low on honesty and dependability. Small businessmen were rated slightly lower in efficiency, but substantially higher in integrity. (Seventy-one percent gave good or excellent marks for the small businessmen's integrity, versus 33 percent to the corporate executives.) Yankelovich, Skelly, and White found similar sentiments: 55 percent thought that corporate executives' behavior was unethical. Lipset and Schneider, reviewing these findings, found good correlations between confidence and these perceptions of ethical practices (Lipset and Schneider 1987, 74–79).

The size of the organization seems to be a determining factor in people's attitudes, a hangover perhaps from the counterculture's disdain for the technocracy, for Moloch. But the public is schizophrenic on the question of size: large majorities from the 1960s to 1979 supported the notion that large companies are essential to the nation's economic health, but at the same time, 60 to 75 percent believed that big companies are cold and impersonal in their dealings with people, and more say they would prefer to work for a smaller firm (Lipset and Schneider 1987, 83). In summary, confidence and trust in the large corporation, the mainstay of the American economy for generations, began to drop sharply in the 1960s and has never recovered. And this is the institution that is so closely associated with corporate loyalty.

What of the other countercultural projects, particularly the quest for community, for mutual trust and brotherhood? And what of the mission to overcome anomie by finding alternate values? Sadly, neither survived the sixties. In fact, things have worsened since then on both these counts: trust in one another continues to fall; levels of anomie continue to rise. Levels of interpersonal trust[3] were surveyed from 1964 to 1978; the results show a statistically significant increase in those who show distrust of their fellows (T. W. Smith 1980, 219–20). And the same depressing trend continues: look at Figure 7-2, derived from the General Social Surveys. (Davis and Smith 1994). With a temporary upswing in the 1980s, the trend that began in the 1960s continues—down; fewer people trusting one another.

The results for anomie are very much the same. Two measures of anomie that the General Social Survey (GSS) uses are displayed in Figures 7-3 and 7-4. "Anomia 5" (Figure 7-3) is the response to the question. "Do you agree or disagree that the lot of the average man is getting worse, not better?" "Anomia 7" (Figure 7-4) asks for agreement or disagreement to: "Most public officials are not really interested in the problems of the average man." As we see, the trends are toward higher levels of anomie.

Other GSS measures of anomie show the same trends: statistically significant increases from 1973 to 1976 in agreement to the statements: "these days a person doesn't really know whom he can count on," and "Most people don't care what happens to the next fellow" and "You sometimes can't help wondering whether anything is worthwhile any more" (T. W. Smith 1980, 13).

FIGURE 7-2
Trust, 1972–1994

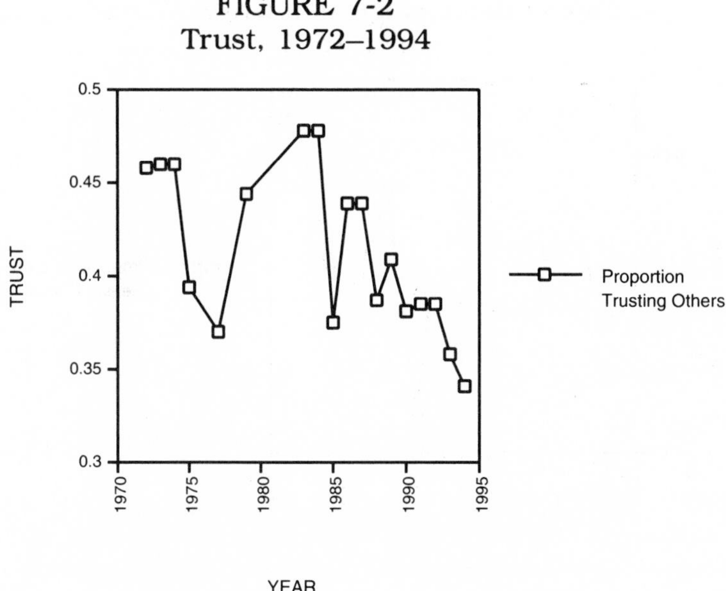

SOURCE: General Social Survey, Davis & Smith 1994

Even the cheerful optimism of Ronald Reagan could not stem the tide of anomie. The Harris poll's index of alienation showed that in 1986 the number of Americans feeling alienated or powerless was at a record high of 60 percent—4 points higher than the previous year, higher than the 1980s average of 58%, higher than the 1970s average of 52 percent, and worlds away from the 1966 figure of 29 percent, even the 36 percent of 1969, at the height of the Vietnam protests.

And so, in the fullness of time, the counterculture—variously denigrated as a freak show, a children's crusade, the voyage of a Ship of Fools—the counterculture left an enduring mark on American social character. In its backwash, people began to look at American society and institutions in a far different, and far more critical way. Not only were morals loosened and tolerance of diversity raised, the counterculture, with its appeal to very old American traditions, made a stinging critique of America's bureaucratic values and corporate culture, and the critique in time spread far beyond the young and the hip. The consumption consensus of the 1950s began

FIGURE 7-3
Fate of the Average Man Grows Worse
1972–1994

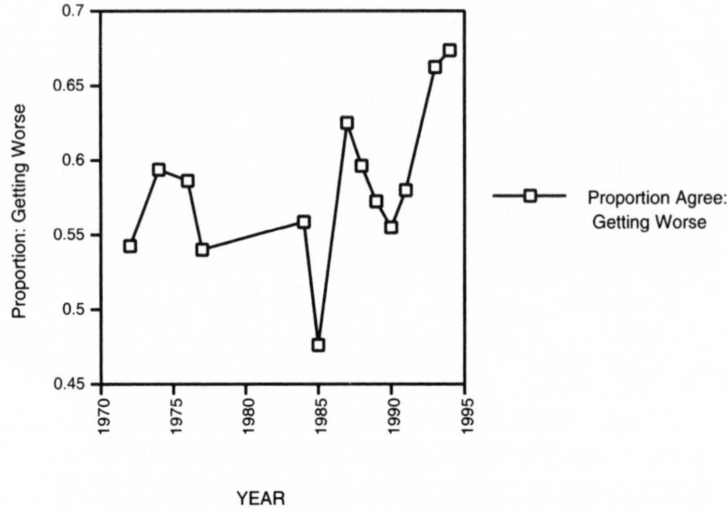

SOURCE: General Social Survey, Davis and Smith 1994

to seem vacuous; people began to feel an enlarged sense of what they wanted from life, from society, and from their workplace (Ladd and Lipset 1980, 6). Through the 1960s, the majority of Americans still held fast to the old corporate culture and its values, which had become traditional. But by the 1970s, the outré attitudes of the kids and the freaks were on their way to becoming dominant American values. Daniel Yankelovich estimated in 1979 that the new values had a 52 percent majority in America, and he described this "New Breed" as having

> a growing disillusionment with the ability of our institutions to deliver the goods, . . . a questioning of whether the values of a consumption society are worth the nose-to-the-grindstone way of life that pays for all the goodies . . . and a further evolution of individualism into the quest for less conforming . . . lifestyles. (Yankelovich 1979, 10)

In brief, the counterculture began the "long unraveling" of that set of bureaucratic values that had sustained American institutions for generations.

FIGURE 7-4
Public Officials Uninterested in the Average Man, 1972–1994

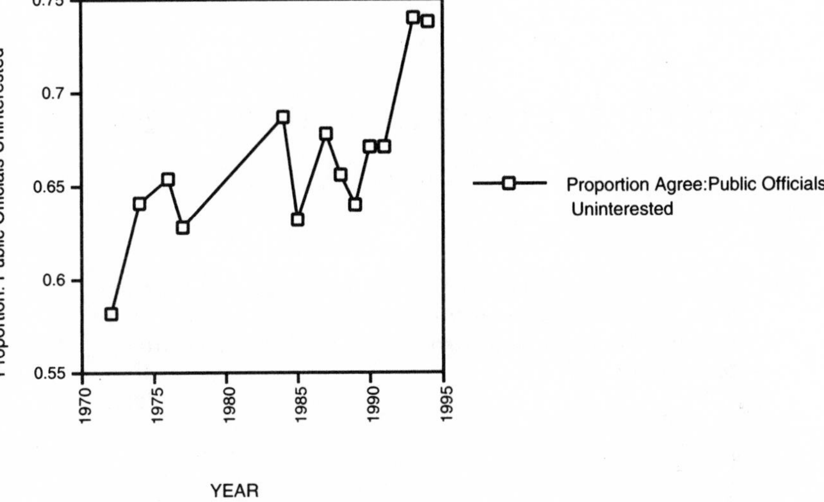

SOURCE: General Social Survey, Davis and Smith 1994

Our discussion of the counterculture's impact necessarily has taken us more than thirty years in time beyond its flowering. Let us go back in the next chapter to the economy and the corporation of the 1960s, for there as well we will find the roots of the present day attitudes that our cohort 2 friends hold.

8
The Sixties: Economy and Management Practices

I have . . . been with RLX since we graduated from college. They've just been family; they paid for our kids to be born, they've sent us around the world, they've always been there.

—Mary Chalmers

LOYALTIES to companies, their waxing and waning, are, I believe, affected by generalized attitudes in society, by what has been termed "social character." We saw in chapter 5's review of the psychology of loyalty that forming organizational loyalty first requires some preexisting norms that are then modified by experiences with the organization. In the last chapter we saw how American social character began to change in the 1960s, and change in ways that moved away from bureaucratic values—including loyalty. We should not be surprised that our younger cohorts are not predisposed to organizational loyalty, as their older colleagues were.

But social character is only part of the story. The set of values and beliefs a person brings to the company are a necessary, but not sufficient, condition for the formation of loyalty. Additionally, the potential loyalist must find a company that is operated in ways that induce a sense of attachment and commitment. Those practices of management are in turn a function of both economic conditions and of the prevalent management ideology of the time. In this chapter we shall look at all of these: the management ideologies of that time, the economy of the 1960s, and the popular management system of the 1960s and beyond "welfare corporatism."

A Brief History of Management Ideologies

We owe to Marx the modern idea of "ideology" and its self-serving roots; Marx's famous dictum spelled it out:

> It is not the the consciousness of men that determines their existence, but, on the contrary, their social existence that determines their consciousness. (Marx 1904, 21)

Marx contended that the economic and social ideas of a time were nothing but a "superstructure" erected upon the base, the prevailing economic conditions, and as such were only a justification for the actions of the dominant class. What Marx had uncovered is an idea we all now sense intuitively, that reality is "constructed" by our position in the social world, that we tend to view the world through the lens of our socioeconomic status (Berger and Luckman 1966, 1–3). Everyone has an ideology, since it is the model we have of the world, the framework within which we can explain that world. An ideology comprises both *beliefs*—how we think the world works—and *values,* how we think it ought to work. And, the way the mind works, values have a substantial effect on beliefs: simply, the way we think things *ought to be* colors how we think things *are* (North 1990, 23). Managers, like all of us, have ideologies and those ideologies color how they view the world, and result in practices to fulfill that vision. Let us look briefly at the ideologies that managers have embraced since the time of industrialization, ideologies that served to justify the essential fact of society: the authority of the few over the many, or as Bendix puts it:

> Ideologies of management are attempts by leaders of enterprises to justify the privilege of voluntary action and association for themselves, while imposing upon all subordinates the duty of obedience and the obligation to serve their employers to the best of their ability. (Bendix 1956, xx)

For some time, managers gave little thought at all to the workers; late nineteenth-century management theorists like Fayol and Weber barely mentioned them. It was not until labor forced itself on their attention with strikes that management began to focus on labor relations as a business issue. If they gave much thought to it, American managers faced an intellectual and ethical dilemma. Preeminent among American values were liberty and equality. But in reality, large masses of workers were being forced to submit to arbitrary authority, enforced by the police and the legal system. How could the managers justify such a state of affairs? Were liberty and equality, the right of free association, to apply only to themselves? The short answer was: yes. The theory of Social Darwinism was the intellectual tool that justified these conditions, rescued the managers from their dilemma. Success and wealth were regarded as the reward for superior ability and one's contribution to society. Samuel Smiles had presented the case to great popular acclaim in *Self-Help*, published first in 1859 (Bendix 1956, 109). Wealth and power were the rewards for those who had proven themselves in the struggle for survival. A contributor to the *American Journal of Sociology* in 1896 asserted that "The struggle is a human battle; the captains of industry were better fighters than most of us . . ." (Perrow 1979, 60). It was rather simple: the successful were entitled to command, the failures lacked the requisite personal qualities. The owners and managers were evidently superior individuals; the workers were biologically unfit to do more than they were doing. (Almost certainly there were racist overtones to this view; at the time a majority of manual workers were foreign-born and considered genetically inferior.)

The managers may have thought they had justified their position and power in this way, but there were still some uncomfortable facts to deal with. For all of their success, they were being challenged by unions in their central activity—the control of their own factories—where their authority was supposedly supreme. And they were being challenged by people who were manifestly unfit. The employers first sneered that the challenge came from collective action, not individual strength. That proved to be an embarrassingly bad argument when the firms had to band together themselves to fight the unions (Perrow 1979, 61–63).

The mythology of the employers' superior wisdom and strength faced another blow, as Scientific Management came to the fore. Management faced a crisis of control on the shop floor; worker dissatisfaction was manifested in strikes, slowdowns, absenteeism, and shirking. It was no longer sufficient to point to the genetic inferiority of the workers; that solved nothing. A means must be found to make the open-ended employment contract beneficial to management. Then on to the stage strode one of the most remarkable and influential management theorists America has produced, Frederick Winslow Taylor. He saw the workers as purely *homo oeconomicus*, without any motivation other than pecuniary reward. Hence, all that was needed was to introduce appropriate financial incentives, once the work had been organized properly so that management and labor could both benefit from the system.

Some of the ideas behind Scientific Management had emerged before Taylor came on the scene. Taylor published his first paper in 1895, applauding the efforts of his predecessors, but adding to their rationalized management the idea of gain sharing for the workers. But, piece-work compensation had been used in the past; indeed, in the late Middle Ages in the "putting out" system. Taylor's contribution was the blending of rationalized management with the old piece-work system. Management's job was to analyze each job in exquisite detail and design procedures to improve productivity. Then, once standard procedures were in place for each task, the workers could be compensated on how well they performed them. In fact, the workers were made a "throffer"[1]: higher pay for exceeding the standard, and reduction in pay for sub-par performance (Chandler 1977, 272–75).

The breakthrough in thinking was substantial and the change in managerial methods was revolutionary. Control of the process of production was effectively taken from the foremen, but also from the top management, and of course from the workers. The engineer was now the master of the shop floor; the foremen were monitors more than task designers, and the workers were essentially de-skilled, becoming a part of the production machinery (Perrow 1979, 63–64).

In our day, "Taylorism" has become a term of opprobrium, signifying impersonal and uncaring management. The 1973 report to the Secretary of HEW is a long philippic against Taylorism (O'Toole et al. 1973). But this is to misunderstand what Taylor sought to accomplish and the conditions he faced. The shop-floor practices of his day were a scandal to Taylor's engineer's eyes. Taylor's solution was to eliminate the brain work of the workers and replace it with that of the engineers. Management's job was to enforce and reward new standards of output which had been scientifically developed by task analysis (Brody 1993, 11–12). The inhumanity of the approach escaped Taylor; his motives were noble. He truly believed that his system would benefit both management and labor, that the Marxist view of an unbridgeable conflict between the two was fallacious. Taylor said: "One of the chief advantages from . . . the system is that it promotes a most friendly feeling between the men and their employers, and so renders labor unions and strikes unnecessary" (F. W. Taylor 1914, 637).

Applying Taylor's methods had several unintended consequences. Most employers embraced the methods without absorbing Taylor's ideology, so bureaucratization and control increased, but the managers were uncomfortable with the ideas behind the methods. The ideology basically questioned management's superior ability and judgment. It implied that workers' discontent and inefficiencies were the fault of management's failure to use worker skills properly (Perrow 1979, 65).

Critiques of Taylorism were not long in coming, on practical as well as theoretical grounds. Elton Mayo summed up the reaction of most workers to the new system, and it was not the blissful enjoyment of higher pay and greater opportunity.

> The result was not discipline and collaboration but disorder and resistance. . . . (it) imposed upon the workers a low level of human organization from which social participation and social function were excluded. (Mayo 1946, 174)

Taylor's new methods reduced the workers to parts of the process machinery, ignoring their human attitudes and creativity. And, quite simply, the workers did not buy into Taylor's belief that they would subsume collective advances for personal ambition. Soldiering, shirking, and resistance continued and the time-and-motion man was universally feared and scorned. Just as uneducated teen-age car thieves routinely thwart the best thinking of Detroit's engineers, the workers found effective ways to undo the work of the industrial engineers.

The employers had sought to change the workers' thinking through the Taylorian system, appealing to the economic motives of the workmen, and hoping to inspire a change in their consciousness such that cooperation with management would be more congenial. It mostly did not work: labor unrest, absenteeism, and shirking continued. But some thinkers began to suspect that the workers' attitudes may have more to do with their "social existence" than an all-consuming need for higher incomes. These currents gave rise to the human relations school of management and also to the system of welfare capitalism.

Taylorism had only confirmed Marx's critique of capitalism: the replacement of genuine human social relations with universal money relations. All human ties had been abolished and human worth had been reduced to exchange value, cash (Hamori 1974, 31). A change in management ideology came about with the social philosophy of Elton Mayo, a Harvard Business School professor trained as an industrial psychologist. Mayo's psychological assumptions broke with the Taylorian tradition of the wage-maximizing, isolated individual. He considered that to be the "rabble hypothesis," the assumptions that: society was composed of atomistic individuals; that each of these atoms acted purely from self-interest; and, that each acts logically, unswayed by emotion and sentiments. Wrong on all counts, Mayo asserted. Rather, people have the desire for solidarity; they are moved by sentiments; they have an instinct for human association; and, their economic self-interest was the exception, not the rule (Perrow 1979, 67).

Mayo came to the new ideology from his review of the now-famous Hawthorne experiments, conducted in the Hawthorne plant of Western Electric in Cicero, Illinois between 1924 and 1927. The researchers, Mayo's Harvard colleague Roethlisberger and the plant manager Dickson, called in Mayo to help explain some puzzling results. The experiments were informed by the Taylorian theory that the workers were complex machines whose output could be aided by "scientifically" optimizing the workplace conditions. Increased lighting levels did in fact increase output, but output increased as well in the control group where the level was unchanged. The researchers came to suspect that simply noticing people, recognizing some human relation, would improve productivity. The notion of wage-maximizing, Taylorian production machines seemed to be of little help to explain this phenomenon.[2]

The research then shifted to a seven-month observation of workers and nondirective counseling. This led to the discovery that workers systematically restricted output and penalized those producing more than the group norm, ostracizing them and threatening physical reprisals. Also, records were falsified to retaliate against the overly productive and to protect or discipline group members. A game was certainly being played, a repeated game in which the work group had arrived at an equilibrium satisfactory to themselves, but with low productivity, quite suboptimal to the company and to the group itself, which could earn more from the incentive system. Why did they behave in this "irrational" way? The counseling sessions revealed the role of sentiments, nonrational lack of cooperation with rational management, and no identification with the rational goals of the company. Mayo did not dwell on the hostilities and group-survival techniques of these workers, but rather stressed that the workers were in a sense tribal, forming social groups with elaborate norms and customs (Perrow 1979, 90–94).

The human relations school emerged from the researchers' publications which interpreted their results. The school, although emphasizing—perhaps for the first time—the human needs of the workers, was nonetheless a pro-management approach. The factory was posited to be a psychological-sociological community, a form of a tribe, and like all tribes, supposedly in need of good leadership by the chief (Kerr 1988, 12). Leadership becomes, then, a mechanism for influencing the behavior of individual members, and the human relations school form of leadership thus never escaped the criticism that it was manipulative—a more sophisticated means to operate the "production machine" than Taylor's methods, but with the same purpose.

The effects of the school on management ideology were profound and its fundamental assumptions informed management thinking in the 1960s era of welfare corporatism, the assumptions that people are tractable, docile, even gullible; that they yearn for leadership; and most importantly, that they want to feel united, seek some cause worthy of their best efforts, a cause that can give significance to their lives and work (Perrow 1979, 65).

The contemporary critiques of the human relations school were not long in coming. Most commonly, the critics noted the absence of conflict in the new model; there seemed to be no grounds for legitimate conflicts of interest. The workers could be brought around to management's way of thinking, and management was presumed to have right and logic on its side (Perrow 1979, 94).

C. Wright Mills, writing in the 1950s, saw the new ideology as just another, more sophisticated way to get performance from the worker without really changing his basic condition: a life of drudgery in a hierarchy with work devalued from the ideal of craftsmanship . Mills sneered:

> Make the chemical in the vial a little different and you have someone who is loyal. He likes you, and when mishaps come he takes a lot from you because you have been good to him. . . . You have to put into his work and environment the things that change the chemical that stimulates action, so that he is loyal and productive. (Mills 1953, 233)

I think a very telling criticism was the one also applied to welfare capitalism[3]: the ideology led management toward manipulation; the recommended face-to-face relations and counseling were really establishing the relation of a parent to a child; a colonizer to a primitive. (Perrow 1979, 94). One analyst even suggests that "the language of motivation may become subtly elitist by suggesting that the employee resembles a captive rodent in a cage." (T. H. Fitzgerald 1979, 277).

But another criticism of the human relations school is more basic and more telling: it does not seem to work. The basic thesis of the school is that good leadership will improve productivity—"good" in this context meaning more democratic, more employee-centered and more concerned with human relations and feelings. This style of leadership is posited to produce high morale and thus, presumably, greater effort and therefore greater output. But empirical research has never shown much evidence for this causal chain; there is no strong link between attitudes and performance—in fact the causal arrow seems to go the other way: good performance leads to good attitudes, not the reverse. The school's tenets suffered yet another blow from empirical research. Mayo et al. fiercely condemned Taylor's methods of breaking jobs down into their smallest components, which the human relations advocates claimed produced boredom and job dissatisfaction. Their remedy was job enhancement, job enlargement: integrating the fragmented tasks back into a larger job which more nearly approached the ideal of craftsmanship. Again, empirical research has not been able to find much evidence to support this thesis.

The work of Chester Barnard was related to the human relations school and in many ways can be seen as a codification of the corporate culture and its bureaucratic values. Barnard went well beyond Elton Mayo's pious statements about the need for cooperation and Mayo's romantic notions of a return to an earlier time of craft labor. Barnard insisted that organizations were per se cooperative systems. He wrote his widely influential book, *The Functions of the Executive,* in 1938, in the depths of the Depression and a time of social unrest. As a former telephone-company executive, he was concerned about the militant attacks on the American industrial system and sought its justification. His solution was, like Mayo's, an appeal to the naturalness of cooperation, but more than that, the central idea that corporations, bureaucracies, were by their very nature vehicles for moral purposes. Barnard parted company with Max Weber here in his model of the nature of bureaucracies. Weber saw them, as did Barnard, as goal-oriented organizations, but for Weber the goals were established at the top, and the various features of bureaucratic organization were means to maintain control in order to attain those goals. Barnard also saw the hierarchy as more rational than individuals, but it was not an impersonal entity so much as it was supra-individual, somehow extracting from individual cooperative behavior the means to achieve *common* goals. The authority relations in a hierarchy, the darling of Marxist theorists, Barnard finessed by his idea that authority really comes from the bottom up: the subordinate has decided to grant authority to his superiors. This had to be, since the organization was almost by definition a cooperative system, and the idea of cooperation was inconsistent with imposed rules and coercion of any kind (Perrow 1979, 70–81). In short, bureaucratic values were good for human beings.

The Hawthorne experiments can be read as confirming Barnard's insights, but with a twist. The work groups seemed to be functioning as cooperative units, and the effects of hierarchical management were peripheral to their actions. However, the dynamics that Barnard expected for the entire organization were not really present: the workers did not share the hierarchy's goals, nor did they have any hand in establishing its common purpose. They had found ways to cooperate, but only with each other, and the goals they pursued were not those of management.

By the 1950s and 1960s, new management theories were built on the human relations school's ideology. We find in the work of Ouchi, Argyris, McGregor, and Maslow that the human relations school's ideals and assumptions survived well into the postwar period. Ouchi acknowledges the influence of Elton Mayo in showing that a careful look at forms other than hierarchy, specifically the social organization of primitives, would lead the way to better industrial organization. Mayo had deplored the fact that social and human factors had been ignored in industrial organization and noted:

> If we seek to know more of the part played by such factors, the simplest situation . . . is the collaboration in work which have been studied in primitive peoples . . . The tribe responds to situations as a unit; each member knows his place and part although he cannot explain it. (Mayo 1946, 72)

This notion fueled the organizational development (OD) movement and inspired the work of William Ouchi, who asserted that some latter-day industrial tribes actually exist. (He called them "Theory Z" firms, and I shall refer to them as "welfare corporatist"). Writing in 1980, he found some firms that appear to rely less on bureaucratic hierarchy and more on conditioned control. Now, 1980 was the heyday of the "Japan is right" movement, so of course Ouchi pointed to Japanese firms as exemplars. But, he also cited such American firms as Kodak, IBM, Procter & Gamble, Hewlett-Packard and Cummins Engines as American industrial "clans." Ouchi made an argument similar to that of Peters and Waterman, that these firms were also perceived to be the most prestigious in America, with the best reputation for managerial ability and the strongest earnings. High performance would seem to follow from Theory Z thinking. One part of that thinking, which I will discuss below, is its sine qua non—the practice of long-term, stable employment. An implicit contract of lifetime employment allows the organization the time to acculturate its people, which presumably leads to more consensual decision making, and much less supervision and coordination (Ouchi and Price 1980, 573–74).

Now it might be said that this is an old idea. The advocates of welfare capitalism from 1900 through the 1920s, to their credit, felt responsibility for the welfare of their employees. But their philosophy was a curious blend of paternalism and instrumentality. The employer knew better than the worker what the worker needed, and took up the duty to provide him security. At the same time, the employer believed that the workers' gratitude would increase productivity, output, and profits. But welfare capitalism never promised anyone a job, even with all its paternalistic concerns for the employees.

As we have seen, welfare capitalism collapsed in the cataclysm of the Great Depression but Elton Mayo and the human relations school proved more enduring. For the first time managers had come to see the social nature of the workplace and sensed that more might be obtained by attending to the workers' attitudes and feelings, not just their material needs. Again, this philosophy was an unstable blend of altruism and instrumentality. The teachings of the school were viewed by many as a more-sophisticated means to control and manipulate the work force. But many tenets of the school have survived into the late twentieth century, in welfare corporatism and in Ouchi's notion of Theory Z industrial clans.

Let us look now at welfare corporatism, the world depicted in Whyte's *The Organization Man*, the product of postwar management ideology and the economic conditions of those times. This was the organizational world that our middle cohort subjects encountered as they entered the workforce, and it was their experience for a number of years, since welfare corporatism survived in Softmatics and its parent the RLX Corporation, as well as many other American companies, well into the 1980s.

As background for the welfare corporatism of the 1960s, we turn first to the economy of those days.

The American Economy in the 1960s

After the Second World War, the fear of inflation was as keen as the fear of unemployment and the postwar administrations of Truman and Eisenhower were preoccupied with that specter. Fiscal policy under Truman was passive: not until the seventh month of the 1949 recession did he abandon his tax-increase efforts designed to reduce the deficit. Eisenhower's terms were also characterized by policies of balanced budgets. Recession came in 1957–58 and again in 1960–61, but the administration continued to eschew Keynesian prescriptions to cut taxes and/or increase outlays.

Only with the election of John F. Kennedy did the federal government shift its economic policies. For the first time, American policy makers explicitly endorsed Keynesian economics and sought to spur economic growth through fiscal policy. With unemployment at 6.7 percent at the beginning of his term, Kennedy asked Congress for a 20 percent reduction in corporate and personal tax rates. He did not live to see his plan enacted; Lyndon Johnson signed the bill in 1964. It seemed to work marvelously, although some pointed to the expansive monetary policy of the time as the critical factor. In any event, by the first quarter of 1966, over seven million new jobs had been created, real per-capita after-tax income was up 20 percent over 1961, corporate after-tax income doubled, and real wages increased by 30 percent. Yet inflation rose only 1.3 percent per year from 1960 to 1965.

It was a prosperity unequaled in American history: GNP growth was 5.5 percent in 1964, 6.3 percent in 1965, and 6.5 percent in 1966, and averaged 4.9 percent from 1962 to 1969. Despite heavy defense spending for the Vietnam War beginning in 1965, inflation was only a moderate 2.3 percent from 1959 to 1969 and civilian employment grew 2.2 percent per annum in this period.

Good economic times characterized the 1960s, but there were signs—almost universally ignored—that America's economic progress might not be the envy of the world. American GNP growth between 1948 and 1960 only averaged 2.9 percent per annum, as compared with Japan's 8.7 percent, Germany's 7.2 percent, Italy's 5.8 percent, France's 4.2 percent and Canada's 3.6 percent. Manufacturing productivity increases should have set off alarm bells. Productivity had fallen disastrously in the slump of 1946 (7.97 percent), but then began a long climb as new technologies and managerial techniques came into their own: productivity grew by nearly 53 percent over prewar levels by 1969. The period 1948 to 1966 were the high points, averaging 3.4 percent per annum in this period, before a secular decline took place. After that, the stage was set for long-term productivity declines through the 1970s and into the 1980s (Galambos and Pratt 1988, 134 and Bruchey 1988, 207).

The decline in productivity advance showed up in the erosion of real incomes. Real income growth rate began to slow in 1965, and then declined by 20 percent between 1968 and 1981. It also showed in America's global trade performance:

U.S. manufactured goods have fallen as a percentage of world trade ever since 1963. The flagship American industries led this decline: steel, textiles, automobiles, electronics, rubber, and petrochemicals. From the end of the Second World War until 1950, the U.S. accounted for 60 percent of world manufacturing output. Of course, America's international competitors had their economies in shambles at that time, their productive capacity shattered by war's destruction. The Marshall Plan injected $13 billion into the European economies in the 1950s, and Japan came on the world stage economically in the 1960s. By 1979, the American share of world production was down to 35 percent and the American export share—29 percent in 1953—sunk to 13 percent in 1976.

The conditions after the Second World War found America in a favored and unique economic position, but it was not seen as a transient advantage; it was seen as an enduring economic superiority, a "boundless cornucopia of growth." The surplus wealth being created could be used to aid the recovery of our friends all over the world, as well as address pressing American social problems. That optimistic era began to end in the late 1960s and was effectively shattered by the oil shocks of the 1970s and the competition from the economies we had helped restore (Kamer 1988, 98). Nonetheless, to those who ran the big companies and those who manned them, the 1960s still seemed a period of endless growth and prosperity. After all, Gross National Product in 1969 was more than three times the 1940 level, and seemed likely to continue to advance (Galambos and Pratt 1988, 134). It was those economic conditions, or at least the optimistic perception of them, which animated the attitudes of both management and employees in the 1960s, and in some cases, right on into the 1980s.

Welfare Corporatism

Alfred Chandler has described how the managerial class was the essential ingredient in the formation of the large, integrated corporation in the late nineteenth century, providing the "Visible Hand" of management to replace the market's invisible hand in allocating goods and services. After the Second World War, this management class proliferated; it was the era of "staffs": headquarters staffs, PR staffs, finance staffs

(Bennett 1990, 97). This was definitively the age of the organization man: white-collar employment, mainly centered in large corporations, rose 61 percent between 1947 and 1956 (Leinberger and Tucker 1991,125–28). Most top managements assumed that the more control the company had over its people and its business, the better; any problem whatsoever called for a new department, so administrative empires grew apace. (I once had an issue with IBM sometime in the 1980s; within days I had a "Director of Channel Conflict" sitting in my office and explaining how he and his fifty-person staff would help me solve that.)

These organizations became so large and complex that organizational "navigators" were needed, skillful people whose only real knowledge and contribution was where to go to get something done in the vast enterprise. I met many such people in my own and other large organizations, people who functioned like harbor pilots, knowing little about the ship's cargo of products or their destinations in the wide world, but knew in detail the shoals, reefs, and snags of their own organization and could bring projects safely through the great harbor of their own company.

But for many years, buoyed by good economic times and largely insulated from foreign competition, these large firms worked marvelously and built a comfortable environment which has been called "welfare corporatism". The practices of welfare corporatism engendered a great deal of loyalty to the firm, they were the "magic helper" for legions of people. We heard Mary Chalmers in this chapter's epigraph: "They've just been family . . . they've always been there." The metaphor of family is commonly employed to describe what if feels like to be in a welfare corporatist firm (Heckscher 1995, 100–101). And, family and community are the standard expressions my subjects used to describe life in the old RLX, a welfare corporatist company. Bill Abernathy said: "I really felt I was a part of that company, that there was a relationship, an honest relationship between me, my fellow workers, my supervisors . . . that there was a camaraderie . . . a community." And Dennis Madison repeatedly referred to a "second family" and an "extended family." Joe Weston of cohort 2, who started his career at welfare corporatist IBM, described the atmosphere at RLX and what he gained from it:

> If I were to put it down to one important thing, I'd have to say a sense that I belong, that I'm a part of this, that I'm not an outsider, that I'm not a Lone Ranger, I'm not in this all by myself . . .

Tony Scalia of cohort 2 expressed much the same sentiment:

> One item that I really liked about RLX, to think that we all felt that we were part of the RLX family and at least in the early years—my early years I would say the 1980 to 1985 timeframe—RLX was a very exciting company to work for. It was a company that you could feel proud of that you worked for and references to the tradition of the company I thought were very gratifying and it was fun to be a part of that environment.

What was that welfare corporatist environment, exactly? Essentially, it was a set of management practices and programs which emerged after 1945. Many large Japanese firms had used such practices, but in the United States the approach was first tried after the war by firms such as IBM, Polaroid, Kodak, AT&T and US Steel. Some of these companies used the methods to ward off union organizers, but in all cases they found that the practices were a better way to manage both manual and knowledge workers than Scientific Management or welfare capitalism.

Its essential purpose was that of Chester Barnard: to ensure control of the work force by creating an atmosphere conducive to cooperation. This can be looked at in two ways. First, it is really immaterial whether one takes a Marxist (or C. Wright Millsian) line of bureaucratic alienation, or one supports the human relations school's assumptions; in either case the conclusion is the same: the formal bureaucratic organization, no matter how efficient, can create an oppressive work environment that does not satisfy basic human needs. Welfare corporatism's essential purpose is to overcome this dilemma and, with appropriately designed practices, instill loyalty and commitment in the employees. The basic difference with the human relations approach is that welfare corporatism's decentralized and participatory forms are a way to motivate and coopt employees, rather than a move toward industrial democracy and a change in basic power relations (Lincoln and Kalleberg 1990, 181). Power remains with the organization, but the power emphasis shifts to conditioned power, the power that operates through internalized norms. Marxists might emphasize the power relations of this new system in calling it "bureaucratic control," thereby highlighting the control processes and showing that the control is embedded in the social structure and social relations of the firm. Hierarchical power is institutionalized; Edwards asserts that this is the defining feature of welfare corporatism: a rule of law—the firm's rules and regulations—replace the rule of supervisory command in the direction of work (Edwards 1979, 131). Ronald Dore, who studied Japanese and British management practices, coined the term "welfare corporatism" to indicate its methods—programs and practices similar to welfare capitalism—-as well as its effects—the creation of a pseudo-state in which the company's rules assume law-like legitimacy. Because,

> A large firm . . . is inherently a *political* (author's emphasis) system because the government of the firm exercises great power, including coercive power. The government of a firm can have more impact on the lives of more people than the government of many a town, city, province, state. (Dahl 1982, 184)

The practices of welfare corporatism are a panoply of welfare programs, organizational structures, and personnel policies. It is important that these be seen as a gestalt. The research of Lincoln and Kalleberg reveals that removing key parts of the system tend to diminish its effectiveness. The measure of effectiveness is first and foremost the development of employee commitment—loyalty. (The posited causal chain is that greater commitment will lead to greater effort and higher overall performance for the firm.) Welfare corporatism can be seen to be characterized by the following features:

1. The linchpin of welfare corporatism is an implicit guarantee of a lifetime job and the consequent creation of an internal labor market.

2. Welfare corporatist firms feature organizational structures such as "tall" hierarchies and a proliferation of relatively small work units.

3. Programs are in place to relieve the fragmentation and monotony of jobs and tasks: job rotation and enlargement that increase the intrinsic rewards of working and build identification with the organization as a whole.

4. Mechanisms have been installed to foster employee participation in decision-making, but without the formal guarantees of high-level access that might threaten management control. No one would mistake these firms for industrial democracies.

5. The companies have created a pseudo-legal structure of formalized rights and obligations that confer corporate citizenship on employees; alienating personal forms of supervisory domination are studiously avoided.

6. Typically, one finds the trappings of a strong organizational "culture"—ritual, ceremony, symbolism. People wear company hats, ties, T-shirts.

7. As with welfare capitalism, there is usually a potpourri of tangible welfare benefits including family subsidies, educational programs, pensions, savings plans and health benefits (Lincoln & Kalleberg 1990, 248).

Effectively lifetime employment, which results in an internal labor market, is a critical element in meeting welfare corporatism's objectives. Dore's study of English Electric and Hitachi underscores the basic differences between Taylorian or welfare capitalism firms and welfare corporatism. The differences can be seen clearly in the way wages are set. The Tayloristic British firm sees itself in an external market for labor, and wages are set by the market price for a particular skill, with the supply and demand for worker types determining their wages. By contrast, Hitachi does not buy skills; their point of view is entirely different: they admit people into the enterprise to serve it to the best of their abilities. Hitachi is not buying a skill, but rather a lifetime of work. They look for development potential in new recruits, not any particular existing skill. Hitachi will train and reassign the worker through his lifetime of work for the company[4] (Dore 1973, 111).

An internal labor market, for that is what Dore is describing, has a number of effects. Market forces are essentially absent, since the company is the only buyer and creates the supply; production workers commonly are hired only into the low-level entry jobs; and upper-level management and professional jobs follow the same pattern. Promotions come from within, very often by seniority. And, as noted above, employment is accompanied by various benefit programs, many a function of tenure. These benefits are increasingly immobile, so workers are reluctant to move on. Additionally, many of the skills they have developed are quite company-specific. In sum, the managers of welfare corporate firms usually did not see themselves as competing with other firms in a market for anything but entry-level labor.

The internal labor markets of welfare corporatism were advantageous for both management and the employees. Management could develop its own labor supply, people with the precise skills the company needed. The long-term—permanent, in practice—period of employment gave management the time to socialize individuals, encouraging cooperation and loyal attitudes. Turnover is, of course, reduced by such a system, enhancing the company's substantial investment in human capital. The employees benefit from the system, as well. They receive training free of charge; they have employment security and good benefits; they avoid the costs and risks of seeking new employment; and, they have the opportunity to work up the promotion ladders that characterize internal labor markets (Lester 1988, 107–8).

Internal labor markets have economic and social consequences as well. Both the management and the worker have sunk costs in the relationship: the company has invested in human capital; the worker faces opportunity costs for the time spent learning company-specific, nonportable skills. Both therefore have the incentive to maintain the relationship (Reynolds 1988, 131).

The permanent relationship could, and did in the ideal cases, create a view of the enterprise as a community. "Time builds up identification; not just time past, the familiarity of long association, but also the prospect of time to come" (Dore 1973, 214). Personal experiences are translated into sentiment by refraction through the shared norms of fellow employees. An employee is imperceptibly socialized, more disposed to feel what he is supposed to feel. Dore noted a distinct difference between his British and Japanese firms—and not just with the employees in this regard; the management similarly had a different point of view. The Hitachi senior management considered themselves elders in a corporate community, not just fiduciaries of shareholders' property, responsible only for wringing the last ounce of value from it. As a result, Hitachi management had a genuine concern for the employees, and an excellent spirit of cooperation with one another (Dore 1973, 260–62). One of Heckscher's management subjects exemplifies this welfare corporatist solidarity: "We are collegial, we work with our brothers. We may make less profit on one plant to help the other . . ." (Heckscher

1995, 29). And in the good times at IBM, managers had been inculcated in the virtue of always first considering the "greater good of the whole" and not merely the benefits to their own units.

In these and other ways, the welfare corporate firm took on the trappings of a polity, with the employees having a species of citizenship in it. Besides the social safety net of any good modern polity, the employees found themselves in a network of rules and policies that took on the force of legitimate law. In the 1950s and 1960s, three quarters of large American companies had formal, accessible personal policies (Selznick 1969, 86). These bureaucratic rules take on the color of laws; inexorably, the notion of due process under these impersonal "laws" emerges (Burawoy 1979, 116). The employee is encouraged to be a good corporate citizen, to practice the virtues of altruism, conscientiousness, sociability. He is even given a type of vote: participation in decision making (Organ 1988, 8). And he is often given the psuedo-legal right of appeal. At IBM and other like-minded firms, an "open door" practice was in place, which permitted the employee—without fear of repercussions—to take his grievance to any level of management, up to and including the chairman of the board. When the practice functions honestly—as it did at IBM—it takes on the aura of law, and the appeal process comes to be seen as a genuine right (Moore 1972, 74). Welfare corporatist firms, by design or by happenstance, had hit upon the most effective means of exercising power and control over their subordinates: the idea that the company's regulations and policies were a matter of "law." As Foucault has pointed out, "In Western societies since the Middle Ages, the exercise of power has always been formulated in terms of the law" (Foucault 1990, 87). People have become socialized to authority that operates in a law-like environment; we are comfortable with it and see it as natural and right.

Not every firm was able to create the conditions of welfare corporatism, but when it worked, it worked very well. The use of the internal labor market (ILM) itself was a powerful influence on loyalty; empirical research has shown that above all things—above participation, communications, above caring supervision—above all these the ILM practices of career-long employment security, upward mobility, and personal skill development are the important determinants of organizational commitment (Gaertner 1989, 975).

What results could we expect from welfare corporatism? Edwards, who views the world exclusively in power terms, sees a sinister trend in its substitution of true constitutional law for Weberian bureaucratic rules. In particular, he deplores the type of person who develops under this regime: the desirable traits are rules-orientation, dependability and loyalty, internalization of the company's goals and values. These of course are the bureaucratic values, and Edwards derides them as constituting the traits of a person who has been seduced to fall under conditioned power. That may be the case, but of course, that was welfare corporatism's principal objective.

Lincoln and Kalleberg performed a massive study of firms in the United States and Japan to test the efficacy of welfare corporatist forms; their summary of its ability to forge loyalty is telling:

> Taken as a whole . . . the findings . . . suggest that organizational designs and management practices which engender "responsible autonomy" . . . as well as participation, integration, careers, and intrinsic rewards foster loyalty and diminish alienation. This, of course, is the rationale for Welfare Corporatist organization. (Lincoln and Kalleberg 1990, 80)

At their best, welfare corporatist firms were able to create a warm and close-knit community, a simulacrum of *Gemeinschaft.* People were expected to sacrifice their short-term interests for the good of the community, to work hard and delay their rewards since they were expected to make a career of the company (Heckscher 1995, 22). As we have seen, our cohort 1 friends, who were socialized in an earlier and very different time, maintained this sense of attachment to the company, in spite of the experiences of layoffs and disruptive reorganizations. Their loyalty trend was found to be flat, unchanged over time.[5] In chapter 2 we heard from cohort 1's Ralph Simmons about the layoffs:

> That was, in a sense, devastating and in another sense understandable . . . But do I actually get mad at the company? Totally, absolutely not. The companies do this corrective surgery to help those that are left and help the company.

Heckscher, in his study of a number of companies working themselves through layoffs and restructurings, found much the same thing and was surprised by the finding. He concluded:

> It appears that the complexity of the system of loyalty is sufficient to withstand simple shocks. If it were supported merely by mechanisms of self-interest, it would vanish as soon as those mechanisms were undermined. That is indeed what most commentators seem to expect. But the reality is that it is also supported by a deeper psychology: it is internalized in the motivations and self-images of the mangers, and therefore cannot be easily abandoned even when the conditions change. (Heckscher 1995, 26)

I believe that Heckscher is precisely right in this (although I am less surprised than he). The "system" of loyalty is far more complex than simple self-interest, and the notion that loyalty is some simple exchange phenomenon—loyalty for security—totally misses the point. As we have seen, our cohort 1 subjects had been through the Fire—demotions, layoffs, reorganizations—their self-interest would suggest they should cut their bonds to the company, but they persisted in their attachment. Yet the cohort 2 folk, who had grown up in another time, faced the same conditions as their older colleagues, and largely let their loyalty lapse. Their loyalty trend is down. They did not have the reservoir of general societal acceptance of bureaucratic values that the cohort 1 folk cut their teeth on. Their loyalty was not "sufficient to withstand simple shocks." They can be said to be "wandering between two worlds, one dead/The other powerless to be born" (Arnold 1986, 161).

Exactly how did welfare corporatism bring about loyalty? Well, its effects may be best illustrated by a comparison of experiences within a welfare corporatist firm and one with a more "modern" view. Just such a comparison presented itself to most of my subjects. They had been part of the RLX corporation, some for many years, and then their division had been acquired by DRI, a decidedly *un*-welfare corporatist company. Tony Scalia saw the contrast in these terms:

> The relationship that I think that we see at DRI right now is the fact that, you know, most people are happy that we're a part of DRI because they are a major technology company which is where we should be. The down side of it is, you (don't) see a lot of humanity. I don't see a lot of logic as far as the way people are

treated, although I think they talk a real good story . . . They seem to be a lot more non-personal, a lot more numbers-driven. . . . I only have warm feelings to DRI because they pay me.

Mary Chalmers talked of the day that she and her husband learned that the acquisition had taken place:

> My husband was sort of a company man. I think today he'd probably go back to RLX, you know, if there was something there. I can remember the day that we saw the video . . . all about DRI . . . We were going to be done and we never even thought or even occurred to us that we would be sentimental but we were. . . . When it was over with we went walking out . . . and we kind of grabbed each other's hands like "This is it" and he was thinking the same thing I was thinking. "Well, like this is the end of it." . . . it was emotional. It really was. . . . You know, it was sentimental that we were leaving; it's kind of like getting married . . . it's terrible to leave that bedroom and that Mom and Dad, you know and that's how it was.

Bill Abernathy saw the change in stark terms, as an abandonment of community and mutual trust, the end of all the rewards he had found in the old welfare corporatist RLX company. Of the new company, he had little good to say:

> They don't even pretend to be a people-oriented company. . . . They are as cold and calculating and cut throat as they come and I'll be frank with you, I don't fit. That's not my way.

Many of the cohort 2 people felt that the sense of family and *Gemeinschaft* seemed to have been lost. One remarked: "I don't feel there is a family there. I don't have the sense (that) they belong to each other." Let us look at how this sense of family had been created by welfare corporatism. If we review its characteristics, we can see that welfare corporatism in its entirety supports the formation of loyalty. First, of course, are the lifetime employment "guarantee" and the accompanying internal labor market. Dore's observation is acute, it is "not just time past, the familiarity of long association, but also the prospect of time to come" (Dore 1973, 214). You simply act and feel differently in the knowledge that you are in a permanent relationship, whether it be a marriage, a family, or a job.

The welfare corporatist practice of breaking into relatively small units also supports loyalty. It is in face-to-face encounters with long time colleagues that the sense of *Gemeinschaft* is formed, that the alienation of a faceless and impersonal bureaucracy can be overcome. The welfare practices themselves give the employee a key consolation: there really *is* a magic helper, someone always there to fall back on. Mary Chalmers said it succinctly: "They've always been there."

There is one other vital aspect of welfare corporatist firms which made them the object of so many loyalties: they stood for something, they had a mission and objectives that people could identify with. Simply, their purpose for existence was a Roycean "cause" that people could relate to, which could give meaning to their work lives. Today, of course, the objective of virtually every American corporation is to maximize shareholder wealth. That may seem obvious and incontrovertible. But it was not always so. In another place I have analyzed the purposes of business that were articulated by its leaders over the years since the corporations first formed (Clancy 1989). In the early days, most leaders supported the modern view: the purpose of business was solely to make money. But with Henry Ford, a new view was put forth: a business was there to supply goods and services for society. He said: "It is the function of business to produce for consumption and not for money or speculation" (Ford 1923, 12). This became a popular view in the 1960s and 1970s, the high-water mark of welfare corporatism. The CEO of the John Deere Company said in the early 1970s: "We are proud because we are engaged in a necessary kind of business. . . . We are feeding the world" (O'Toole 1986, 233). And most corporate leaders of that welfare corporatist time had similar sentiments: IBM stood for excellence in customer service; du Pont for "Better living through chemistry"; Johnson & Johnson for attending to the world's medical needs. These were all "causes" that could animate people, causes they could rally around and become loyal to, values that could be internalized.

Let me give you an illustration which makes the point: Safeway, the California supermarket chain, had started as a family business and had grown nicely under a management that believed in treating the public and the employees with dignity and respect. Their old motto said it all: "Safeway means security." A clever, but certainly not contrived, message to the public: they would get food at reasonable prices. It was also a clear signal to the workforce: they had lifetime jobs if they did their work well.

All of this was washed away when the new generation of Safeway managers caught the gold bug. Everyone else was doing it. Although business was good, they were soon convinced that a leveraged buyout (LBO) of their public company would make them rich beyond the dreams of Croesus. All they had to do was saddle the company with a huge debt, readily financed by the hot money all around in the 1980s. But to pay off that debt, costs must be severely cut. Now, that's a business euphemism: "cost cutting." What it usually means, and did in this case, is fire people and close stores. So, people who had dedicated their lives to the old company were out in the street. Neighborhoods which had supported the firm for generations no longer had a convenient place to shop. Not coincidentally, Safeway got a new motto: "Targeted returns on current investment." Not to put too fine a point on it, but I ask you, could anyone feel the slightest loyalty to an organization with a slogan like that? Exactly how do you make a "cause" out of "targeted returns on current investment"? How could you internalize that one? Nonetheless, paradoxically—a paradox I have been attempting to unravel in these pages—paradoxically, it is even money that there are still loyalists at Safeway, almost certainly people of cohort 1 who stubbornly hold on to the "old dispensation," despite the worst that management can do. But the future is clear to me as well: the younger cohorts would find the notion of loyalty to Safeway an odd one indeed.

We saw in our discussion of the psychology of loyalty[6] that the process of company loyalty formation follows a typical course. A person comes to the workplace with norms developed from his earlier socialization. On the job, he finds some goals and values of the organization, which, if they are congenial to his own values, he in time internalizes and takes the company's values as his own. From this perspective, it was the most natural thing in the world for the cohort 1 people to develop an enduring sense of loyalty. They were socialized in a time when the prevailing social character embraced bureaucratic values, when confidence in business as an institution was at its zenith. And, they joined companies which largely had values that could be reasonably internalized. Even when the companies shifted course and abandoned their social purposes, they held fast to their loyalty. The cohort 2 people, socialized in a time when antiauthoritarianism was high and confidence in business plummeting, had a much more fragile base to build on. When Corporate America said baldly that its sole raison d'etre was to make money, when that became clear, then the edifice of their loyalty, built on sand, collapsed. They were left wandering between the two worlds, that of the old dispensation when corporate loyalty and bureaucratic values were the norm, and the world of the new generation, when such things were definitely passé.

Let us turn now to our youngest cohort, the new generation, and see how they dealt with these issues.

Part Three
"All Wars Fought, All Faiths in Man Shaken": The Youngest Cohort

9
The New Generation: The Seventies

As an endless dream it went on; the spirit of the past brooding over a new generation, shouting the old cries, learning the old creeds . . . destined finally to go out into that dirty gray turmoil . . . a new generation . . . grown up to find all Gods dead, all wars fought, all faiths in man shaken . . .

—Fitzgerald, *This Side of Paradise*

The New Generation Speaks

As we have seen, our cohort 1 friends of the old dispensation grew up in a time when the corporate culture was intact, when bureaucratic values of solidarity and loyalty to institutions were the social norms. When they joined large corporations, they found the welfare corporatist environment congenial, seemingly right and natural. Even when those forms passed into history, their loyalties, forged in an earlier time, remained largely intact. Their younger colleagues of cohort 2 were less fortunate: wandering between two worlds, their own upbringing and socialization were in the turbulent sixties, when all was being questioned and new values being proposed. But they, like their older colleagues, joined welfare corporatist firms and found there the relics of the old corporate culture. When that culture came tumbling down in the layoffs and restructuring of the eighties, their reaction was dismay, disillusionment, a sense of betrayal. Their earliest socialization had been incompatible with the forms they first faced in their work lives, and no strong foundation had been laid against the day when those forms would disappear.

Our youngest cohort, the new generation, had quite a different historical experience. They were socialized in the seventies, a time when the debate on the corporate culture was largely over: confidence in institutions, social trust, social cohesion—all were failing. They too began their work lives under welfare corporatism, but when that edifice crumbled, they were undismayed: it was as though that is just what they expected from Corporate America all along. And so in my interviews with these younger people, I found little angst, little disillusionment. Bob Dylan said it: "When you ain't got nothin', you got nothin' to lose." Scott Fitzgerald, in our epigraph, describes the young people in the 1920s and the world they would face as adults. Our cohort 3 friends seem to have much the same response, they too had "grown up to find all Gods dead, all wars fought . . ." They too would confront the world with a new set of values, and make an accommodation to a new way of living and doing business. And, largely I found that their accommodation was successful. There is, as I said, little sense of angst; there is none of the "hard and bitter agony" their elder brothers and sisters went through when the old dispensation passed. For them, that war had been fought, that God was dead. And so we shall find a matter-of-fact, clear-eyed assessment of the new realities of Corporate America, an acceptance of that and an accommodation to it. Let us listen to some of these people.

Gene Evans is fairly typical of the younger subjects I interviewed. Born in 1960, he is at the midpoint of my cohort 3. Gene was just eight years old when the Vietcong launched the Tet offensive, and gave the lie to the U.S. government's claims that the war was being won. He was ten in 1970, when U.S. troops invaded Cambodia, sparking nationwide antiwar demonstrations and tragically concluding with the death of four students at Kent State, shot on 4 May by Ohio National Guardsmen. He was eleven when the *Pentagon Papers* were published, revelations of U.S. duplicity which further undermined public confidence in the integrity of government. There was more and more bad news that year of 1971: more than one thousand New York State troopers stormed Attica Prison to end a hostage crisis, and nine hostages and twenty-eight convicts were killed. The economy was in trouble as inflation rose precipitously; Nixon responded with a wage, price, and rent freeze. In 1973, the landmark *Roe vs. Wade* decision endorsed new American attitudes on abortion. That year as well saw the end of the American involvement in Vietnam as the last troops left in April. But more shocks and bad news were in store. The U.S. Senate began its Watergate hearings in May and the Justice Department appointed Archibald Cox special prosecutor in the same month. Nixon's long struggle against his fate continued before a fascinated/horrified nation until the denouement: his release of incriminating tapes under a Supreme Court order on 5 August 1974 and his resignation three days later. Gene was fourteen. He was nineteen when the Three Mile Island nuclear plant spewed radioactivity around Harrisburg, and the oil crisis had Americans on long gas lines. He was twenty when the Iranian hostage crisis—a bitter blow to American pride—began in 1980.

Gene is a native Californian who has been with Softmatics only two years; this is his fourth job, at age 34. He has been laid off twice; it doesn't seem to have bothered him. His job satisfaction measurement is quite high, but his organizational commitment is more than one standard deviation lower than the Softmatics mean. On his work, he says:

> I don't feel I've found a new calling or anything like that, but I do enjoy helping people, trouble-shooting their problems . . . I've always realized that it is a job. I want to enjoy my job and look forward to it, but I've been laid off twice so I know that in most cases there's not a whole lot of loyalty by the company. When times are tough and they're not bringing in any money, they're going to lay off. That's just a given fact. So I try, you know, I try to stay there. I don't take it too personal and I look at a company as to what I can learn or what I can gain from the company. . . . But I don't have blind devotion. I mean I want to gain something out of it too. Hopefully . . . the company will also.

Note his insouciance about layoffs: "It's a given fact . . . I don't take it too personal. . . ." And note as well the relationship he sees with a company, a pure exchange: he hopes to learn something for another job elsewhere, and he trusts that the company will gain something as well. A very impersonal, rational contract—worlds away from the emotional attachment we have seen with our older subjects. Recall Bill Abernathy from cohort 2 before his disillusionment: "There was a relationship, an honest relationship between me, my fellow workers, my supervisor . . . there was a camaraderie. . . . a community." I should note here that Gene's stance—that he has made a conscious and voluntary contract—is the stance that many contemporary writers assume to be the stance of all employees. I think I have shown that this may be true for cohort 3, but it is most definitely not true of the older cohorts.

Gene's views on loyalty confirm his new and minimalist idea of the relationship. He told me that his loyalty had neither diminished nor grown in his career (as is the case for the preponderance of cohort 3), but listen to his definition of loyalty, an almost comical reductio ad absurdum of Royce's noble virtue:

> I feel that I've got a set of values that pretty much go down the line with all of my employers that I've been with. You know, to be honest with them and not steal, or you know, try to take advantage of the company.

Gene's pragmatism—if that is what it is—and his minimal sense of loyalty are generally echoed by his coevals. Here is Dave Schneider, 31 years old and already a veteran of four professional jobs before he came to Softmatics two and half years before our conversation. He first distinguishes between loyalty to a person and loyalty to an organization:

> Personally . . . loyalty probably means hell or high water, where I'm loyal to that, be it a friend or a significant other; and that's kind of unconditional. . . . I think professionally loyalty has taken on a, maybe a narrower meaning. I think that (it) means to have a vested interest in that organization and to do everything ethically, . . . to see it go forward and to stick by it as far as that goes, but in these days of corporate layoffs and cost-cutting—I'm not trying to make any subjective statement about whether that's good, bad or indifferent—but you know, you got to kind of watch out for number one . . .

Linda Altmeir, 35 years old, spoke of the irrelevance of loyalty in the new exchange relationship with a company:

> Well, it gets back to feeling like I was a factory worker type there. You know, I didn't feel like I had any particular value, like I could just be replaced by anybody just out of school . . . That's what the position was. So I'm sure that was realistic, but, you know, it didn't feel much like loyalty to me. I didn't feel like it would have mattered one way or another if I left.

One of Linda's colleagues noted "Loyalty is not going to send my kids to college." And yet another seemed honestly to fail to grasp the very meaning of the word, when I asked him what loyalty meant to him:

> I don't know. To something? I'm trying to think of a word here to put it in—like for work-related? Like if you have a relationship or something like that? That's one aspect. (It means) trust them. Don't lie to them and stuff like that.

Many of this age group also echoed Gene Evans's insouciance about layoffs and said they were not surprised or angered: it was what they expected from the company. This is thirty-eight-year-old Peter Dennison; I have just asked him if the layoffs had any effect on his attitudes:

> Not really. I mean those are business decisions that had to be made. I mean we have to recognize that the industry has changed. It's constantly changing. It's something that if you don't change, you'll be out of business. If you don't do some of the things that have to be done, everybody will lose. . . . Gone are the years of what I would call golden handcuffs and not only are corporations not as loyal to their employees, the employees can't be as loyal to their corporations for life either because there's just no guarantee.

One of his thirty-year-old colleagues was similarly nonchalant about layoffs, the very experience which had shattered the older Bill Abernathy and many others:

> The layoffs seemed like normal life to me. It wasn't terribly unusual . . . I've never been afraid of a layoff in my life. . . . There's one of these little self-help business books and one line in there was you should start planning for your next job the moment you start your current job and I've always thought like that. . . . So layoffs, they don't bother me and the way I see it is the layoffs get rid of a lot of the dead weight and we have layoffs now because it's . . . too complicated to fire people . . .

Peter Dennison touched on a pillar of the welfare corporatist system, the "golden handcuffs" of a lifetime job, and he noted that now there are no guarantees. Many of his colleagues also implicitly attacked another welfare corporatist feature that they found still alive in Softmatics. We have seen that a cornerstone of that old way was a sense of family and community, a *Gemeinschaft*, the bonds of past time shared and future time together anticipated. "We are collegial, we work with our brothers." To the new generation, those treasured bonds were nothing of the sort: they were some kind of conspiracy; it was the "buddy"system, the "good old boy" network.

One put it in the context of the differences between their old and new parents, the welfare corporatist RLX and the "modern" DRI:

> I have nothing against RLX. The only thing I see, there's a lot of promotions within because of the buddy system, because we go drink beer or play golf or something like that. You're promoted because you know someone. With DRI it's the opposite. You have to prove yourself, then the promotions come and that's kind of a hard thing to take because you go from one end of the spectrum to the other end and there's no in-between happy medium it seems like.

Another said:

> It's still the good old boy network . . . hasn't changed . . . the old style of management, old attitudes are still around. . . . Moving your friends and your acquaintances up the ladder.

In general, for these younger people, the job is not a mission; they do not serve a cause; they are not in some kind of *ersatz* community, some latterday Brook Farm. Rewards should come from merit alone, not from loyalty or past time shared. And the essential thing is to build your resumé, for the inevitable day when you will move on. This is a consistent theme in this younger group. A few examples:

> If I was in a position to manage people . . . the first thing that I would want them to do is: "What's your resumé saying . . . You need to be prepared at all times to find where else you can go, to be prepared to go somewhere else, I encourage you to be that way, I want you to learn because I think ultimately that would contribute back to you . . ."

Another told me what he had learned from the layoffs:

> The job I'm working on right now, the opportunity I'm getting is . . . I think good experience for me, for my career. . . . you know the reality of it all is that it's a business . . . Everybody is waking up to that fact . . . So what I know now and what I have done since then is always . . . constantly build up more skills so that if you ever do get laid off again, you know you'll have the skills

> set where you would be valuable to somebody else. You know it (the layoffs) did teach me something: Don't ever sit tight; don't ever get too comfortable. Always improve, always build on your skills, always make sure you are marketable.

It is interesting that this stance, using the job as a base for another, building skills for future marketability—essentially taking more than giving to the company—it is interesting that this stance was deprecated by an older employee, Joe Weston from cohort 2, whom we met earlier. He calls the new people "surfers." Here's how he puts it in the context of the new attitudes in sales, and contrasts it with his own loyalty:

> I never thought of it as a loyalty issue, but we talk about sales people who depend upon selling the best products in order to sell. We say, "Well what happens when the product they're selling isn't the best"; and I have a couple other acquaintances who are sales people who are that way and I tease them, I call them surfers, because they ride the waves . . . They're just riding the top of the wave of each product, but they don't have the loyalty to the product to ride the product down. . . .

Let us look now at some of the background for these attitudes, the 1970s, the time of their socialization. We will look first at the economic conditions of the 1970s, which helped spell the end of welfare corporatism. Then we move on to the social character forming in the 1970s, as traced by public opinion polls.

The Economy of the 1970s

We saw earlier how the United States sailed through the 1960s on a tide of fortunate circumstances: world trade domination, low inflation, a consumption-mad society. And with the institutionalization of Keynesian economics, policy makers had come to believe that they understood the economy and could run it like a machine. But then in the 1970s the supreme confidence of the Keynesian interventionists was badly shaken by an unexplainable phenomenon: stagflation. The Keynesians held the Phillips curve as an article of faith: inflation and unemployment were inversely related; orthodoxy knew it was impossible to have both high inflation and high unemployment, but of course denying it did not make it go away. This was the opening for the monetarists who asserted that national income and the money supply were strictly correlated. But monetary policy itself seemed of little use under the "supply shocks" of the 1970s; the impact on inflation of higher energy and food prices seemed more relevant than changes in the money supply. After 1973 and well into the early 1980s, the economy was marked by rising inflation and unemployment, with episodes of high growth (e.g., 4.9 percent in 1976) followed by recession.

At the beginning of 1973, Nixon dropped controls on agriculture and farm prices exploded. This, with the quadrupling of oil prices from OPEC actions, drove the economy down while at the same time driving inflation to 11 percent per year in 1974. From a GNP growth rate of 5.2 percent in 1973, the economy lost 0.5 percent the following year, and lost 1.3 percent in 1975. The government's response was "halting and feeble" (Galambos and Pratt 1988, 205). Like the Nixon years, Carter's watch was accompanied by record inflation, trade deficits, and oil prices, and then a severe slump that proved the longest in postwar history, continuing until 1983. Oil prices were one of the prime culprits. After nearly quadrupling in 1974, prices stabilized but then hit $30 barrel in 1980 with the aftershocks of the Iranian revolution. In only ten years, the price of this vital commodity had increased tenfold (Galambos and Pratt 1988, 220). The U.S. government seemed unable to do a thing about it.

One thing is clear from the record of government attempts to manage the economy: they had failed to achieve stability, to tame the business cycle. The dream of the Keynesians had failed. The most that could be said is that the measures mitigated the business cycles; the built in stabilizers of the New Deal appeared to have prevented a new Great Depression (Bruchey 1988, 188–97).

But a long-term trend of lagging productivity was perhaps the most disturbing feature of these times. The rate of productivity improvement fell to 2.3 percent during 1966–73, then to 1 percent in 1973–77 and to 0.4 percent during 1977–78. In 1979 and 1980 there was no growth at all and productivity actually declined (Galambos and Pratt 1988, 134 and Bruchey 1988, 207). The reasons for productivity decline are complex but the result is clear: an erosion in the standard of living. Various accounts have been given of the American decline in productivity improvement, ranging from the demographic one (more women and young people in the workforce), to declines in investment rates. It is a fact that the proportion of GNP invested in R&D dropped in the late 1960s and early 1970s. Some pointed to the enervating burden of government, which raised costs and discouraged investment. Others made the case for management responsibility: the risk averse school of management, which avoids new products and processes. Many more innovations seem to have been made in tax avoidance and other financial management than in technology and improved techniques. Rather than creating new wealth, we have seen paper innovations which just rearrange industrial assets. The merger and acquisitions movements of the 1960s, and then again of the 1980s, are illustrative.

Before the 1960s, in the great merger movement of the late nineteenth and early twentieth century, the imperatives had been to increase market share by horizontal integration and to rationalize the business by vertical integration. In the 1960s, the conglomerate movement was born; firms like Gulf & Western, ITT and LTV grew vastly by acquisitions in totally unrelated fields. ITT, for example, at one time owned a baking company, a hotel chain, an insurance company, publishing companies, and various unrelated manufacturing companies. In place of intelligent investment and attention to cost reduction and product enhancement, conglomerate managers were bent on short-term profits from the market manipulation of company assets (Bruchey 1988, 207–8).

It has been said that America has been on a long course of deindustrialization since the 1970s, a profound structural shift from manufacturing to services. Not all agree that deindustrialization has actually taken place, pointing to the fact that manufacturing has the same share of national output as it did in the 1950s. The employment figures tell a different story: manufacturing's share of nonfarm employment declined from 37 percent in 1960 to 24 percent in 1985, although this can be explained by increased productivity. But there is a sense that this loss of jobs and slower growth in manufacturing output poses a threat to the American economy. Between 1960 and 1986, services industries accounted for 89 percent of total employment growth.

Manufacturing jobs have gone abroad in a massive way. Management's response to strong foreign competition in the 1970s was to shift capital and plants to low labor-cost areas; partly as a result, U.S. manufacturing lost one and a half million production jobs from 1977 to 1983. This was a different kind of investment than that of the early days of industrialization, an investment in rationalization (cost cutting), not in growing the nation's industrial base with new products and new output capacity.

All in all, the 1970s were a very difficult time for American industry, and the millions who depended on it for jobs and stable prices. In the 1970s and early 1980s the United States experienced three recessions, double-digit inflation and unemployment rates, 20 percent mortgage rates, two oil embargoes and a halving of its saving rate (Light 1988, 44). Surprisingly, welfare corporatism survived the 1970s—barely. The old management ideology that saw benefits to the system of lifetime employment (at least for white collar workers) weathered the economic storms of the 1970s and its practices continued. But the effects that the economic upheavals had on attitudes and social character may be seen as we explore the public opinion data from that era.

Social Character and Public Opinion in the Nineteen Seventies

The trends in opinion that we saw earlier in the 1960s continued unabated in the 1970s: confidence and trust down; anomie rising. These sentiments were only exacerbated by the events of the 1970s: the staggering economy, and most importantly, Vietnam and Watergate. As we have seen, mistrust in government had grown alarmingly from 1964–70; a vague sense of something gone wrong seemed to be confirmed by the Vietnam escalation in 1965, the student protests, and the Watts riots of 1965. Michigan's Survey Research Center's survey on trust in government showed marked change from 1964 to 1970: on government waste, agreements went from 47 to 59 percent; on the influence of big interests, from 29 to 50 percent; on mistrust of Washington "to do the right thing," from 22 to 44 percent. But on cynicism about the integrity of officials, there was little change in this period: in 1964, 29 percent thought there were "quite a few of the people running the government who are a little crooked", this moved up only to 32 percent in 1970. Watergate changed all that. By 1974, after the Watergate revelations, this measure increased to 45 percent. The condition seemed to be permanent: neither the accession of the honest Jerry Ford, nor the election of squeaky-clean Jimmy Carter had any effect. The level of mistrust stayed about the same in 1976 under Ford, and in Carter's time, between 1976 and 1978, the indicators of mistrust increased again from an average of 61 percent to 63 percent. By 1978 mistrust was at an all-time high, and by 1980, fully two thirds of Americans distrusted the government (Lipset and Schneider 1987, 16).

Corporate America was tarred by the same brush. There was both the spillover of the odor of corruption emanating from Watergate, and of course the frustrations from the "stagflated" economy. Confidence in business leadership had begun to decline in the 1960s, but with a lag in time compared to the government confidence figures. Attitudes toward business were actually improving a bit up to 1965, then began to fall after 1968. As the Watergate tale of corruption unfolded and the economy worsened, confidence in business skidded: by 1975, a year after Watergate but in the midst of a recession, antibusiness sentiment was at 81 percent, and reached 86 percent in 1977 and 1978 before a modest rebound occurred. But never since has business reached the 70 percent approval ratings of 1968, nor even close to the 58 percent of 1969 (Lipset and Schneider 1987, 32). Stagflation was eating away at the social fabric. In 1978, fully three quarters of those surveyed had the sense that the rich were getting richer and the poor poorer (Russell and Megaard 1988, 142).

Lipset and Schneider's study of confidence in American institutions emphasizes that the decline in confidence was not confined to government nor business—those actors reasonably and logically culpable for Watergate, Vietnam, and stagflation. No, every source of power and influence in American life went down the long slide, losing public esteem in a general rout: medicine, science, organized religion, Congress, the courts—and the melancholy list goes on.

> the collapse of confidence was general. The period of the most rapid increase in alienation and cynicism was 1965 to 1972. Events since that time—Watergate, and other scandals, the energy crisis, recession, and inflation—have done nothing to reverse the trend; rather, faith in institutions tended to move down gradually in the 1970s and at the start of the 1980s to a level much lower than that of the 1960s. (Lipset and Schneider 1987, 383)

Lipset and Schneider are very much of the opinion that the loss of confidence in institutions is directly a product of events: particularly Watergate, Vietnam, and the 1970s economy. I believe this is mistaken. The very poll data they cite belies this view as a complete explanation; there is something deeper afoot. Antiauthoritarian and antibureaucratic stances were on the rise in the 1960s, sparked by the counterculture's critique of the entire corporate culture that had slowly become dominant by that time. Lipset and Schneider point to the comparative experiences of the 1930s and 1940s versus the 1970s and make the legitimate point that in the earlier days of crisis, government had responded admirably, fighting the Depression and winning the war. In the 1970s, government appeared weak and corrupt: the debacle of Vietnam, the Watergate scandal, the complete ineffectuality before the miasma of stagflation. This is all certainly true, but attitudes had begun to shift well before the worst of Vietnam, well before anyone ever heard of the Watergate complex, and in the good economic times of the 1960s. The sad events of the 1970s were, I believe, a mediating variable, merely confirming the antiauthoritarian sentiments of the 1960s and rallying more people around that banner. For confirmation of this point, an analysis of the General Social Survey results for 1973 and 1974 revealed that it was the middle-aged and middle-income Republican Nixon supporter who was more likely to have lost confidence in government leadership than all others. The young had very little confidence to begin with (Dunham and Mauss 1976, 485). Lou Harris summed up the general population's sense of what the kids of the 1960s suspected all along: there were two kinds of people, the insiders in Washington, Wall Street, and Corporate America—and everyone else. The real lesson from Watergate was: if you are powerful, you don't go to jail (Harris 1989, 33).

What was the response to this loss of confidence? We saw in an earlier chapter the rise in the sense of anomie that began in the 1960s, and is still unfortunately on the rise. Nine separate measures of anomie show a statistically significant rise in this sense of futility and normlessness from the 1960s through the 1970s (T. W. Smith 1980, 9–13). In polls from 1973 to 1976 nearly 70 percent thought that "a person these days doesn't know whom he can count on"; Fromm's magic helper had decamped (Russell and Megaard 1988, 143). And we saw Robert Merton's idea that one reacts to anomie characteristically in one of several ways: ritualism, retreatism, rebellion (Merton 1968, 195). Clearly, the young chose rebellion in the 1960s; they chose the attempt to remake society with their own values and lifestyles. That failed; the technocracy was not overcome, and the rebels went to work like everyone else. The 1970s showed a shift toward a different strategy: retreatism, or disengagement. The philosopher Peter Marin, writing in 1975, thought he observed a

> growing solipsism . . . the world view emerging among us centered solely on the self and with individual survival as the sole good . . . a retreat from the world of morality and history, an unembarrassed denial of human reciprocity and community . . . The denial . . . of the claims of others upon the self. (Marin 1975, 46–48)

Another observer said: "A quest for personal fulfillment within a small community . . . of significant others: this strikes me as the dominant thrust of American civilization during the sixties and seventies" (Clecak 1983, 9). This general sense of these observers has been confirmed by polling data; Norval Glenn's 1987 review of the relevant poll data concludes:

> It seems possible, even probable, that most of the trends shown by . . . survey data for the past 3 or 4 decades reflect in some way one basic trend, namely an increased tendency for individuals to withdraw allegiance from social groups, institutions, traditional religion, and anything outside themselves. (Glenn 1987, S124)

We shall have more to say in a later chapter on this general retreat from institutionalized society, from the bureaucratic culture itself. For this disturbing trend has continued into our own day, has worsened in fact. More and more people have "checked out" from major governmental and private institutions, using them as needed, but shunning them if at all possible—certainly not granting them their loyalty, as had their elders under the old dispensation.

The 1970s were marked not only by a loss of confidence in institutions; there was a loss of confidence in the future as well. As I noted in chapter 3, even in the bleakest days of the Great Depression Americans retained their old faith in a brighter tomorrow. By 1979, this faith had evaporated: public opinion about confidence in the future was at its lowest ebb since scientific polling began in the 1930s (Ladd and Lipset 1980, 3). It was actually worse than that: not only did Americans no longer think the future would be better, they thought it would be worse than the present (Lipset and Schneider 1987, 137).

Other attitude changes marked the 1970s, changes which had a direct effect on the social character of our youngest cohorts: the traits that parents valued in their children. In 1954, fifty-seven percent agreed that "a child should conform"; the agreement was half that by 1973, twenty-seven percent. Sixty-five percent believed in 1954 that it was "wrong for a child to talk back"; only forty-one percent thought so in 1973 (Niemi et al. 1989, 267). Similarly, a comparison of polls from 1964 to 1973 showed that parents' valuations of child qualities associated with obedience or conformity declined, while those associated with autonomy or self-direction increased (Alwin 1989, 95). If we look at the results from the General Social Survey, we can see these same trends. For example, the trait of "getting along with other children" showed a statistically significant decline in importance from 1973 to 1976; the value of honesty, good sense, and judgment increased in the same period (T. W. Smith 1980, 155–59). What I believe this shows is that the bureaucratic values were no longer prized by parents in the 1970s; the old corporate culture which valued conformity, loyalty, and collective effort was no longer believed in, no longer seen as a fit set of values to inculcate in children.

Let me try to summarize what was happening in the 1970s, when our youngest group was growing up.

- Confidence in institutional leadership in general continued to fall. By 1980, two thirds of Americans distrusted the government; antibusiness sentiment stood at 86 percent in 1977 and 1978.

- The sense of anomie reached new heights in the 1970s. In the middle years of the decade, nearly 70 percent thought that "a person these days doesn't know whom he can count on." And, in 1978 seventy-five percent felt that the rich were getting richer and the poor poorer. The old American belief in Adam Smith's "Invisible Hand"—that private interest would lead to public good, that the rising tide would lift all boats, the faith that the economy was not a zero-sum game—had evaporated.

- Parental assessment of desirable child traits had changed dramatically in the 1970s. More and more parents stressed autonomy and fewer and fewer valued conformity. The bureaucratic values were no longer prized, and parents taught children to be more ready to go it alone.

And so, we find a different social character among these people when we encountered them as adults in the mid-1990s. Gene Evans valued his job, but "I've always realized that it is a job . . . I don't have blind devotion. I mean I want to gain something out of it too." Dave Schneider remarked "I think professionally loyalty has taken on a, maybe a narrower meaning . . . in these days of corporate layoffs and cost-cutting . . . you know, you got to kind of watch out for number one. . . ." These people of the new generation have accommodated themselves to the world they grew up in and the new management practices they have encountered. Their faith is not in major institutions of any kind, least so in large businesses. Their faith is in their own skills and experiences, their ability to take what they can from their work experiences, move on and find something better elsewhere. We heard them: "What's your resumé saying? . . . You need to be prepared at all times to find where else you can go, to be prepared to go somewhere else." And, "I've never been afraid of a layoff in my life. . . . You should start planning for your next job the moment you start your current job and I've always thought like that. . . . So layoffs, they don't bother me."

The new generation's stance carries with it a new view of company loyalty; its value is discounted, the disciples of the old dispensation scorned. One said:

> My personal opinion is the people that feel the company is being disloyal to them by not providing a job to them or guaranteeing a job to them are the ones that probably aren't as productive . . .

In the next chapter we shall look further at the cohort 3 generation and its attitudes. We shall also tell the tale of the end of welfare corporatism, the end that the old dispensation folk of cohort 1 weathered, the end that shattered the fragile hopes of the middle cohort, and the end that failed to surprise the new generation.

10

The Shipwreck of Welfare Corporatism

The duty of management is to make money. Our primary objective is not to make steel.

—David Roderick, former chairman of U.S. Steel, cited in O'Toole 1986, 145.

Welfare Corporatism Passes

All of our subjects were touched by welfare corporatism. For those of the old dispensation it was a way of work life that seemed as natural as rainfall. For the middle cohort it was different; they found themselves between two worlds. Socialized in an antiauthoritarian age, they began their careers with welfare corporatist firms, and for ten years or so, worked away in them. In time, they gave allegiance to these firms, then watched in dismay as the corporatist system disappeared. For the new generation, cohort 3, the experience of welfare corporatism was brief and they seldom paid its loyalty-building mechanisms much attention. One of them expressed his distaste for the very idea of the welfare corporatist "magic helper": "I can't stand people that expect the company—this mythical entity that doles out punishment and benefits—to hand them a career and lead them through it at every step."

When welfare corporatism collapsed, the youngest cohort shrugged. For collapse it did, beginning mainly in the 1980s. By the 1990s, firm after firm had left the vision and the practice of welfare corporatism behind it. Even some of the most stalwart welfare corporatist corporations spurned its practices, eschewed their traditional paternalism; old-line corporatists like IBM, Eastman Kodak, duPont—and the former parent of Softmatics, RLX, which began layoffs in the mid-1980s.

The drain of human capital from Corporate America continues apace, and seems to have taken on a life of its own: no longer are cutbacks associated with hard times—good times and bad times, layoffs continue. When the economy picks up, workers are not hired back, in fact more are let go. Job losses in January 1994—a good economic period—were over 108,000, a new record for a month. It was the prosperous companies reducing staff along with their less-fortunate brothers (Uchitelle 1994, A-1). In July 1993, Procter & Gamble announced that it would eliminate 13,000 jobs, twelve percent of the work force; in the same announcement, the company said they expected record profits. General Electric, AT&T, NYNEX, GTE, Gillette, Eli Lilly, Johnson & Johnson—all profitable, all laying off (Chilton and Weidenbaum 1994, 8).

Nor is this strictly an American phenomenon. Since 1990, Siemens, Daimler Benz, and Phillips have eliminated tens of thousands of jobs (*Economist* 1993, 63). Even the storied Japanese commitment to lifetime employment is under siege. Nippon Telephone and Telegraph announced it would eliminate 30,000 jobs over the next few years; Nissan announced the closing of its Zama works, once a symbol of Japan's economic miracle. It was not only the factory workers who were being let go; as in America, it was the university-trained managers and professionals, the loyalists, who now dreaded the *kata tataki*, the tap on the shoulder (Sanger 1993, A-1).

The reaction from the investment community? Enthusiastic approval, unmixed with any concerns about the write-offs of human capital. Wall Street simply loves layoffs. The Standard & Poor's index rose just eight percent in 1993, but when Boeing told the analysts it would layoff 21,000 people on 18 February 1993 it was rewarded with a 31 percent run-up in its stock by the end of the year. Similarly, IBM announced on 27 July 1993 that it would cut 60,000 jobs; the stock rose 30 percent by year-end. Cummins Engine, a bastion of welfare corporatism, announced the layoff of 2000 employees on 30 October 1995: the stock rose the next day (*The New York Times* 10/31/1995, C-3).

What has happened here? Why did Corporate America, and its counterparts around the world, begin to cut staff with abandon? The conventional answer is competition, and I will address that, but I believe there is something more basic at work here: a fundamental shift in management ideology. A change in ideology should not really surprise us: after all, managers are no Janissaries, cultureless people: they grew up in the same society as everyone else; they absorbed the historical experiences of their generation, and perceived them in their own generation's unique way; managers too shared in the decay of the old bureaucratic values that began to change American social character in the 1960s.

But, in any event, American management ideology did shift; in some sense it has returned to much older views about the purpose for business, and much older means to accomplish that. Alfred Sloan, who headed General Motors from 1923 until his retirement in the 1950s, spoke for an old strain of business thinking when he said: "The primary purpose of the corporation . . . was to make money, not just motor cars" (Sloan 1965, 64). As I have noted earlier, Sloan's great rival, Henry Ford, scorned this idea, saying "It is the function of business to produce for consumption and not for money or speculation" (Ford 1923, 12). Ford's view became the more popular one in the 1960s and 1970s, the heyday of welfare corporatism, when firms tended to ascribe noble purposes to their activities, purposes that many employees internalized and forged into loyalty. But Sloan has won out in the end—or at least so far. We saw David Roderick in this chapter's epigraph mouthing Sloan's words in the 1980s—almost a paraphrase: "The duty of management is to make money. Our primary objective is not to make steel." That is a vision that an employee would find difficult to internalize as a treasured goal in the best of circumstances; under the threat of termination, it would be impossible.

What has happened is that a new generation of management has caught up with academic thinking on the purpose and governance of business. As early as 1932, Berle and Means had shown that the American companies had become effectively unmoored from their nominal owners, the shareholders. Stock ownership was so diffused that the shareholders could not exercise their rights of ownership, leaving it to the salaried managers to run the companies as they wished (Berle and Means 1932, 2–3). And "as they wished" in time inevitably became serving their own interests. (Ackoff 1986, F-2). Berle and Means's critique was ignored until the late 1970s and early 1980s, but then it was received as a thunderbolt: managers controlled large corporations but were oblivious to the claims of the legal owners. Three developments assured that something would be done about that: academic theory, concentration of stock ownership, and a new species of financier, the "raider."

Beginning in the 1970s, business schools had begun to preach a simple mantra: the purpose of a business—and the sole guide to management—was to maximize shareholder wealth. For a public corporation there was a single metric for this: stock price. Forgotten, or scorned, were other purposes for a business: providing employment or serving society. Ideals such as "feeding the world" or "better living through chemistry" might still remain as PR slogans, but the new orthodoxy dismissed them as puerile.

At about the same time, shareholder concentrations came about by the great rise in "institutional" investors. Managers of pensions funds, mutual funds, and insurance companies had in time accumulated great hoards of company securities. These managers were rated on the performance of their funds, and rated generally on short-term results. Only the prices of their holdings could matter to them. The idea of a corporation serving any purpose but maximizing wealth seemed as anachronistic to them as the principle of divine right.

The raiders saw their opening. Many American corporations were simply not deriving the maximum return from their assets. The raiders could borrow money and launch a hostile bid for the companies' securities and, if successful, dismember the corporation, selling off assets to repay the debt. If unsuccessful, they could still win: those companies that still had fragmented ownership and a board made up of the CEO's friends and employees would buy off the raider with "greenmail," a premium price for the raider's holdings. The actions of the raiders were applauded by Wall Street, the institutional investors, and much of the academic community.

For those on the losing side of these transactions, the reaction was dismay and anger, a feeling that some sacred trust had been violated. The chairman of GenCorp articulated the concerns of the old dispensation: "It's one thing to have something that is financially attractive to shareholders, but at the same time . . . managers have responsibilities to other interests—to customers, suppliers, and to employees" (Bennett 1990, 130). But, for an emotional response, none can top Walter Kissinger's. Listen to the former CEO of Allen Group's *cri de coeur* on the passing of welfare corporatism under the blows of the raiders:

> The victims may range from well-known consumer names to our leading defense contractors . . . None is sacred or immune from

> the onslaught of the financial wizards who move companies like pieces of paper and casually trade their "Boardwalk" and "Park Place" with junk bonds as payment. . . . It is of no interest or concern to these individuals that they touch the lives of tens of thousands of workers who may become unemployed; that they destroy the careers of dedicated individuals who have devoted their lives to building a company; that they frequently destroy communities, that they undermine the vitality and creativity of a company. (Kissinger 1986, 15)

But Kissinger was fighting a rearguard action; the old dispensation was losing that war. All of these developments—the sanction of theory, the concentration of ownership, the success of the raiders, and another: competitive pressures—-all together brought down welfare corporatism. The idea that the company was there to serve anyone but shareholders became more than passé, it became idiotic. Any CEO who would seriously voice such a view—other than as PR—faced summary dismissal.

American management ideologies have been on long trajectory which, in the end, has proven circular. In the early days of industrialization, the workforce was viewed simply as a resource, a means to generate wealth. This attitude was shored up by Social Darwinism, which taught that the workingmen were biologically unfit to do more than simple tasks and were fortunate to have the superior management class to direct them and provide a livelihood. Scientific Management had a less contemptuous philosophy and gave the men credit for ambition, at least in material terms. But, the assumption of the superior ability of management to design the work remained from the days of Social Darwinism.

The advocates of welfare *capitalism* from 1900 through the 1920s—to their great credit—felt responsibility for the welfare of their employees. But, their philosophy was a curious blend of paternalism and instrumentality. The employer assumed that he knew better than the worker what the worker needed, and took up the duty to provide him security. At the same time, the employer believed that the workers' gratitude would increase productivity, output, and profits. Welfare capitalism collapsed in the cataclysm of the Great Depression, taking with it the sense of paternalistic concern for the blue-collar workers, when the men opted for unions rather than industrial charity.

Elton Mayo and the human relations school proved more enduring. For the first time managers had come to see the social nature of the workplace and sensed that more might be obtained by attending to the workers' attitudes and feelings. Again, this philosophy was an unstable blend of altruism and instrumentality. The teachings of the school were viewed by many as a more sophisticated means to control and manipulate the workforce. But, many tenets of the school survived into the late twentieth century, in welfare corporatism and in Ouchi's notion of Theory Z industrial clans. And, we see much the same thinking in the precepts of Total Quality Management (TQM) which proposes job enrichment and an "empowered" work force. Let us take a closer look at TQM, since it will illustrate the current mindset of American managers, and also expose the contradictions in the ideology.

TQM is a phenomenon of the 1980s and 1990s, a movement accompanied by an extraordinary level of evangelical fervor from its supporters. It is billed as nothing less than the salvation of American manufacturing, perhaps even the salvation of American civilization. At the very least, it is offered as the answer to America's productivity problems. Like Taylorism, TQM is a set of techniques, but also an informing philosophy. The techniques are statistical approaches to quality control, tools that originated at Western Electric and Bell Laboratories in the 1920s. These methods were refined into a a variety of tools: control charts, sampling techniques, and cost-analysis methods.

TQM in its current form is the brainchild of W. Edwards Deming and Joseph M. Juran, both American industrial engineers. Deming and Juran found few American companies interested in these techniques, since quality was not high on the list of issues for American manufacturing after the Second World War. But the Japanese were interested, and in the early 1950s Deming and Juran convinced them that quality improvement could open world markets to them and insure Japanese national survival. The Americans introduced their statistical quality control techniques in Japanese plants and all the world knows the result: Japanese quality—and Japanese world-trade volumes—-improved at unprecedented rates while American quality levels—and trade dominance—slipped (Dean and Evans 1994, 5).

The Japanese use of the quality issue as a strategic weapon came home to American business generally with an NBC broadcast in 1980, a program entitled "If Japan Can, Why Can't We?" American firms woke up to quality; Deming and Juran became celebrated, widely consulted figures; the rush was on to implement a new management orthodoxy. Like Scientific Management, there was more to TQM than shop techniques. A new focus on the customer was the byword, with "quality" newly recognized to mean satisfying the customer's needs. As the Japanese had done thirty years earlier, quality was moved into the center of American business strategy (Dean and Evans 1994, 6–7).

But the edifice of TQM was still not complete. The theorists believed that the Tayloristic methods must be blended with a human relations school approach to the workplace. "Empowerment" and "teamwork" became the watchwords. Teamwork must be created within the work groups, but that is an old human relations story. The new concept went further: vertical teamwork must be developed as well, cooperation between management and the workers. This could be accomplished by empowering the workers to make decisions affecting quality and to allow them to develop new and better systems and procedures. We can see here a radical departure from Taylorism, in which such decisions were the province of management, acting through its industrial engineers (Dean and Evans 1994, 17–18).

The vision of TQM is that of a partnership, a partnership between the company, its customers and suppliers; but, also a partnership with its employees, even with its unions. The assertion is made that these practices will remove the age-old stain of adversarial labor-management relations; they will show the union the benefits of being a partner and stakeholder in the firm (Dean and Evans 1994, 20).

In many ways, the philosophy behind TQM is that of welfare corporatism. The employees are made to feel a part of the company, to share its goals and values. Cooperation is the talisman, the magic that will set all aright. The old management ways of competition between individuals and groups is scorned; in the new world that will disappear. "Competitive behavior—one person against another—is not a natural state in TQM" (Dean and Evans 1994, 22).

TQM is definitely the current fad in American business thought and practice. Fifty-five percent of American firms use at least a portion of the system: specific measurements of quality in evaluating monthly business performance. (The comparable Japanese figure is 70 percent.) The notion of quality as a strategic issue has certainly penetrated management's thinking. Whether the social and organizational practices become as widespread as the statistical ones, is a question for the future. The rhetoric is certainly there.

But Ouchi and the TQM fraternity have run aground on the reefs of the new, overarching management ideology. The keystone of Theory Z and TQM is a guarantee of lifetime employment for good service, that essential ingredient of welfare corporatism. No one is willing to make that guarantee any longer and the vision of happy clans and empowered, innovating workers falls to the ground in its absence. (How exactly do you encourage someone to innovate himself out of a job?) The ideologies have come full circle: labor is seen again as a variable cost in the Profit & Loss statement—and the P & L statement is the ultimate measure of effectiveness. "Empowerment," "partnership," and "mutual interests" are on everyone's lips, but in no one's practices. A company is seen simply as a money machine; no other claims are allowed. That is the stark reality. Today's management is driven by two interrelated motivations: preeminently, increase shareholder value, the favored means to doing which is satisfying customers. As one of my subjects said: "That's all we hear, the shareholders and the customers. What about us?"

The conventional view of welfare corporatism's shipwreck is that it foundered on the shoals of economic pressures and global competition. (See, e.g., Beth Rubin's *Shifts in the Social Contract* (1996) for one presentation of this case.) There is some merit in this view; those factors certainly gave credence to the new orthodoxy of shareholder wealth. But the competition argument fails to explain that America's most feared competitor, Japan, had not cut back on management employees in the 1980s, when the American layoff trend gathered steam. In fact, many of the leading American downsizers did not act out of a sense of crisis at all. In 1988, less than half of those surveyed by the AMA cited a business downturn as even a contributing factor. Most cited the desire to increase productivity, but not from any looming crisis (Heckscher 1995, 5). So, ideological changes seem the most likely causes of the revolution. Nonetheless, let us look further at competitive developments, which certainly sharpened and help justify the new ideological stance.

American global economic hegemony began to erode in the 1970s and has not made a comeback. In the 1980s, falling American productivity and an inflated U.S. dollar gave foreigner competitors an abundant opportunity to build market share in the American market. They took it. By 1981, America imported 26 percent of its cars, 25 percent of its steel, 60 percent of its consumer electronics and 53 percent of its numerically controlled machine tools. Twenty years earlier, imports had accounted for less than 10 percent of these items. And, not only were traditional European and Japanese competitors now at our throats, newcomers have joined the fray. The world economy has undergone a vast structural change. Less-developed countries had gained access to capital and technology; access to markets followed naturally. The American domestic market—the largest in the world—was the target for every strategy of every industrialized or industrializing country. America's once-secure domestic market was a battleground of competition: a startling 70 percent of goods made in the United States were the objects of foreign competition. Old-line American companies were not up to the challenge in their present forms and with their present cost structures. Many American industries had become stable oligopolies, unaccustomed to price competition, managing the corporate commonwealth with administered pricing, guaranteed wage increases and, effectively, guaranteed employment (Bruchey 1988, 213–15).

Looking at the historical record, we feel a sense of *déjà vu.* Precisely the same thing happened in the 1930s, when ruthless firms cut wages and benefits, laid off thousands and put enormous pressure on the paladins of welfare capitalism. They found they could only compete by matching the practices of their merciless competitors, and they followed suit with their own layoffs, wage cuts and of course, the elimination of employee benefits. We see the same today, but most significantly the end of employment guarantees, that linchpin of welfare corporatism.

American industry had unfortunately made a pact with the devil. Lifetime employment had converted the wage bill from a variable cost to a fixed cost and none believed that could be sustained under competitive pressures and turndowns in the business cycle (Edwards 1979, 157). It may not be the message the old dispensation wanted to hear, but recent developments indicate that the market is telling us something. The economic justification of both welfare capitalism and welfare corporatism is simple: firms with such practices will outperform those without them. The faith is that better worker attitudes, an atmosphere of trust and cooperation, will translate into improved productivity and output. That faith seems to have been misplaced. At the very least, the faith has been lost among American managers in the rush to forsake welfare corporatism. I fear they are right; after all, it appears that the younger generation has little interest in loyalty in any event, so the loyalty-engendering practices of welfare corporatism are not just expensive—they are pointless.

Staff reductions, like so many management practices in the past, have become fashionable. Not just layoffs to reduce costs in bad times: as I noted, we are now seeing healthy companies paring back with abandon. The motives are usually two: bringing cost structures in line with foreign competitors and eliminating bureaucracy (*Business Week* 1986). The dismantling of those bureaucracies is another historical irony: as we saw above, the current round of cutbacks is not just affecting production workers; the layoffs are eliminating the managerial cadres, the pride of Alfred Chandler, the "visible hands" that were assembled at great cost over the years to manage the complexities of modern corporations. These cadres were first built after the turn-of-the-century merger wave and were set to work to integrate disparate units into the modern industrial enterprises.

America had a recurrence of merger mania in our own time as well. The merger forest fire of recent years has not disappeared, although it slowed in the late 1980s and early 1990s when its fuel supply—junk bonds—dried up. But mergers are on the rise again: from the peak year of 1988 ($340 billion), through the trough of 1991 ($140 billion), the value of mergers and acquisitions set a new record in 1994 ($347.1 billion.) And 1995 is shaping up to break that record: through the first ten months, the figure was $346 billion. Many buyers are foreign companies taking advantage of the dollar's weakness in the mid-1990s to access American markets and technology (Zuckerman 1994, A-1). Other buyers are American firms trying to find cost savings through staff reductions. Chemical Bank and Chase Manhattan combined and now plan to layoff 12,000 employees. The CEO of Kimberly Clark promised Wall Street that his acquisition of Scott Paper would be be accompanied by "significant staff reduction" (Strom 1995, A-1).

The result of the latest mergers will certainly be more cutbacks in both production and management, but probably most especially in management. The current orthodoxy is that "flat" management structures are the ideal. These will presumably decrease bureaucracy and make decision-making more rapid and more informed, since the top management will be closer to where the work is being done. This is just one more instance of dismantling welfare corporatism, which featured "tall" hierarchies. A tall hierarchy is the natural result of organizing by numerous specialized subunits, a strategy that in theory creates individual paths to rewards and enmeshes the workers in strong bonds with their immediate managers (Lincoln and Kalleberg 1990, 233). One of my cohort 2 friends remembered how it was in the old days of welfare corporatism.:

> The organization was very structured. There was a definite . . . leadership . . . ranks all the way down and you typically knew the people for a long time. You've worked with them, so there was a relationship with them and you trusted them and they trusted you and so, you wouldn't mind going an extra yard for them, for the organization, to do what they wanted you to do. So that's loyalty from that sense.

Again, the "tall" hierarchy, the smallish groups of long term associates—those loyalty forging elements of welfare corporatism—they are not seen as a benefit today; certainly not seen as worth the cost.

These thoughts lead us to a basic—and troubling—question: does a company have any obligations to its employees over and above those prescribed by law? Both welfare capitalism and welfare corporatism, of course, answered this in the affirmative. But, more and more we find American top management is answering "No." I wondered if the old affirmative stance, the old sense of obligation, could make sense to some of today's employees, so I posed the question to each of my subjects.[1] Content analysis of their responses showed a monotonic decrease in the belief that a company should have obligations, decreasing from cohort 1 to cohort 3. In other words, those of the old dispensation were more likely to think a company owed something; those of the new generation more likely to think not; and, those in the middle with a good deal of ambivalence. Here is a 32-year-old member of the new generation's response to the question:

> I don't think a company should owe anything to an employee any more than an employee should owe something to the company. . . . I don't think they owe me anything. You know they've hired me to do a job for them. I will do that job for them and if they don't think I'm doing that job for them, then I don't think they owe me anything but saying: "We don't think you're doing this job for us and we don't want you working for us anymore."

When I asked Gene Evans of cohort 3 if the company owed anything, he replied:

> No I don't. I believe that . . . they provide a service and we help provide that service for a fee. The same thing if I was to hire a plumber. I don't owe him anything. I'm hiring him to do a service just like I feel a (customer) is hiring Softmatics to do a service. When they don't need Softmatics anymore, then they won't hire Softmatics and then when Softmatics doesn't need me, they—you know, it just escalates down. But no, I don't feel that way at all.

It would be interesting to hear what Walter Kissinger ("Dedicated individuals who have devoted their lives to building a company") or the chairman of Deere ("We are feeding the world") would have to say to this: their lofty vision of the purpose and social role of a corporation, reduced by a latterday employee to comparing their firms' missions to hiring a plumber.

To see the different views of the different cohorts most clearly, look at the following accounts from two Softmatics officers, James Kessler who was born in 1953 (cohort 2); and, Art Merrill, born in 1938 (cohort 1). First James Kessler's response to the question of company obligations:

> all I think this company owes me . . . is (at) the time that they don't want my services that they try to make it as dignified as possible and be equitable . . . I'm not asking them that they owe me a job for life. I don't believe that's true. . . . It's clear companies are there to make money . . . and they can be sympathetic to a point, but the reality of it (is) most of them are driven towards the bottom line. . . . So, do they owe me anything? Probably not. No. . . . If I'm the obstacle, you got to get rid of me. It's just a fact of life and that happens. Sometimes we all kind of go beyond our

> useful life, but I hope they would be nice about it. I'm not sure they would or wouldn't.

We see quite a different response from Art Merrill of the old dispensation. He is struggling with the same business conditions as Kessler, but brings to the problem a different set of values and assumptions. He thinks the company owes a great deal more than being "nice about it" when it lets you go after you have passed your "useful life." Listen to him as I ask him if the company owes anything:

> Yes. I'd like to think the responsibility of the company . . . is once you've hired somebody . . . the company has some responsibility to utilize that talent. . . . We're talking about people who can perform, and for whatever reason, either the job that they were performing is no longer a necessary job or business conditions or things that go beyond their responsibility. I think we owe people . . . something to help them adjust to the changing environment.

Art sees clearly the responsibility he and the company have, but his sense of duty and loyalty to the people runs up against some harsh business realities. Yet he does not take the easy way out and just cite the bottom line; he feels personally responsible for the need for layoffs and is ashamed that it came to that pass; he feels powerless to help the people he feels responsible for.

> I've never gone through a layoff where I haven't blamed myself for not making decisions that could have avoided this. I mean I could have been smarter. I could have gotten new business. Believe me, to maintain sanity I try to rationalize all that, but it's still a thought and obviously when you lay somebody off you say: "Well . . . if I'd only known I could have put him into something else or trained him differently." . . . But you challenge your own rationalization. There's no question we have an obligation to deal with that. The question is how do we fulfill that obligation? But we try.

As I noted, cohort 2 folk varied in their opinions on this question. One said flatly:

> No, it shouldn't have any obligations to its employees. The only obligation I think they have is to provide a work environment and a steady paycheck.

Another was blunter, if less grammatical in his denial that the company is some sort of commonwealth in which people are invested with rights:

> A company don't owe an employee nothing. You give them forty hours and they pay you for forty hours. That's how I feel that it should be. You have no rights to the company and the company has no rights to you.

Not all my cohort 2 friends were as convinced that the company had no obligations. For example, forty-four-year-old Stuart Gregory had a quite different view, a sense that the human value of the employees was being discounted in the rush for profitability. Note his evocation of the old Marxist theory of surplus labor value as he responds to the question of company responsibilities:

> Well, I think so, yeah. The employees here are spending eight hours at least a day. Well, they are getting paid for it, but they're not getting paid what they deserve and they're not getting paid the value of what they make and I definitely think that if people give away a large portion of their lives to an organization that that organization needs to take care of its people . . . to see to it that they get compensation, that they get the respect that they need, that they get the opportunities to grow and to learn and that they have the power to basically set up their lives here at work the way they want it.

Stuart's concern with human values comes out in his musing on the sacrifices the employees make, and the obligation the company has to respect that. He uses the metaphor of "society," the old welfare corporatist belief that the company is a type of polity:

> As I said we are spending a lot of hours here . . . part of our happiness is dependent on the relationships and the environment that we have here at work and it is a very large investment to work at a place like this. People spend sometimes sixty hours a week doing this which means it's their life and so you can think of this as a mini-society and in that respect you really need to use the intelligence of the people that work here for making this mini-society one that is well functioning.

Another from cohort 2 also framed the issue in human terms:

> We often talk about heads and headcount and resources, but I mean, after all, these are people you're dealing with and they've got wives and families and dogs and cats and mortgages. . . .

I found that cohort 2 opinion could be found on both sides of this issue. But, cohort 1 folk had a distinctly different view. They showed little ambiguity on the question; the old dispensation, those with bureaucratic values, believed as a matter of course in the company's definite responsibility. Let us meet Frank Hoskins, fifty-five, a twenty-four-year veteran of Softmatics, and a true loyalist: his organizational commitment score is more than one standard deviation above the company norm. He explicitly rejects the notion that all the obligations lie with the employee. Should the company have any obligations?

> Yes it should. . . . I don't buy the philosophy that . . . companies express these days . . . "You owe it to yourself to stay marketable so that if we want to get rid of you at 55 . . . when you're too expensive, we want you out. You should have maintained your ability to be marketable."
>
> I don't buy that . . . You give to the company. . . . I think the company does owe some loyalty to people who have put in 20 or 30 years of sweat for them and helped them through some good development . . . and helped develop a hell a lot of good people . . . I think there ought to be a different solution instead of throwing them out on the streets, forcing them out of their jobs. . . . So I think they owe something to people who devote their lifetime to them other than to turn them out at 55.

And 55-year-old Joe Hirschfield, whom we met before, also stresses the human factor, the notion that the job is more than an economic relation, but a social one as well:

> (It) can't be a faceless thing that you work for. . . . I think that . . . the company needs to think in terms of they've got some real people out here, not just faces, doing the job . . .

Another of cohort 1 articulated the old welfare corporatist ideology in this way:

> Yeah I believe that a company should have an obligation to employees in terms of offering them a career . . . they need to con-

sider what the employee has done for them and . . . treat them that way.

But, welfare corporatism is as dead as Caesar, taking with it much of the old concern for people and their careers. Let us look further at the effects that welfare corporatism's collapse had on people, and also the effects on the corporations themselves.

Effects of Welfare Corporatism's Demise

Welfare corporatism's "tall" hierarchy is an abstraction; the reality is the human beings in those positions, those in Chandler's managerial cadres, Whyte's Organization Men. The economic results of dismantling Chandler's cadre lie before us in time to come; the personal effects on the organization men are clearer. In yet another historical irony, the problem that Whyte saw in 1956 has solved itself. Whyte feared the loss of autonomy and individualism that the Organization Man was undergoing in the welfare corporatist firm. He saw his Man deluding himself, believing he was in a polity of sorts, with lifetime membership, pseudo-legal rights, and an ability to exercise the civic virtues of cooperation, to harness his individuality to the group's goals. Whyte deplored those effects on the American character, the precious heritage of American individualism submerged in group-think and collectivism. We can see now that his fears were groundless, although the form of the Organization Man's liberation was not as Whyte hoped, not a new stirring of individualism. The decision was made for the Organization Man when welfare corporatism went to the wall. Whyte would applaud this rescue from the flirtation with collectivism, his Organization Man's illusion that he lived in a corporate pseudo-state and could find there his meaning and his freedom. Stripped of his *ersatz* citizenship, he could perhaps reassert his individualism—but often at the price of eating the bitter bread of banishment.

The new orthodoxy is clear: "The company's assets and franchise are primary, the people are secondary." It is as though the ideal would be to run the company without any people (Bennett 1990, 136). But what effects has this had on the people who are still there? One veteran of layoffs spoke of his epiphany: he was not a valued member of a corporate polity at all; he was just "casual labor":

> you aren't part of a group anymore. There is no group. You are casual labor. Suddenly, you realize you might as well be a coolie digging a trench, and when the trench is finished, they don't need you anymore. (Bennett 1990, 217)

As we have seen, my subjects' reactions were not uniform. They reacted in most cases differentially with age due to the different perspective they brought to events as well as the different access they had to their own historical experiences. Most observers have not attended to this age factor, but nonetheless provide some valuable insights into the results of welfare corporatism's ruin. *Fortune* saw a "Morale Crisis" in 1991: "Legions of supervisory types, their livelihoods endangered by cost cutting and recession, are angry, distrustful, stressed out, and scared" (Fischer 1991, 70). I found the anger and fear only, in the main, among my cohort 2 subjects: recall Bill Abernathy's words: "I felt I was betrayed." and ". . . when things started to unravel, it was devastating . . . it was frightening." Anger and fright may be confined to cohort 2, but distrustfulness appears to be a general phenomenon, and that has disturbing consequences. *Fortune* asserts that employees generally have soured on management, are resentful of the management's generous pay, "perks," and golden parachutes, while everyone else just gets by—or gets laid off (Fischer 1991, 71).

Take one example: IBM, an old-line corporatist firm. The edifice of welfare corporatism began to crumble at IBM in April 1991 when Chairman John Akers belabored a group of managers about IBM's slack work ethic. His remarks were soon on everyone's e-mail screen and even leaked into the media. One IBM friend—an old loyalist in his fifties—flatly denied to me that Akers would ever have said such things. But he had. The reaction was not what Akers had hoped: rather than a new dedication to the company, most employees voiced contempt for top management, complaining about Akers big pay raise and "The Big Gray Cloud" of managers who couldn't see what was going on in the world. One IBM'er said: "We have a vast hierarchy of management whose singular talent is that of career advancement" (Carroll 1993, 268).

It should not have surprised anyone, but the end of welfare corporatism bred distrust. Even my own interview project was suspect for one cohort 3 subject: "I hope that this isn't a secret plan by somebody to assess how they should treat the upcoming imminent announcement (about downsizing the Division) . . . ." We'll talk more about the general erosion of trust in the next chapter, but distrust of management—their abilities and their motives—seems to have reached crisis proportions. One 1993 survey of 400 managers reported that 33 percent distrust their immediate superiors and a full 55 percent do not believe anything top management says (Yates 1993, 1). The Hay Group's survey of middle managers in over 1000 big companies found that between 1987 and 1990, assessment of top managers' abilities fell from "generally high" to "awful." One middle manager in a "downsizing" company said of the CEO: "If it were my choice I wouldn't follow him to the men's room" (Heckscher 1995, 61).

Well, we certainly have distrust and angst among employees, but other than some personal concerns of management, what effect could that really have on the corporation's performance? I believe that potentially it has a great effect. No company ever operated as an ideal Weberian bureaucracy, in which all knew precisely their roles and the actions required of them. Every company has depended on discretionary effort from its managers and professionals, doing what is right for the company in ambiguous circumstances, not sliding by with minimum effort, but making an all-out effort. Loyalty makes this happen; loyalty and mutual trust are the keys to reducing transaction costs in the hierarchy by guiding the employee to right behavior (Simon 1961, 2–13). One of those right behaviors is risk-taking, the essential entrepreneurial spirit that takes risks with company assets in the expectation that the company will benefit. More and more, that makes less and less sense in the new environment. Managers are simply afraid to make decisions for fear of the consequences of a misstep. One of my cohort 3 young managers told me: "They are living under fear here now. . . . They don't want to take risks because it puts them out on a ledge." Bennett, in her study *The Death of the Organization Man*, reports that:

> The end of loyalty meant the end of a manager's willingness to go the extra distance for the company. . . . Middle managers won't

> make decisions. They won't make a move without passing it through upper management. That reduces creativity. . . . (Bennett 1990, 220)

Dennis Madison of cohort 1 remembered how it used to be at Softmatics with regard to risk-taking, and how it is now:

> You weren't afraid to make a mistake. You know, you make a mistake, you'd get your ass chewed out, but there wasn't fear there; it was more of . . . you needed it and you did something wrong and they'd tell you about it, but you just enjoyed being there. It was almost like going to your father's house or something like that and you know that's what it was all about to me. . . . Some of our people don't think that [now] because . . . they don't trust the management enough.

I have been giving you anecdotes and theory. What does the overall economic record say about the effects of dismantling welfare corporatism? In fairness, it may be too soon to tell, but the early returns are not promising. Increased productivity was the essential rationale, but some companies found that layoffs did not even attain their budget reduction targets. Wyatt and Company found in a 1991 survey of 1005 companies that fewer than half met their cost targets despite the staff reductions: they cut the people but not the workload, misjudged the consequences, and had to bring in expensive contract workers. Only 32 percent of these downsizers raised their profits appreciably; only 21 percent improved their ROI to any extent. Tellingly, 87 percent of those companies that offered early-retirement packages saw their star performers gleefully exit (Fischer 1991, 71). Of course, those were the people whom they most needed: those with brains and initiative. And naturally, they would be the first to leave: they had the assurance of finding new positions, and a nice bonus from the old company to cheer them on their way.

The Wall Street Journal reported in 1993 that in most cases—counterintuitively—productivity fell after layoffs.[2] Of 531 companies reporting layoffs, *The Journal* found only 46 percent achieved increased profits after two years (Lublin 1993, A-1). The new management ideology has far to go to prove that it will be better than welfare corporatism. Old and trusting networks have been uprooted; morale is low; risk-taking is avoided. In time, these problems may solve themselves, but for now, the jury is still out. Yet there is no going back; a divide has been crossed. Neither in management practices nor in the hearts of employees is there the will or the desire to forge bonds of loyalty.

The New Employment Contract

We hear a good deal of talk today about a "new employment contract," a new relationship between employees and companies. Now, I could quibble with the "newness" of the relationship: it is hardly different from the days of Andrew Carnegie and Henry Frick, when men were fired for the slightest cause. But, that aside, the "contract" is certainly a different relationship from that we found in the halcyon days of welfare corporatism. The "old" contract was best described by Whyte in *The Organization Man:*

> Be loyal to the company and the company will be loyal to you. After all, if you do a good job for the organization, it is only good sense for the organization to be good to you, because that will be best for everyone. There are a bunch of real people around here. Tell them what you think and they will respect you for it. (Whyte 1956, 181)

The relationship has been described as a "social contract," with the obvious implication that this is a pseudo-political agreement, with rights and obligations for both parties. In the old dispensation, the employee was expected to have satisfactory attendance, display an acceptable level of effort, and exhibit a generalized loyalty. The company for its part was to provide fair pay and fringe benefits, steady advancement, and—critically—job security.[3]

Well, if there is a "contract" at all today, it is a one-sided one, one without mutual obligations. It has been described, tongue-in-cheek, in these terms:

> You're expendable. We don't want to fire you, but we will if we have to. Competition is brutal, so we must redesign the way we work to do more with less. Sorry, that's just the way it is. And one more thing—you're invaluable. Your devotion to our customers is the salvation of the company. We're depending on you to be innovative, risk-taking, and committed to our goals. Okay? (B. O'Reilly 1994, 44)

One item here, "do more with less," has had profound implications. When a firm downsizes, the work does not go away: the people remaining just have to do more. For the blue-collar workers, this means more compensated overtime. In fact, the work week in 1993 set a postwar record: 41.7 hours (Chilton and Weidenbaum 1994, 8). But for the managers and professionals, it just means more work without additional compensation. Pat Flaherty of Cohort 3, thirty-five years old, told me what it was like with reduced staffs:

> It's having an effect on my personal life and the negative effect on my personal life is increasing, not decreasing. . . . Yeah, a lot of hours and a lot of stress. So I'm not compensated for that negative effect with anything else positive coming out of it. But not a lot of good feelings at work. I'm not getting paid a whole lot more. There's no extra benefits coming from it. I'm not getting more vacation time, you know. I'm still working harder and harder and there is more and more stress and the harder you work, the more demanding things become.

Long hours have been the staple for many years in investment banking, Wall Street law offices, and Silicon Valley start-ups. But there is a crucial difference: there, people had the opportunity for very large payoffs. Nowadays, as a friend of cohort 2 age told me, the underlying assumption of the new management is that employees are as risk-taking and as aggressive as the managers are—ignoring the disparity in rewards. Common sense belies that. Most people are not the start-up or investment-banking types; they are only after a comfortable life and less stress, but are caught in jobs in which the "reward" for all-out effort is that you get to keep your job. One example: after a five percent layoff in 1993, the president of Sprint wrote to his employees: "I ask each of you to be introspective about the adequacy of your commitment to Sprint . . . Forty-hour workweeks are a relic of the past" (Schellhardt 1993, B-1).

The somewhat playful account of a "contract" that we saw above ("You're expendable. . . . And one more thing—you're invaluable") is the invention of a *Fortune* writer, but we have an example of a contract from a real CEO, McDonnell Douglas's John McDonnell. The fall 1994 issue of the company organ, *Spirit*, featured a memo from then-chairman McDonnell to all employees titled "The New Employment Contract." Here are some excerpts:

> Almost five years ago I wrote a controversial *Spirit* article about the need for a new kind of loyalty at McDonnell Douglas. I advocated abandoning "unquestioned" loyalty and replacing it with a "ruthlessly performance-driven" loyalty where the company provides' training, education, coaching, mentoring and support . . . but each of us must take responsibility for our own self-development." . . . Now across American business there is a growing realization that the former relationship between companies and employees has changed. Employees had come to expect that if they did what they were told and performed acceptably, the company would provide lifetime employment, unless there was a major disaster. In its place there is now emerging a new job compact in which companies provide demanding, challenging assignments, more freedom to perform, and opportunities for self-development. Employees have the responsibility for their careers so that when the company no longer needs their skills, they are employable elsewhere. . . . It is painfully obvious to all of us that the old job expectations are no longer workable, if they ever were. . . .
>
> We . . . have an extensive education reimbursement program and growing after-hours voluntary training courses. . . . Simply put, I believe that intrinsic to the new relationship is the company's responsibility to develop an environment that enables high performance and rewards it.
>
> Employees must accept the responsibility to take advantage of the opportunities to develop their skills and manage their careers so that they are always satisfactorily employable somewhere. (McDonnell 1994)

The message is clear: you are on your own, no guarantees. But, the message is also softened by the promise that the company will provide the skills for employability elsewhere—tuition reimbursement and after-hours training programs. Why? It is not clear; probably, it is a holdover from welfare corporatist practices and old dispensation thinking. (McDonnell was born in 1938 and is the son of the corporation's founder, a man noted for his paternalism.) In the strict logic of the new faith, investing in human capital for some other firm's benefit hardly makes sense. Training was part and parcel of welfare corporatism, but there was logic there: much of it was firm-specific, useless to outsiders; and even general-skill development investments would be expected to yield a return, given the long tenures of the old way. Average tenure for managers and professionals has fallen from 8.5 years in 1968 to 6.3 years in 1991 (B. O'Reilly 1994, 46).

The seemingly generous offer of training for future employability is often spurned by employees, baffling management which sees that as a helping hand. But interpreting it as help requires that the employee trust management, and that is a poor assumption nowadays. Pat Flaherty of cohort 3 did not exactly see an offer of training as a management conspiracy, but certainly a trap for him:

> And as soon as you take on one of the new competencies . . . now you've learned something new. . . . Well, it just increases the load. Because now people expect you to be able to do this because you know how and other people can't and you can, so you have to.

In any event, John McDonnell has articulated a "contract" for his company, one-sided as it may be. Sun Microsystems has an even more one-sided contract, and they make sure that all employees are aware of it. It runs as follows, in two parts:

> 1. Your career is your responsibility, not the company's.
>
> 2. You have a job here so long as your work is acceptable *and* your project is active. Once the project ends, we make no guarantees of employment.

That is as plain a statement of the new way that I have heard, so I asked all of my subjects simply: "What do you think of that?" Let's look first at our youngest cohort. You will recall Gene Evans and his *insouciance* about layoffs and job-hopping. He was unequivocally in favor of Sun's approach, seeing it as the expression of a self-evident fact:

> I would appreciate someone telling me that. It's very straightforward. It's a fact. Just because a company doesn't tell you that coming in the door that if work gets slow, you're going to get laid off, everybody knows it's a fact. (A company) cannot afford to pay paychecks if they're not bringing in a profit. So I would accept that and appreciate that statement.

This point of view was also noted in a recent study of Chase Manhattan, where the observer concluded that younger workers thought that the company—once affectionately known as

"Mother Chase"—now only needed to provide a place to work and a paycheck (Kleinfield 1996).

My cohort 2 subjects in general reacted more ambivalently. Andy Freese, whom we met before, agreed with Sun, but by changing the conditions so it more resembled a promise like John McDonnell's, i.e., that the company would also provide training.

> On the other side of the coin, Sun has also publicly stated . . . they will invest in the employee and the training . . . There is no contract for life (as it was) in the 50s and 60s and the early 70s . . . that if you're loyal, you do a good job, the company is successful, you're here for life. You know, the Japanese concept . . .
>
> I like that attitude (Sun's) because it doesn't necessarily mean that you're gone at the end of that project. It means . . . that the company has the option. If you've developed competencies that can be used elsewhere, then you're going to be used elsewhere. If you have not developed those or if they're not required, then you're going to move on.

In contrast, another from cohort 2 rejected Sun's approach out of hand:

> Well, every employee that's working there is always looking for the next opportunity, so they've got one foot in their current job and one foot looking somewhere else.
>
> (*Would you like to work there?*)
>
> No. No. No loyalty in the organization. The person that you're working for is just a temporary fixture.

And, 48-year-old Evelyn Glavin of cohort 2 saw clearly the one-sidedness of the Sun "contract":

> First of all those companies would be the first to tell you: "You better be loyal to me for the time that you're with me, but we don't owe you anything." I think that's an injustice. You cannot promote any kind of feelings of trust. . . . Why would someone want to invest in something like that? I mean you're investing your life and putting everything else on hold to try and get something done and I don't care how important it is, if you know that there's nothing long-range, then why do it?

Forty-four-year-old Stuart Gregory (cohort 2), whom we met earlier, was even more scornful of Sun's approach, which he thought typified the new outlooks in business:

> I'm not surprised. I don't think that is a good thing to do. I would not work at a place like that. We're not just machines working. We are humans and I think Sun should realize that. . . . These human beings have families. . . . They have hopes and aspirations and they have dreams and if you would just be here one hour a day. . . . I think that you might justify that, but we're giving our lives to this company and certainly the people here deserve more than that kind of attitude. . . . Since the overriding concern in this society is profit, I mean we've no regard whatsoever for the human aspect. That is the basis. Then whatever comes out of that I'm not surprised. I'm more surprised when I hear the companies are actually acting in a human way . . .

Virtually all of my cohort 1 subjects, those of the old dispensation, reacted to the Sun "contract" with distaste. Mike Jennings struggled somewhat with the idea. He is the man, you may remember, who also found himself holding to the old values in his behavior, but mouthing the new orthodoxy in telling his children "life is competition." On the Sun statement he said:

> I would find it difficult working for a company who said that . . . When they tell you you have no security, then that probably is a big problem.

When I asked him if Softmatics operated that way, he thought probably they did, but God forbid they should articulate such a coldhearted policy:

> As a matter of fact, (Softmatics) may actually believe that and that might be . . . a principle of the top management . . . They haven't told everybody that . . . Really, if you think about the issue that the bottom line is what executives are measured on and they had to make business decisions, there really is no such thing as security (for us). But gee, you don't have to tell people that, do you?

Another from cohort 1 framed the issue, nostalgically, in terms of the old dispensation, loyalty:

> I guess in terms of no longer relationship and the company says: "OK, we're paying you for this job and after the job's over there's

no guarantee," then the company is not being loyal to the employee and if the company expects the employee to be loyal to them or have the same attitude because if the company has the attitude that "This is just a job . . . when this job's done there may be another job for you or there may not be." If that's the way a company was, I would have my resumé on the street . . . There is no loyalty. There's no . . . relationship beyond that job . . .

It is still an open question whether the new approach, as exemplified by Sun's statement, can achieve a stable equilibrium. Some think it is easy: A *New York Times* article on the new practices was subtitled: "Loyalty? Security? Just Cut Jobs" (Moskowittz 1993, C-1). Charles Heckscher has explored this question more deeply in his 1995 study of companies dismantling welfare corporatism, *White-Collar Blues*. He found the new ethic of the marketplace, the "free-agent" approach to be:

extremely meager: the obligations of employees and companies are limited to specific legally binding contracts. In this view there is nothing wrong with leaving for a little more money somewhere else, and there is nothing wrong with laying off people on short notice. (Heckscher 1995, 152)

Heckscher divides his interview subjects into "loyalists" and "professionals," what I would categorize as my cohort 1 of the old dispensation, and cohort 3 of the new generation. He finds that the loyalists view the free-agent ethic "with contempt and horror". Even the professionals are critical of pure individualism and tend to stress job challenge over personal gain (Heckscher 1995, 153).

Perhaps the biggest effect of welfare corporatism's downfall is the loss of community, *Gemeinschaft*, and the concomitant loss of trust—loss of trust in management, as we saw, but also loss of trust in one's peers. I found this theme in a number of my interviews. Charles Pearson of cohort 2 reflected on the new Softmatics environment, noting that his recourse to "voice" was gone; distrustful, he would no longer give management the necessary feedback he once did out of loyalty to the company:

I don't trust management like maybe I should be able to trust. I'm just very leery of what I say and what I do because as I said earlier repercussions, "Do as you're told, not as I do"-type philosophy and it makes me very leery to really say what I really feel . . .

The shipwreck of welfare corporatism rather clearly and deliberately did away with company obligations to employees. But, as a surely unintended consequence, it also fractured the trust that employees had in management; and, at the same time, American society at large experienced a loss of mutual trust. This general erosion of trust in one another is a serious issue in today's companies, and a serious issue to society. Let us explore that further in the next chapter.

11

The Old Dispensation Withers Away

Ha, ha, what a fool Honesty is! and Trust his sworn brother, a very simple gentleman.

—Shakespeare, *The Winter's Tale*

Trust: "A Very Simple Gentleman"

As we saw in the last chapter, trust in management has substantially eroded in the last twenty to twenty-five years. I noted that a survey of managers in 1993 reported that a third distrusted their bosses and more than half were skeptical of anything top management said (Yates 1993, 1). This is a phenomenon I found at Softmatics as well. Dennis Madison of cohort 1 bemoaned this departure from the old dispensation; he could not understand the attitudes of younger people: "We got a lot of people . . . They don't trust the management enough." Dennis told me of one company officer's problems:

> He would never, never break confidences if they told him anything, but they just don't trust him. They look at him as either a (parent company) spy or (the CEO's) hatchet man or whatever, but he's just not accepted.

And, we have heard cohort 2's Charles Pearson say: "I don't trust management like maybe I should be able to trust. I'm just very leery of what I say and what I do . . ."

The distrust of management of course is related to loyalty lost[1] and many of my subjects made that connection. One of the cohort 2 people defined loyalty precisely in terms of mutual trust:

> When I say that I'm loyal, it really comes down to (that). I earn the trust of Softmatics and Softmatics earns the trust back to

FIGURE 11-1
Trust, 1972–1994

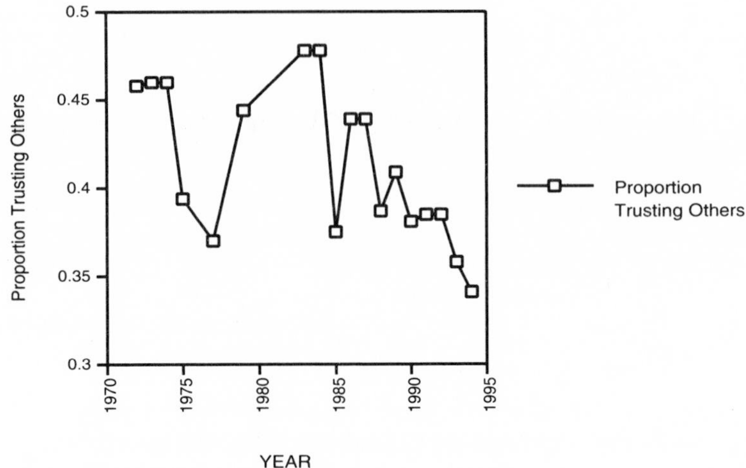

SOURCE: General Social Survey, Davis and Smith 1994

> myself, until I've proven or they prove you can't be trustworthy. And by that I mean there's a lot of things that take place between employee and company and it develops, what I would say, is a binding relationship.

Jeff Myers of cohort 2, whom we met before in our discussion of welfare corporatism, linked loyalty and trust, and linked both to the corporatist experience of time shared. He speaks, as you see, in the past tense:

> You typically knew the people for a long time. You've worked with them, so there was a relationship with them and you trusted them and they trusted you.

My cohort 3 friends also associated trust with loyalty when I asked them to define loyalty for me. One—characteristically for cohort 3—put loyalty in terms of an exchange, "a two-way street":

> I'll be loyal to something if I know that they're going to be loyal to me. Loyalty probably means that you—let's see—that you . . .

FIGURE 11-2
Trust by Cohort, 1974–1986

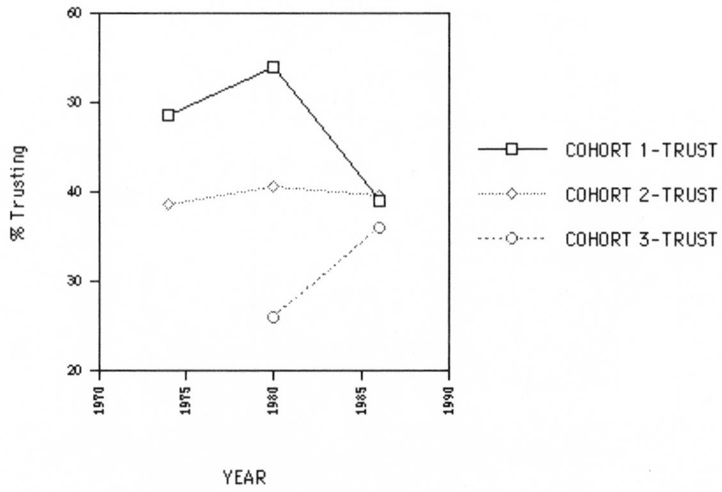

SOURCE: Wood 1990, 314-5

have some amount of trust with the organization . . . You trust that they will do certain things for you if you are in need . . .

Many see a necessary linkage between trust and loyalty. But the problem is that few anymore have that degree of trust in companies, or in each other for that matter. Trust more and more is cynically seen as "a very simple gentleman," as Shakespeare's rogue Autolycus puts it. Look at Figure 11-1[2] and note that the falloff in trust was not confined to the 1960s and 1970s. It continues to this day. Figure 11-2 shows the levels of trust by cohort, a picture that should not now surprise us: lower trust as the cohort age decreases (Wood 1990, 314–15).[3] Figure 11-2 gives a picture of the change in trust over one time period, and I should note that the apparent upswing in trust in 1986 was a false harbinger of better things; as you see in Figure 11-1, after 1986 trust continued its relentless decline. For a look at the average level of distrust over the period 1972–86, look at Figure 11-3 (Russell and Megaard 1988, 158).

And of course, the workplace reflects the same melancholy picture of social bonds fraying. A 1996 poll found that 70

FIGURE 11-3
Distrust by Cohort, 1972–1986

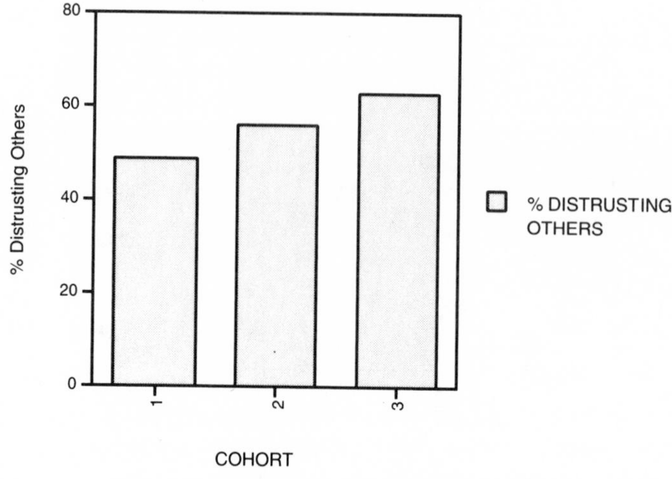

SOURCE: Russell and Megaard 1988, 158

percent believe that workers now, more than in the past, compete more than cooperate with one another. And 53 percent found their coworkers "angrier"; only 8 percent found them "friendlier." (Kleinfield 1996).

What is the real concern about trust levels dropping, and particularly the low levels among young people? There is a societal concern of course, a threat to democratic institutions: "Democracy requires a degree of trust that we often take for granted. . . . The heritage of trust that has been the basis of our stable democracy is eroding." (Bellah et al. 1991, 3). But there is also an economic concern. Royce saw the connections clearly in 1908: "The single act of business fidelity is an act of loyalty to that general confidence of man in man upon which the whole fabric of business rests" (Royce 1908, 141). In a commercial civilization the norm is dealing with strangers, and a general reservoir of trust is vital (Jacobs 1992, 34). The economist Kenneth Arrow is most insistent about an economy's need for trust:

> Trust is an important lubricant of a social system. It is extremely efficient; it saves a lot of trouble to have a fair degree of reliance on other people's word. . . . Trust and similar values, loyalty or

> truth telling . . . have real, practical, economic value; they increase the efficiency of the system, enable you to produce more goods . . . (Arrow 1974, 23)

Distrust of management is one thing, but distrust of one's peers may be an even more serious problem. In a modern economy with its highly complex division of labor, economic efficiency demands a good deal of cooperation and mutual trust. But there is less and less of that every day. The Roper Poll periodically asks people if they are satisfied with "the kind of people" with whom they work. Fifty-two percent were "completely satisfied" in 1976; the current figure is 37 percent. Roper reports as well that morale is lower, but the form of the question really solicits an opinion about the respondent's peers. In March 1994 only 27 percent said the morale of "fellow workers" was excellent. That is down from 38 percent as recently as 1990 (Chilton and Weidenbaum 1994, 15). Trust was one of those "bureaucratic values," a value associated with loyalty, confidence, and the sense of community, a community in which its members wanted to cooperate with each other. The importance of those values to business efficiency is illustrated by a conversation I had with a cohort 3 manager. He talked to me about the problems he had managing a group of new-generation people:

> There's always been some distrust amongst groups. Just jokingly, but at the same time there's some truth to it . . . There was a lot of blame and there still is today. In fact, there's a meeting down the hall where there's a lot of finger-pointing and you just can't stop it anymore. Even when you try to get a small group of people together . . . we still can't pull people together. . . . In my group I basically turned over 90%. . . . And that's extremely expensive and it's very frustrating for me. It costs a lot to retrain the employees. . . . I have been searching for ways to build team-work inside my own department . . . Trying to build a spirit of teamwork in the department is really difficult to do. I spend a lot of my time that I didn't ever have to before. That costs me. . . . I've been burning the candle at both ends now for four years and it's wearing on me, it's wearing on my personal life. It's got to get easier fast.

Our young manager gives us a revealing picture of the costs to the business—and the personal burden on managers—that the lack of trust and cohesiveness brings. Trust in management, trust in one another—trust is fading along with the other components of the old dispensation. Today's younger employees are more likely to eschew loyalty and mutual trust, and be content with an inward-looking attitude toward their careers, an attitude that has been called "professional." We saw earlier Heckscher's distinction between "loyalists" and "professionals." Heckscher did not make an age differentiation in his categories, but my data show that those of the oldest cohort (cohort 1) are much more likely to be loyalists, and those of the youngest (cohort 3), far more likely to be "professionals." A loyalist from a downsized company framed the issues of loyalty, trust, and professionalism in this way:

> There was a time when the attitude was, you do your job, and the company will take care of you; it was a situation of trust in the company. Then the word "professionalism" came in, and you . . . do your job, you do it in a highly professional manner. Never mind the word "trust" . . . And with professionalism came mobility, so loyalty and dedication went with it. The highly skilled professionals didn't care about trust, they didn't care about where the company's been, what kind of family relationship we've had here. They say, "Hey, I'm a professional, I do my job, and if it works out, fine; if it doesn't work out, hey, I'll go to another company." (Heckscher 1995, 34)

The professionals' attitude is not perhaps as cynical as Shakespeare's Pistol, but there is certainly a family resemblance:

> Trust none;
> For oaths are straws; men's faiths are wafer cakes,
> And hold-fast is the only dog, my duck.
>
> (*Henry V*, 2.3)

Daniel Yankelovich, whose polling has for some time concentrated on the shift to new values, characterizes the new generation in ways which fit my data and Heckscher's observations as well. Yankelovich finds that the younger people have no aspirations for a lifetime job, nor do they think employers would proffer any loyalty nor show any concern for them. But more than that, they appear to be losing confidence that they will be rewarded for building their skills; they fear the corporation's emphasis on "quality" is no more than shorthand for "downsizing." And, as we have seen in the poll data on job satisfaction, the younger people think that the workplace is not a reliable source of satisfaction, other than in strictly monetary terms (Yankelovich 1994). In all these things—lack of mutual loyalty, confidence in the corporation's ability to provide rewards and job satisfaction, an exclusive focus on money—in all these we see the stark contrast with the bureaucratic values and corporate culture which nurtured their elders. The poll data gives us sanitized summaries, abstract numbers. Here is a concrete human expression of some of today's attitudes, from 43-year-old Charles Pearson:

> There needs to be more fairness. To me, there's not that fairness in this country and I don't think it's been there for a long time and it's not just with corporations, it's with the government and everything else in general. There's too much lying, backstabbing . . . .

Trust and Confidence

We see it in the workplace, and we see it in the larger society. We see a fraying of the social fabric, an erosion of trust, loss of the sense of community, and waning confidence. "Trust none / For oaths are straws." Earlier we looked at confidence in institutional leaders and Figure 11-4 shows that continued downward trend between 1966 and 1986. Trust and confidence are both part of the old dispensation's bundle of values, and the connection can be demonstrated statistically—levels of interpersonal trust have been found to be correlated positively with confidence levels (Lipset and Schneider 1987, 119). What is particularly disturbing in the decline of trust is that one would expect that better-educated people would find the world less threatening and be more inclined to trust others. But the educational levels in America have been rising steadily for generations, yet trust has declined precipitously. Also, there is evidence of an increased feeling of alienation and anomie, again a trend one would not expect from a more-educated society. The questions posed by the pollsters to measure these things in effect seek to reveal the respondent's view of reality, such questions as: "Is the lot of the average man growing worse?"; "Do most people try to be helpful or take advantage of you?"; "Can most people be trusted?". Oddly, a more highly educated American public is more distrustful and feels more

FIGURE 11-4
Confidence in Institutional Leaders, 1966–1986

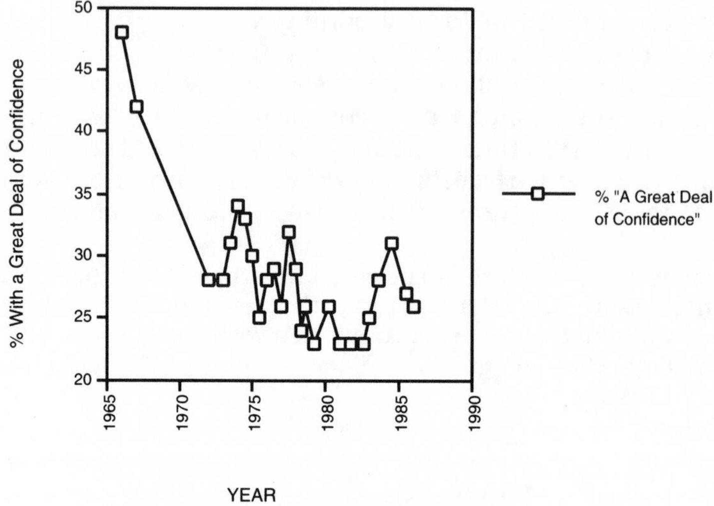

SOURCE: Lipset and Schneider 1987, 50

powerless. And when these worldviews are tested against confidence in institutions, the correlations are strong and consistent. This, I believe, demonstrates that the old dispensation of confidence, trust, and loyalty, was a complex of attitudes and beliefs which supported one another, and which all began to lose their hold, beginning in the 1960s. The correlation results can be summarized as follows:

> People who trust others, who think that most individuals try to be fair and helpful, and who express a sense of optimism about the present and the future also voice higher confidence in those running our major institutions. (Lipset and Schneider 1987, 119)

Opinions about the Market Economy

Distrust of institutions, particularly large corporations, could be interpreted as general dissatisfaction with the entire economic system, the American brand of a free-market economy. But—at least to date—this would be an unwarranted generalization. Despite the dramatic loss of confidence in big business which began in the 1960s, as late as 1979 80 percent of the public believed that free government is necessarily associated with a free enterprise system (McClosky and Zaller 1984, 133). Yet, there are sharp differences of opinion about the ideology of unfettered capitalism among my subjects, and the differences are rather clearly correlated with cohort.

I found these differences when I asked my subjects about a recent press release by Mattel Toys. Just before Christmas 1994, Mattel announced record sales and earnings for the sixth year in a row; further, its balance sheet was strong and growing stronger. Stockholders would be rewarded with an increased dividend and a 5-for-4 stock split. Yet, Mattel announced in the same press release that it would eliminate 1000 jobs, about four percent of the workforce (Rosenthal 1995). I asked my subjects: "What do you think about that?" and, if appropriate, "Do you see an ethical issue there?"[4]

In general, the youngest cohort subjects (cohort 3) were able to justify Mattel's actions and saw few, if any, ethical issues. One 29-year-old professional said:

> I think they must be working terribly efficient[ly]. . . . If they can determine that's going to keep them working profitably, that's what they should be doing. Yeah.
>
> Absolutely. I see no reason for companies to have people working for them that aren't producing or helping the company . . . If I'm an employer and I have 3000 people and 50 of them I don't really need and I'm profitable, I don't see a problem with that.
>
> *(Do you see an ethical issue?)*
>
> Well, I suppose there would be some, but again I really don't think the company owes the people a salary so I wouldn't have a problem with that.

Pat Flaherty, the 35-year-old manager we met before, favorably compared the Mattel action to the wise business practices of Softmatics' new parent, DRI.

> On the surface it doesn't necessarily sound stupid. I think the way you succeed in business over the long run is looking ahead, not looking at what you just did. . . . At a corporate level it seems like DRI is looking ahead. . . . Even though every year is better than the previous, that they're always looking for areas (in) which

> they're deficient . . . It seems like they're not sitting on their laurels.

Asked if there were any ethical issues here, Pat sarcastically referred to the Marxist theory of surplus value: "Maybe it's sort of like Karl Marx's thing where these people are sucking the labor out of these poor workers and cashing in on it and then just cutting them free."

The middle-cohort subjects were mainly ambivalent, recognizing that there were human as well as business issues in the Mattel case, and that a proper course of action would have difficulty reconciling the two. One cohort 2 person addressed this:

> It's difficult because . . . you want to put human qualities or human values on an organization and that may or may not be a good idea, particularly if you're trying to run an organization that meets the expectations of your investors.

The Mattel case raises an age-old issue with a market economy, the balance between public and private interests. Free-market economists and their many business followers celebrate Adam Smith's teachings on the efficacy of the market, conveniently forgetting that Smith had many reservations about the actions of business people. For one, Smith was opposed to joint-stock companies. "Corporate executives . . . who cite Smith today as the source of all sanction and truth without the inconvenience of having read him would be astonished and depressed to know that he would not have allowed their companies to exist" (Galbraith 1987, 43). And, despite Smith's optimism that the "Invisible Hand" of the market would assure growing benefits to all of society, he recognized that "The interest of the dealers . . . in any branch of trade or manufacturing is always in some respects different from, even opposite to, that of the public" (A Smith 1974, 358). One of Smith's twentieth-century disciples, Friedrich von Hayek, was much more sanguine about self-interested economic actors. In *The Road to Serfdom* (1944), Hayek argued that a free-market economy is not only the most efficient economic system, it was the bulwark against totalitarianism and the guardian of political liberty. "If 'capitalism' means . . . a competitive system based on free disposal over private property, it is . . . important to realize that only within this system is democracy possible" (Hayek 1994, 77–78). As I noted above, in 1979 some 80 percent of Americans agreed with Hayek's connection between free markets and freedom.

Nevertheless, today's paradigm of economics is a market system which ignores social life, ignores both the human responsibilities of business and the potential economic gains that attention to human factors might bring. This restricted view of business is not just the worldview of conservative economists and business leaders, it is the conception of many in the general public and in much of the media (Bruyn 1991, 4). And it is the conception of some of my subjects, particularly those from the youngest cohort.

It was certainly not so in the heyday of welfare corporatism. But, the idea that it might be good business to care for employees was jettisoned in the shipwreck of welfare corporatism. Younger managers, nurtured in the same culture, found their younger employees little disposed to become loyal, and they themselves little disposed to offer loyalty. Both turned to the main chance, to the idea that business was simply money-making. And so I found in many of my subjects, especially the younger, the view that business was an autonomous sphere, without any moral connection to the rest of society and its human values. Here is one example from a 35-year-old member of cohort 3, trying to square the circle, trying to look at the Mattel question from both the business and the human standpoints. He said on the one hand, he'd feel abused if he were one of those laid off:

> I'd say: "I've worked hard, right? . . . the company's made record growth. I've been doing my part. You know, what did I do wrong? Other than the company's been successful. I've done everything you've asked me to do."

Yet when I asked him about the ethics of the situation, he recognized the conflicts between the norms of two quite different spheres, but was inclined to let the logic of the marketplace override human concerns:

> It kind of conflicts doesn't it? However, I'll put my business hat on . . . and my people hat. I've put my business hat (on) and (it) says: "Where am I in relationship to the rest of my competitors in this industry? . . . Do I know there's something going on that the rest of the world doesn't know about?" You know, maybe there's a slump coming . . . (My) people hat? . . . I feel that's prob-

ably unethical. My business hat says there were probably some good reasons for it.

The middle cohort was more likely to see something amiss with Mattel's actions, but some were still willing to show some support and justification for it. Here is a 45-year-old Softmatics software professional. He veers between the two spheres, on the one hand citing the logic of business, and on the other a social concern, finally coming down on the side of the human factor:

> It doesn't sound right, but . . . if these people are doing a job that's no longer a function, then just because they're making money they can't keep people, . . . (But) If they're making money . . . these people obviously contributed . . . that's what I'm saying. These people who were contributing to their profits, they should try and retain them because . . . if you're trying to make money for the company, the company should try and take care of you.

Jeff Myers of cohort 2 saw the issue much the same way, first justifying Mattel in business terms, but then adding some further thinking about the function of business in society. He evokes the old ideology of welfare corporatism in words that Walter Kissinger would have endorsed, except that Jeff's valuation is confined to the personal sphere, rather than a unified concept of business within society:

> If it's a fact that . . . they don't need these people . . . then that's a logical decision for them to make . . .
>
> *(Do you see an ethical issue?)*
>
> As a person probably, yeah. I would think as a person . . . I think if these people are the people that helped make this company, make it what it is . . . If it's just for the sake of making money, I think there's more to a company than just making money, you know. Companies have an obligation to society. They have an obligation . . . to use their money or to use their influence to better the society in which they live. I don't think just throwing people out is a part of that picture."

Cohort 2's Jerry Austin rather explicitly espoused welfare corporatism ideology, the notion that loyalty and long-term employment were not simply good human relations, they were economically productive. Note that Jerry asserts that Mattel's actions were not only unethical, they were bad business decisions.

I think that there's a crisis in American business today with the lack of corporations valuing people and their employees. I think employees are the greatest asset that a company has. . . . And there's obviously too much Harvard Business School influence on America's businesses' bottom line. . . . People are not commodities and . . . treating people like a commodity (is) just not right in my book, . . . and very few people can deal with being treated that way.

(But is it a good business?)

No. Not good business at all. . . . I think something that's missing so very much: experience is not valued in corporate America any more. . . . It's more of a general knowledge and experience that I think all too often companies . . . do not see a value in it, for the sake of the bottom line . . .

Our oldest group, cohort 1 of the old dispensation, generally had a strong aversion to the actions that Mattel undertook, although as old loyalists they understood the business reasons. Joe Hirschfield's reactions are typical; he understands the business rationale, but finds layoffs by a healthy company unpalatable:

once you get the labor dollars down, of course your profits are going to go up. . . . So it doesn't surprise me at all to see that in any industry. Basically what they're doing is they're getting rid of a percentage of people who are surplus. . . . I mean Barbie can be made just as easily in Central Mexico as she can in Torrance, but a lot cheaper. So of course they're going to do it. . . .

(Do you see an ethical issue there?)

A lot of it. . . . I really feel that a company owes something to the people that work for it. They don't owe them a livelihood forever, but I think they owe them the opportunity if they are going to make a serious change, to either retrain them . . . instead of just coming to them and a person . . . feels they have contributed and all of a sudden they're surplus for whatever reason. And the company seems to be healthy . . . it's kind of about: "What have you done for me lately" attitude. . . . it's a profit-driven attitude.

FIGURE 11-5
Anomie, 1972–1994

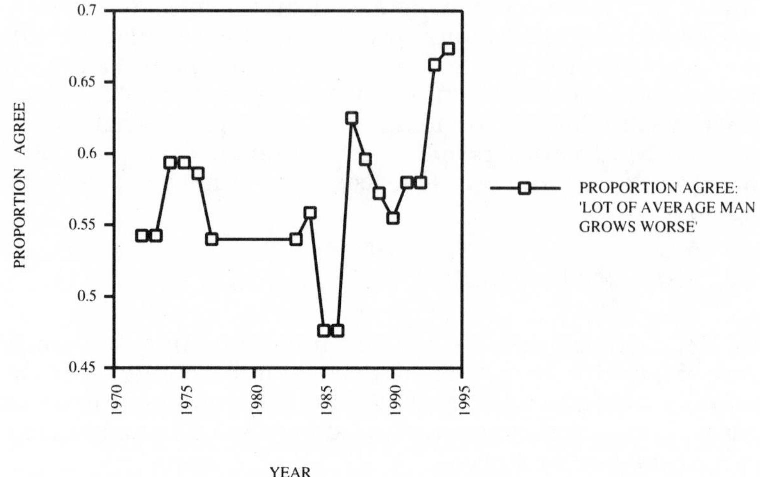

Disengagement

Mutual trust is fading, confidence in institutions of all types is down, and furthermore, as shown in Figure 11-5,[5] levels of anomie are on the rise.

And, it is the younger cohorts who are leading in the overall rise in anomie. What course of action could we expect people to take, given these widespread attitudes? Earlier, we saw Robert Merton's thoughts on anomie, which he defined as "the deterioration and, at the extremes, the disintegration of value-systems, which results in marked anxieties . . ." (Merton 1968, 217).

I believe we are in the midst of such a deterioration of value systems, as the old dispensation, the corporate culture, withers away. Merton thought there were three possible ways to deal with anomie: ritualism, or acting as though one's values meshed with society's; rebellion, the countercultural impulse, the attempt to change society's values; and, retreatism, the strategy of Candide, retreating into one's own private world (Merton 1968, 140). More and more it appears that Americans are choosing the strategy of retreatism.

We have now seen opinion-survey data on a number of attitudes, and how they have changed over the last thirty years or so. Can some "master trend" be found in this data? The sociologist Norval Glenn undertook that task, using as his hypothesis the assertion of Bellah et al. in *Habits of the Heart* (1985) that a new form of individualism is replacing the older American social character, replacing that set of values which had stressed civic duty and obligations to society. Modern individualism in its extreme form, by way of contrast, undermines allegiance to social institutions, religion, and abstractions such as the "state" and "society." Glenn found a long list of survey results that suggested that the hypothesis had value: lessened political-party affiliation, voting rates down, a decline in traditional Christianity, increased support for abortion rights. Most of these shifts in attitudes began in the 1960s. The "master trend" underlying all of these changes is a withdrawing of allegiance from "social groups, institutions, traditional religion, and anything outside themselves" (Glenn 1987, S109–S124). Merton's prediction appears to be coming true in present day America; many have chosen "retreatism." And there is yet more evidence from the sociologist Herbert Gans.

Gans asserts that we are seeing today nothing more than a very old strain of the American social character. In the America of the 1830s Tocqueville found a decided tendency toward an isolating individualism, a tendency for:

> each citizen to isolate himself from the mass of his fellows and withdraw into the circle of family and friends; with this little society formed to his taste, he gladly leaves the greater society to look after itself. (Tocqueville 1988, 506)

Tocqueville saw menace in this tendency, as "each man is forever thrown back on himself alone, and there is danger that he may be shut up in the solitude of his own heart" (Tocqueville 1988, 508). But this threat was averted in early America by Americans enmeshing themselves in a dense network of civic and private associations, which kept the citizens in constant contact with one another, overcoming the impulse toward a solipsistic individualism (Tocqueville 1988, 510–13). But this network is fraying badly, according to Gans. Rather than rugged individualism—the entrepreneurial spirit so celebrated by politicians and business theorists—Gans finds a dominant "popular" individualism, which aims to "live mainly . . . in a small part of society, the array of family, friends, and informal relationships: the microsociety" (Gans 1988, 3). Sharing time with family and friends is hardly to be scorned, but Gans finds that popular individualism goes beyond that. The ties to the wider world of institutions are loosened, a withdrawal from the larger society ensues. Our friend Charles Pearson of cohort 2 is representative of this distancing, this strain of paleoindividualism that Tocqueville saw:

> To me, as long as I got a nice roof over my head, I can put food on the table, I can watch my television, I can go play golf, I don't bother anybody else, but I don't like—my main objective—I don't like somebody telling me I have to do something.

Charles wants to live his own life unimpeded by anyone, but also without the demands of outside obligations, particularly those of large institutions. His stance fits Gans's findings; an attitude toward large institutions reminiscent of the medieval prescription for the plague: flee as far and as fast as you can. Some institutions are minimally acceptable, such as retail firms, since one can deal with them impersonally as a customer. Politics and political organizations are seen as corrupt and self-serving, and are avoided: witness the sharp drop in voting rates and in party memberships. The workplace is unavoidable for most people, but if physical withdrawal is impossible, emotional withdrawal is a sound strategy. As Charles Pearson put it:

> To me more companies look at people not as individuals, but as numbers and I think a lot of people look at companies as a place to go work, you get a paycheck, you go home.

With the end of welfare corporatism, companies seem to be actually encouraging their employees to keep an emotional distance, and workers respond with suspicion and cynicism if any attempt is made to lure them into some bond with the organization (Gans 1988, 52). The poll data on confidence in business leaders and trust in management bear out Gans's contention.

Gans believes that current attitudes reveal the survival of Tocqueville's early American individualism, the lone individual, shunning participation in affairs, avoiding, if at all possible, contact with large organizations, "shut up in the solitude of his own heart." Remember that Tocqueville saw this disengagement as a potential danger, not a reality. He saw that Americans of the 1830s in fact had a robust social life through active participation in local politics and a myriad of voluntary associations, which served as the antidote to a lonely "retreatism." What Tocqueville was describing is now termed "social capital." Let us turn to this now, and see what has happened to America's social capital.

Social Capital

Classical and neoclassical economics posit self-maximizing individuals in atomistic competition. As unreal as this picture of social reality might appear, the model can explain a good deal of economic life. A good deal, but far from all. A better model must show how social factors are entwined with individual self-interest, show how in fact the much-acclaimed market system actually rests on a social foundation (Bruyn 1991,4). This is the project of the theory of social capital.

We saw earlier Arrow's assertion that trust is the lubricant that smooths economic activity. But how is trust developed and maintained? It appears to be formed in the personal relationships developed from recurrent transactions. In fact, recurrent transactions—social interaction—can be shown to create the norms of trust and the spirit of cooperation and mutual obligation. These recurrent transactions are the repeated games of game theory. As Axelrod has shown, in a game that one knows will be repeated indefinitely, the best strategy is "Tit-for-Tat," retaliate if attacked, cooperate if offered cooperation. Rational egoists—self-maximizers—will cooperate in a repeated games once they see that the long-run benefits of cooperation outweigh the short term gains from opportunism (Bradach and Eccles 1989, 108).

In effect, the theory of social capital offers a solution to a fundamental problem, one termed the "social dilemma": should one pursue self-interest or cooperate with others and thus achieve a better outcome for all? But even when people are disposed to choose a rational strategy of cooperation, there is no guarantee that the other players will not renege. After all, there are usually no verifiable, enforceable commitments made. Therefore, it is necessary to trust others and to have them trust you for the "game" to be successful (Putnam 1993, 164). Hobbes' solution was, of course, Leviathan—enforced cooperation, the coercive power of the state (Hobbes 1988, 87). But quite obviously a great deal of voluntary social interaction goes on without the policeman standing by. How does that happen? The answer appears to lie in the idea of social capital, which is nothing but norms of trust and reciprocity, networks of interpersonal engagement—in other words, social relations of a particular kind.

It is important to understand that economic transactions are embedded in concrete personal relations and these relations are the source of our expectations, including the expectation of trustworthiness. These personal relations create and enforce norms of behavior. This idea is incorporated in game theory's "Folk Theorem": the rational player cooperates only if he is convinced that the other players are committed to cooperation as well. But norms and expectations do not spring up spontaneously to fulfill the economic function of Arrow's "lubricant", they are structures independent of economic activity, they are rooted in the history of a social system, be it a market, a corporation, or a community. This social structure can be viewed as a capital asset for individuals or groups; they possess social capital, and like other forms of capital, it is productive, making it possible to achieve objectives impossible in its absence. But unlike other forms of capital, social capital inheres in the structure of relations among people. And also unlike other forms, it grows with use. It seems self-evident that a group enjoying mutual trust will be able to accomplish more than a group not so fortunately endowed. It also seems self-evident that such accomplishments will foster further cooperation (Coleman 1990, 302). The result is that, in economic terms, the transaction costs for these people, particularly information costs, are lowered. They need not spend time and energy trying to verify the trustworthiness of their partners.

An example of this phenomenon will serve to clarify its workings and its value. In the 1960s, South Korean student protesters achieved a good deal of political influence, and were a highly organized and disciplined group. They did not begin as a political cadre, but rather first formed as study groups comprised of young men from the same hometowns. The study groups were in themselves a form of social capital—

allowing their members to perform better than if they acted alone. But, transforming the groups into a political-action organization made possible the achievement of even more difficult and important goals.

It is important to note that the ultimate beneficial use of the social relations was not the original purpose of the group at all. This seems to be the common experience in the formation of social capital. Dennis Madison talked to me about this, about how it had once been, how the close social relationships in the old days of RLX had helped the business, and how, sadly, it all seems to have dissipated:

> We don't have the team, see, that we had at RLX, like when we had the (old) group. I mean we had Joe, Bob, . . . all the guys. . . . We used to go out. We'd go fishing, we'd go play ball, we'd go drinking. We're doing everything together. It was a big group. . . . If anybody had a problem, they didn't have any problems going to see (the boss) because he was part of the group. Suddenly I don't know what happened . . .

When we look at social reality in the light of such relationships, it would appear that social capital is ubiquitous, on tap for use for any occasion. But that is not the case. Indeed, every society is characterized by networks of interpersonal relations. Some of these networks are "horizontal," linking people of the same status and power. Others are "vertical" networks, linking unequal people, in other words, in hierarchies. Networks of civic engagement are excellent examples of horizontal linkages: neighborhood associations, choral societies, sports clubs, mass-based parties, cooperatives. These networks are an essential form of social capital and such networks are the very thing that Tocqueville saw as the antidote to withdrawal and solipsism. It is membership in such formal and informal groups which:

> induce a great number of citizens to value the affection of their kindred and neighbors, bring men constantly into contact, despite the instincts which separate them, and force them to help one another. (Tocqueville 1988, 511)

The key to effective social capital is that the denser the networks, the more likely that people will cooperate in other, unrelated, activities. But not all societies, or firms, are equally endowed with dense networks. Putnam has examined this in modern Italy and shown that areas with such dense, voluntary networks have far superior economic performance than regions that lack these horizontal structures. How does this work, why do the networks have beneficial side effects?

First, the networks increase the iteration rate and the interconnectedness of social "games" and increase the costs to an opportunist in any particular transaction. Opportunism is a high-risk strategy, risking future benefits in that game, or the many other games the player is certainly engaged in within a dense network.

Secondly, the networks foster norms of reciprocity. Mutual expectations of trustworthiness and reliability are reinforced in the many interpersonal encounters. These norms will carry over into new activities. For example, the man whom you have dealt with in the sports club or neighborhood association will be rather automatically deemed a reliable partner in a business transaction. The potentially threatening boss that Dennis Madison talked about is, after all, one of the "group" you drink and play with, an approachable person you have learned to trust.

Third, the dense networks facilitate communication and the all-important creation of reputations for trustworthiness and cooperativeness. It is often not necessary to have dealt with someone personally; a good reputation precedes an individual. Knowing and trusting someone who knows and trusts another is usually sufficient warrant for the third party.

Fourth, past successes at collaboration build the confidence that future collaboration will succeed. This is the phenomenon that leads to the transference of relationships formed for one purpose to an unrelated activity, as we saw with the South Korean students. These successes become embodied in cultural norms: it is believed that cooperation works (Putnam 1993, 173).

As I have noted, social capital, unlike physical capital, grows with use. But being embedded in social relationships that have formed mutual trust, social capital is exceptionally fragile. As the human resources vice president of an erstwhile welfare corporatism company told me, the trust of employees, laboriously built up over generations, was effortlessly dissipated in a month when the layoffs and benefit cuts came. The insights of game theory are helpful to explain this. Recall the folk theorem from the structure and strategy of repeated games. The rational strategy for players in repeated social dilemma games is to cooperate only if they are convinced that the other will reciprocate. Axelrod's Tit-for-Tat strategy can result in a stable equilibrium, but it is knife-edge equilibrium. Once one player—in this case, the employer—wavers in his cooperation, trust is destroyed and the players fall into a new, stunted equilibrium, a wary and distrustful state.

We saw Dennis Madison's description of earlier times, when socialization led to an efficient business environment in the firm. Joe Weston of cohort 2 also was nostalgic for halcyon days, when the bonds were tighter:

> We were a very close group. The social interaction, especially in the beginning . . . I mean we did everything together. . . . We always kind of look back on those days and reminisce as the golden years . . . Boy, we don't realize how good we had it back then.

Is this just the normal nostalgia of maturing people, or has in fact social capital been waning in the larger society, as it manifestly has in the corporations? The disheartening answer is that it has. Social capital is subject to measurement, if we assume that the number of private organizations and the size of their membership is an indicator of social capital's basis: the density of informal interactions. Tocqueville was impressed with this density in 1830s America, and as I noted, he saw this network as the bulwark against the tendency to withdraw from society:

> political associations are only one small part of the immense number of different types of associations found there. Americans of all ages, all stations of life, and all types of dispositions are forever forming associations . . . of a thousand types—religious, moral, serious, futile, very general and very limited, immensely large and very minute. Americans combine to give fêtes, found seminaries, build churches, distribute books, and send missionaries to the antipodes. (Tocqueville 1988, 513)

The unfortunate truth is that these associations are losing members at a rapid pace. Figures 11-6 and 11-7, from General Social Survey data, show the decline in the number of people belonging to three or more voluntary associations, and the rise of the number belonging to none at all (Davis and Smith 1994). Robert Putnam has analyzed the GSS data and much more, and has concluded that American social capital is in serious decline. In addition to the fall off in voting and the

FIGURE 11-6
Social Capital: Three or More Memberships
1972–1994

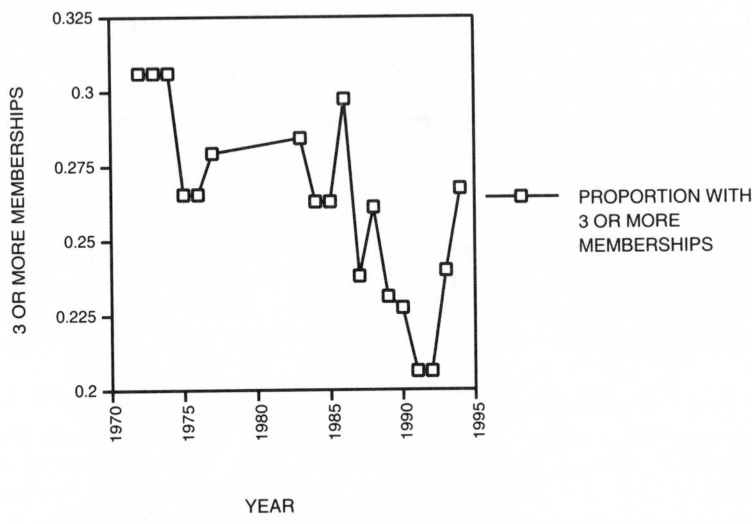

SOURCE: General Social Survey. Davis and Smith 1994

general distrust, alienation and loss of confidence in institutions, Putnam finds that

> participation has fallen (often sharply) in many types of civic associations, from religious groups to labor unions, from women's clubs to fraternal clubs, and from neighborhood gatherings to bowling leagues. Virtually all segments of society have been afflicted by this lessening in social connectedness, and this trend, in turn, is strongly correlated with declining trust. In sum, American social capital has badly eroded in the last quarter century. (Putnam 1994, 1)

The symptoms of this dissipation of social capital are all around us. Voter turnout has declined by nearly a quarter in the last thirty years; the numbers of people attending public meetings is off by a third since 1973. And the figures for political disengagement and alienation are mirrored by the numbers for voluntary associations. Weekly churchgoing rates began to fall in the 1960s, and have not recovered. PTA membership also began to fall in the 1960s and, even cor-

FIGURE 11-7
Social Capital: Zero Memberships, 1972–1994

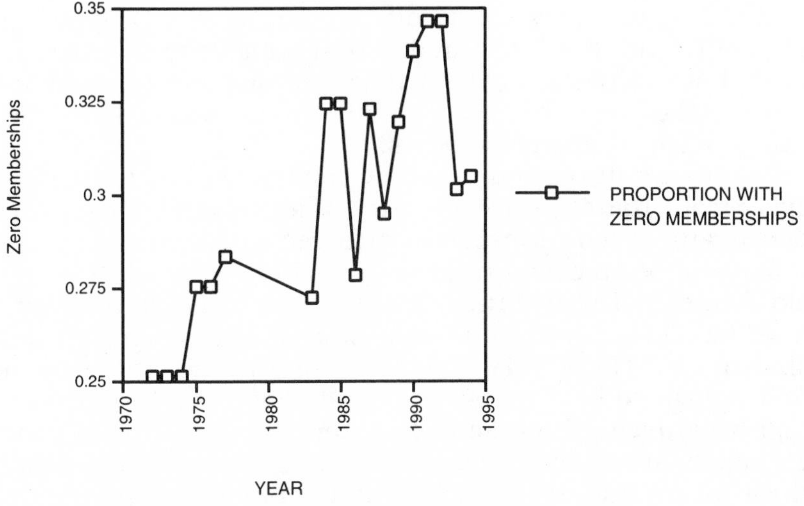

SOURCE: General Social Survey, Davis and Smitht 1994

rected for demographic shifts, the number of actively engaged parents dropped by more than half between 1960 and 1975. The list goes on: volunteering declined by one-sixth from 1974 to 1989; membership in fraternal organizations such as the Lions and Jaycees is off in the same period. After expanding for most of this century, as the old dispensation, the bureaucratic values of cooperation and community increasingly took hold, membership in key civic organizations has declined precipitously in the last decade or two.

And there is significance in another statistic: while more Americans than ever are bowling, league bowling memberships have plummeted in the last ten to fifteen years (Putnam 1994, 8–15). American social capital, amassed over generations, is rapidly depreciating in our day. Social capital is one component of the old dispensation, the bureaucratic values. Clearly it is in serious decline. And, all other components of that complex of values are declining as well. The old dispensation stood for loyalty, cooperation, trust in one another, and it stood as well for a great deal of confidence in American political, social, and economic institutions. Large organizations were seen as efficacious, they worked for society, and they worked to satisfy individual aspirations. The old atomistic strain of American individualism had been largely held at bay (Galambos 1975, 261). If this is to be scorned as the "other-directed" personality of Riesman, or the Organization Man of Whyte, the fact remains that a majority of Americans held these values for generations, and achieved a high level of societal cohesiveness as a result. Anomie was not an American problem until recent years.

But, as we have seen, the new generation has led America away from the old bureaucratic values; loyalty, trust, confidence, and social capital have withered as anomie has grown. It may not be an overstatement to see here what Scott Fitzgerald found in the twenties, a new generation: "grown up to find all Gods dead, all wars fought, all faiths in man shaken . . ." (*This Side of Paradise* 306). And, this does not now appear to be a transient phenomenon. A 1995 survey of highly achieving high school students indicated that cohort 3's values are shared by an even-younger generation. Among these future leaders, confidence in the president and the Congress were 11 percent and 9 percent, down from 31 and 26 percent for similar students in 1971. While in 1971, 20 percent of high potential teenagers had confidence in the media, that number is 5 percent in 1995 (Sanchez 1995). We can conclude, first, that the old dispensation has definitively passed away, and secondly, that the new generation's views are likely to hold sway for some time.

The next two chapters conclude this work. In chapter 12, I will review the origins of the old dispensation in American history and the course that it ran, in order to find explanations for its passing. Then, in the last chapter, I will conclude with some speculations about the direction in which we seem to be heading, the possible consequences of the momentous value shift we have been reviewing throughout this work.

Part Four
Conclusions

12

The Natural History of Loyalty

Is it (loyalty) a thing that really doesn't have any value? Is it one of those religious things that never really had a foundation and physical reality?

—John Francisco, cohort 2

Social Change

I believe that I have shown that the "old dispensation"—that set of bureaucratic values which included corporate loyalty—has given way in our time to the quite different values of a new generation. In that argument the question of causation has thus far been ignored. It is time to address that. But to do so, we must first ask: where did the "old dispensation" come from in the first place? How is it that Americans adopted a corporate culture? To answer that we must first look at the social character of Americans before the corporate culture emerged. In the breakdown of an even older set of values we can then perhaps see the way to explain the demise of the old dispensation in its turn.

Social character, as I noted in an earlier chapter, has been defined by Fromm as "the essential character structure of most members of a group which has developed as the result of the basic experiences and mode of life common to that group" (Fromm 1994, 275). Fromm's definition betrays his social-change model; he asserts that a new social character is formed as an adaptation to new social and economic conditions, that "by adapting himself to social conditions, man develops those traits that make him *desire* to act as he *has* to act" (Fromm 1994, 281). This is of course the position of Marx who famously stated:

> The mode of production in material life determines the general character of the social, political, and spiritual processes of life. It

is not the the consciousness of men that determines their existence, but, on the contrary, their social existence that determines their consciousness. (Marx 1904, 30)

This might be called the "demand" theory of social change, the notion that new economic conditions call forth new character types. Opposed to this are the theories of Comte and Weber, which turn the causal arrow about: changes in cognitive states, that is to say, changes in social character result in changes in society and the economy. Thorstein Veblen subscribed to this view as well, noting that when values change, economic thinking must change as well, and the consequences of, for example, a disvaluation of economic growth would result in the fulfillment of that prophecy (Yankelovich 1979, 4).

As we think through the changes in American social character, we will find that the Marxist/Fromm explanation seems to fit the formation of the "new" middle class—or "old dispensation," if you will. Profound changes in economic organization, spurred by technological change, led to great corporations and created positions in hierarchies which were staffed by people who, almost by necessity, had values quite different from those of the old middle class. The demand for such character types can be seen to have in some sense created such a social character.

But the cognitive change approach seems to explain better the formation of the old nineteenth-century middle class, as well as the transformation in values we are experiencing today. Rather than rising from technological change, these developments seem to have sprung from new ways of thinking about the world. Let us look first at the old middle class, then move on to the formation of the new middle class, which seems more a matter of changes in economic organization creating a new social character.

The Old Middle Class

Eighteenth-century America was a rural, agricultural society. In 1790, only about five percent of the four million Americans lived in towns of more than 2500 people, and almost three quarters of the workers were farm laborers. The little manufacturing that was done was the work of artisans in small shops; institutionally, production was accomplished in a holdover from the medieval guild system, with an artisan assisted by journeymen and apprentices, who were treated as part of the family. Some larger enterprises existed in the port cities, such as shipyards, candleworks, and rum distilleries. There were small coal and lumber industries and a growing iron-forging industry. Distribution was accomplished by the merchants in the port and river towns, who bought and marketed the output of the small manufacturers and also supplied them with raw materials and tools (Chandler 1977, 17). It is from this social and economic base that the old middle class began to form.

From its earliest days, America was marked by an ethos of worldly success. Like their European counterparts, American Puritans came in time to regard economic success as the certain mark of election for salvation. But Americans were also from earliest times characterized by individualism. When the religious element of Puritanism waned in the late eighteenth century, the drive for success did not lose its power; economic success became a major cultural goal. Yet, in the largely agricultural society, the independent farmer and property owner were the main models of success (Stivers 1994, 21). But the conception of exemplary occupation was to change as new men with new values appeared, men with an entrepreneurial spirit who brought industrialization into being.

The era of accelerating industrialization began in the 1820s; by 1830 the age-old system of home manufacturing had virtually disappeared, replaced by shops and factories. Between 1809 and 1839, manufacturing output rose an average of 59 percent per decade, then reached a staggering growth rate of 154 percent in the 1840s and, from a much higher base, 60 percent in the 1850s. By 1860, the United States manufacturing sector ranked second or third in the world (Bruchey 1988, 58–59). Until about 1875, though, firms were mainly small. The merchant was the dominant force in the economy, the essential link between production and the consumer and the provider of capital and transport as well (Chandler 1977, 17).

It is in this merchant class that we can find the values of the old middle class. Their values were those of the Protestant Ethic, the same values that Max Weber attributed to the earliest capitalists in *The Protestant Ethic and the Spirit of Capitalism* (1904–5). Weber asserted that it was the transmutation of Calvinism to a secular faith in worldly success, that it was this cognitive shift which had created capitalism and the ensuing social change. Weber pointed to Benjamin Franklin as the exemplar of this capitalist character type. In his autobiography, Franklin portrays himself as a poor boy who rose in the world by dint of hard work and careful calculation. He tells of his youthful list of virtues, virtues which can now be seen to form the value set of the old middle class.[1] Among these moral standards Franklin counted willpower, industriousness, ambition, thrift, neatness, and sobriety. Above all there was the virtue of *individual* striving, celebrated in a key aphorism from *Poor Richard's Almanack:* "God helps those who help themselves." It is this belief—the notion that all have the chance to succeed through their own initiative—this belief characterized the old middle-class. Closely connected to initiative and striving is the value of work itself; hard work and meeting challenges were considered ends in themselves. There are of course vestiges of the old middle-class values alive in our society today. They are not nearly the dominant view that politicians' speeches might have it, but they are nonetheless alive. I found some of my subjects expressing such values, particularly in the importance of work and challenge. I asked forty-one-year-old James Kessler from cohort 2 what he valued most about his job. As an officer of the company, he had been moved around a good deal to serve as a troubleshooter, but he spoke not of the rewards of solving problems, nor the material benefits, but the inner need to confront new challenges:

> Challenge is probably a big part of it. I'm one of those people that has absolutely no fear of going into something that looks as though it's tough. I have no fear whatsoever. I will also say, though, if you get into those situations, it's extremely taxing because generally everybody hits you with everything. It's overwhelming as to what the magnitude of the problems are . . . I like the challenge; I like the opportunity.

James's score on the Protestant Ethic metric that I used was more than one standard deviation greater than the mean; his Protestant Ethic allegiance is thus unusually high for the Softmatics sample.[2] But I should note that the overall mean was 3.08 on a five point scale, i.e., the mean is near neutrality for Protestant Ethic attitudes, so there are not many traces of that old middle-class value left, at least in my sample. Forty-four percent of the sample were either neutral towards or disagreed with the Protestant Ethic values. Only three-tenths of one percent scored even as high as "somewhat agree." The sample also showed a cohort effect for the Protestant Ethic metric. The oldest, cohort 1, was significantly higher, and Protestant Ethic allegiance then declines monotonically with the younger cohorts.[3] So whatever relics of the old values remain, they appear to be disappearing with the succession of the generations.

My data are confirmed by other researchers. The General Social Survey data from 1972 to 1994 indicate a decline in the number stating they would continue working if they had sufficient means to maintain their lifestyle. This downward trend is particularly marked from 1985 to the present, the time when cohort 3 began to come of age (Davis and Smith 1994). Some earlier data on a related aspect of the Protestant Ethic show the same trends; comparing 1947 results to 1977, fewer people (48 percent versus 60 percent) wanted to own their own business in 1977, and half preferred to work for someone else in 1977, versus only 24 percent in 1947 (Furnham 1990, 204–5). Thus the bureaucratic values have for some time been replacing the old middle-class orientation toward work, especially independent work.

If we look again at James Kessler's statement, we see something missing, and it was generally missing from the old middle-class values; I refer to a healthy social concern, the attention to the needs of the organization or the larger society. Rather, the orientation is exclusively inward. Although Benjamin Franklin may have inspired many to the path of independent success, in fact, he himself did become a public man after his entrepreneuring days. But many whom he influenced lost the focus on the larger social context in the pursuit of individual self-interest (Bellah et al. 1985, 32–33). We can see that the dominant belief of the old middle class accorded with the teaching of Adam Smith: private and public interests would coincide if all were free to pursue self-interest.

Let us look further at the economic backdrop to the rise of the old middle class. The industrial economy of antebellum America was still quite primitive by our standards. A relatively large manufacturing firm might have no more than sixty employees, and in many respects the face of manufacturing was little different from the Dutch textile industry in the fourteenth century: an individual entrepreneur and a single factory. Even the putting-out system, in the form of hiring a contractor to operate within the firm using his own workers, was not uncommon. Chandler has noted that in the period from 1790 to 1840, the volume of goods produced increased enormously, but there was little institutional change; the same traditional business enterprises handled this increased volume comfortably. Chandler's work is informed by the technological imperative, and he asserts that the institutions did not change because there was little pressure to innovate; the same, ancient sources of energy were employed: muscle and wind and water power (Chandler 1977, 14).

In this period, we can find people who exemplify the old middle class, merchants like the hardware store owners in Pennsylvania who were much more than shopkeepers; they were preeminently entrepreneurs, engines of the local economy, who engaged in construction, development, and investment in local companies. These merchants were also the distributors for regional producers and the essential economic link between production and consumption (Zunz 1990, 15–16).

Asa Sheldon was a prototypical old middle-class man, witnessing in his lifetime the transformation of society from an agricultural economy to merchant capitalism. Indeed, he helped make the transformation. Born in 1788 in New England, he grew up on a farm and had an early encounter with Franklin's teachings. As a young boy he plunged into a cash economy, seeking out odd jobs to earn cash and saving all he earned. Significantly, in his autobiography he refers to his first "contract" for a day's work, filling a cart with stones. As Graff notes:

> His calling these informal arrangements "contracts" was one sign of the spreading market economy's impact on the culture and language of everyday life. Significant, too, is the cash basis of these transactions. The shift from traditional unpaid apprenticeship to paid work was under way. (Graff 1995, 64)

Sheldon rose in the world from farm laborer to apprentice and servant, saving his money all the while. Still in his twenties, he was able to buy a sawmill and from there branched out into distribution and transportation. He invested in multifarious activities and even participated in the building of New England's first railroad (Graff 1995, 65). But the days of individual entrepreneurs like Sheldon as a dominant social class were not to last long, as American industry grew in size and scope, and new types emerged along with this transformation.

The New Middle Class: "The Old Dispensation"

Technological progress, rather than cognitive change, led to the next step. When anthracite coal became available, steam power was feasible and the first steam-powered mill went on stream in 1828, although as late as 1832 most manufacturing was still powered almost exclusively by water (Chandler 1977, 58–60). But after the Civil War, the American economy was transformed into the world we largely experience today. The change was dramatic. Asa Sheldon would have found the thirteenth-century world of Venetian commerce more familiar, and more congenial, than he would his own country in the 1860s. Economic growth soared in the decade after the Civil War, reaching a gross annual rate of 4.95 percent from 1869 to 1879, and 2.56 percent per capita in this period (Galambos and Pratt 1988, 27).

Once the railroads appeared, this cheap and reliable transportation greatly increased demand for manufactured goods. Cheap steam power from anthracite coal lowered costs and the factory system spread rapidly during the 1840 and 1850s, then expanded mightily after the Civil War. Mass production came to some industries in the 1870s and 1880s, with machines that not only replaced manual operations, but integrated several stages of production (Chandler 1977, 245–49).

The vast increases in production created by mechanical processes moved the enterprises toward integration of distribution channels. The volumes of goods to be distributed simply broke the old merchant-oriented distribution networks. The manufacturers found the transaction costs in distribution too high, both the direct costs as well as the uncertainty of moving the goods. Manufacturers integrated forward and internalized distribution. Similarly, reliance on a scattered network of suppliers proved costly and these too were internalized. The modern industrial enterprise—the type of firm we are now accustomed to—resulted from this forward and backward integration, the combination of mass production and mass distribution. Such firms were almost nonexistent at the end of the 1870s, but in thirty years they came to dominate many of America's vital industries (Chandler 1977, 283–85).

American industry was thus rationalized and able to attain the economies of scale needed to serve a large market. And most important for our interest here, the vertically integrated firms also created large managerial hierarchies which could do a more effective job than the market in managing the flows of raw materials, through the production process, and out to the ultimate consumer (Chandler 1990, 71–79). Something new had happened, a new form of economic organization had come into being. Before, firms were small and generally specialized: a manufacturer relied on the market, the merchant, to move his goods. With poor transportation, markets were small. When technological progress brought steam power and the railroads, very large markets opened up for the products of mass production, and very large, integrated firms were formed to manage production and distribution. A new economic actor also appeared: the salaried manager, the "occupant" of the offices of the Weberian bureaucracy. A new economic institution, what Chandler calls the "managerial business enterprise," sprang into existence, manned by a new species of economic man, the salaried manager (Chandler 1990, 1–2). It was this new salaried class which embraced the bureaucratic values of order, group effort, and of course, loyalty to the firm.

It is difficult to see how this new class formed—as the old middle class had—from cognitive change. Of course the men who led the new economic developments were old-style entrepreneurs who seized on the new opportunities that technology offered. These men retained the old middle class's Protestant Ethic values of individual effort and striving for success, a taste for risk-taking and the ability to use other people (Furnham 1990, 15). The new middle class of salaried workers can be seen to have developed in response to the demand for their services, the work available in these new enterprises. But the transition to new values was not rapid, nor easy.

The period of the 1880s and 1890s was critical to the formation of new values and a new middle class; the older American values of self-help and community action were rooted in the face-to-face relations of small-town America. In the space of just a few years, urbanization and industrialization spread, and the value system had not yet caught up with the radically new situation. Accordingly, Wiebe finds: "The United States in the late nineteenth century offered a peculiarly inviting field for coarse leadership and crudely exercised power" (Wiebe 1967, 37). The inhibitions on the entrepreneur attendant to operating in a local milieu did not have force when decisions affected distant and anonymous people. Absentee ownership was the rule, and men in New York or Philadelphia made decisions dispassionately which were translated into violence by their agents in remote western mining towns or midwestern factories. Rockefeller, for example, reportedly a kindly man in private life, never saw, nor probably even envisioned, the scenes his orders had precipitated. But there were also, as in any age, genuine rogues. Henry Frick ruled the Pittsburgh iron and steel business with ruthless and savage power; an acquaintance said "He should not be allowed in the same room with children."

Frick may have been especially ferocious, but the incomplete value transition Wiebe describes led to a segmentation of morality: Christian virtue in private life, the law of the jungle in business (Wiebe 1967, 37–40). And the late nineteenth century was certainly an era of cutthroat business competition and ruthless practices of every description. Labor was treated brutally. In their competition one with another, businessmen routinely resorted to bribery and extortion, dirty tricks of every nature. State legislatures were especially corrupted. It was said that Standard Oil had done everything to the Pennsylvania legislature except refine it.

Yet our interest is not really with these rogues; we seek the new middle class, the salaried employees of these corporation builders. The old middle-class values of individual responsibility and risk-taking might still serve their masters well, but the new men in new bureaucracies had new problems to solve. There were both social and business issues demanding attention. The new urban areas required social planning, the government and corporate bureaucracies must be organized and managed. In general, there was a growing recognition that society and the corporation both needed a cooperative effort, that the problems needed less individual initiative and more collective effort (Cochran 1985, 10). As Robert Wiebe has shown in *The Search for Order* (1967), in the period 1880 to 1920 American life was largely bureaucratized, as hierarchical organizations were formed for a wide variety of governmental, economic, and social purposes. Most Americans were increasingly exposed to bureaucracies in some aspect of their lives.

The first large scale organizations and bureaucracies were the railroads, which first appeared in the 1830s, and then grew in size and importance through the 1840s and 1850s. Effective operations of the roads required a sizable cadre of managers to coordinate and control the widespread operations of the railroad. A hierarchical administrative apparatus was required to supervise the large numbers of salaried men who operated the road. The first bureaucracies in American business thus formed, comprised of men with specialized skills who in general had no ownership in the enterprise. These men had developed skills and experience which were company-specific, or at least industry-specific, and their outlook increasingly became professionalized. They now saw their work as a career, in contrast to the old merchant orientation which had men moving from activity to activity as entrepreneurial opportunities were grasped.

By 1870, over 70,000 miles of road were in place and the mechanisms had been developed to coordinate and control thousands of employees, enormous amounts of equipment, and the movement of mountains of goods. The men who manned these administrative hierarchies were a new type, salaried men without a financial stake in the company. They were often specially trained; civil engineering was a common educational background. The engineering training forged a mentality which prized analytical method, the orderly process of solving problems by analysis and rationality (Chandler 1977, 79–95).

As early as the 1850s the general manager of the Erie Railroad had published the general principles of administration, the essential workings of a Weberian bureaucracy: division of responsibilities, authority commensurate with those responsibilities, reporting systems to alert management to problems and to evaluate subordinates. By the time of the Civil War, the essentials of the American large-scale business enterprise could be found in the railroads. In the railroads of that era we could find large numbers of salaried managers, a central office commanded by top managers reporting to a board of directors, and financial and statistical controls providing the information to manage a large and dispersed organization (Chandler 1977, 101.)

It was here in these new bureaucracies that the new middle class had to slough off the dominant values of the old society and learn to be custodians of others' property, to obey orders, and limit their initiative to enhancing the value of the company's property, not their own. This could be a wrenching experience, abandoning the older values which favored working for one's own advantage, having more rights than duties and allegiances, and living in a society which celebrated social equality, not subservience (Cochran 1985, 64). From loyalty to one's self and family, and a few individuals, an adjustment had to be made to giving loyalty to a large and impersonal organization. Yet, the adjustment was made, and in many cases made with a will.

By the 1880s, spurred by the development of the rail networks and the telegraph, American producers and distributors began to consolidate and these new large-scale enterprises adopted the administrative systems of the railroads, the large cadres of white-collar workers. America came into the new century with an economy and a society which would have seemed a fantasy seventy-five years earlier. Revolutions in transportation and communication had created a continental market; vast enterprises employing thousands dominated the economy; millions of immigrants were being absorbed into the society. America had achieved global economic preeminence: from the 1890s on, the United States was the world's leading industrial nation with the highest gross domestic product and the highest per-capita income. On the eve of World War I, the U.S. produced 36 percent of the world's industrial output. Germany and Britain were far behind, with 16 percent and 14 percent, respectively. There were (and are now) a great deal more modern, integrated industrial firms in the U.S. than anywhere else and these firms dominated a number of basic industries (Chandler 1990, 47). The United States was further differentiated from other economies in that these giant firms were managed by large cadres of salaried managers which had effective control of the firm.

At first, work in a bureaucracy was a relatively rare experience: in 1870 no more than one percent of the workforce was in clerical positions. But by 1900 it was three percent and by 1940, ten percent (Zunz 1990, 126). The growing number of white-collar workers created a split in the middle class, which did not go unnoticed at the time, and was seen as a social problem. The old middle class of entrepreneurs now was challenged by a new class of salaried workers. Publications around the turn of the century decried the corporations' luring potential entrepreneurs into salaried work, blocking their chances for economic independence and individual judgment. In less than thirty years, control of the American economy had passed from the merchant/entrepreneur to huge, impersonal corporations, and the valued old middle-class characteristics of independence, risk-taking, and the Protestant Ethic seemed to have passed as well (Zunz 1990, 13).

Why did young men who once would have clerked in stores or become artisans and entrepreneurs join the ranks of the new bureaucracies? Oliver Zunz makes a strong case that the attraction was far more than the security of a salary. In this age of corporation building, the lure was not merely money; it was the opportunity to participate in a vast enterprise, to build something new, build the railroad or the automobile industry. Comparing a life in a small town with its limited horizons—however independent one was—comparing that to the excitement and fulfillment of great accomplishments perhaps explains the rush to join the new hierarchies (Zunz 1990, 39). Zunz relates many tales of young men who eschewed the old middle-class path. We learn of a Thomas Doane, a railroader who traveled to Fort Kearney in 1870 and built towns in a wilderness to prepare for the railroad's coming (Zunz 1990, 54). Or consider the career of W. S. Perry, born in 1851, who gave up the life of an independent farmer to join the railroad. He rose to a middle-management position and in his time was:

> responsible for building, maintaining, and improving the road itself, and, it can be said, played an important role in the settling of the frontier and in pioneering new technology. These challenges were available to him only as a member of the expanding railroad bureaucracy. (Zunz 1990, 57)

These men of the early corporation were already organization men, generations before Whyte thought the type had emerged. Whyte described his mid-twentieth century Organization Men as those who not only work for the organization but "belong to it as well—(they) have left home spiritually as well as physically, to the take the vows of organizational life . . ." (Whyte 1956, 3) Already in these early days of the railroad bureaucracies we find the formation of organizational loyalty. The internalization of the organization's goals can be seen in the reaction of the white-collar employees to the Burlington Railroad strike of 1888. The middle mangers were often from the same backgrounds as the strikers and might be expected to take their part. But they uniformly backed the company in its struggle with the workers. Regardless of their relatively low incomes and their middling position in the hierarchy, they saw themselves as part and parcel of the company, as a distinctive class quite separate from the working men (Zunz 1990, 63–64). They had left home spiritually as well as physically, their true fatherland was the corporation.

By 1918 at the latest, the importance of corporate loyalty had been grasped by top management and its formation carefully addressed. At du Pont, corporate training for salesmen included a formal pledge of loyalty which "reinforced personal ties to the organization and imbued the corporate salesman with a sense of corporate identity that distinguished him from ordinary drummers" (Zunz 1990, 188). In this period, roughly from 1870 to 1920, the corporate culture, the bureaucratic values, formed. This was a fundamental shift from the small-town, entrepreneurial values of the old middle class to a bureaucratic outlook suitable for corporate life (Wiebe 1967, vii.). This is the set of values that I have termed "the old dispensation." A new work culture was created within the large corporations, one that emphasized order and rules, that prized loyalty, and that valued technical—usually firm-specific—knowledge. Additionally, the new jobs offered young men a much-enlarged scope, an opportunity to participate in great enterprises, far beyond the scope of an individual entrepreneur (Zunz 1990, 64).

The changeover to bureaucratic values can be glimpsed in the changing conventional views of desirable management characteristics. In the mid-nineteenth century those qualities had nothing to do with collective effort or loyalty; they were a catalog of Protestant Ethic virtues straight from *Poor Richard's Almanack:* The list included the virtues of industry, calculation, prudence, punctuality, and perseverance. A list from 1918 was different, but still touched little on the manager as a social agent. The prized qualities were said to be intelligence, enthusiasm, honesty, and fairness—the virtues of Scientific Management, an orderly and rational approach to a large bureaucracy. But a dramatic change could be seen in the list from 1928. Here we find that the leader should be worthy of his authority; be eager to acquire new information; willing to learn from subordinates; able to take criticism and acknowledge mistakes (Perrow 1979, 66). It was about this time that Chester Barnard stated that "The most important single contribution required of the executive, certainly the most universal qualification, is loyalty. . . ." (Barnard 1950, 220). The social content of the favored qualities is clear; the manager must have many of the skills of a social worker along with a fundamental commitment to the organization. The workplace was seen as primarily a social milieu, a cohesive community needing intelligent leadership, but also demanding a great degree of loyalty among all its members.

Were it only the relatively few white-collar workers who embraced these new values, the emergence of a dominant new value system would not have occurred. But in time, the mindset of these bureaucrats spread throughout the society and the old middle-class merchant/entrepreneur culture necessarily faded. Louis Galambos has traced this long transition from a minority attitude of the pioneer organization men to a dominant mindset of the American middle-class. Galambos reviewed American middle class publications—those targeted to craftsmen, clergymen, engineers, and prosperous farmers—to determine the changes in opinions about large business enterprises. His crucial assumption is that a favorable attitude toward big business reflects an adherence to the corporate culture, to the bureaucratic values of order, hierarchy, and organizational loyalty. Galambos finds, as Zunz has, that by the 1870s the engineers had already formed a favorable attitude, an attitude which persisted throughout his research period, 1879 to 1940. As we have seen, the new type had emerged along with American industrial concentration, first in the railroads and then in the large production companies spawned by the railroads' opening of continent-wide markets. David Riesman and William H. Whyte, Jr., writing in the 1950s, thought they had discovered a new "other-directed Organization Man." In fact, such types could have been found working for Standard Oil in the 1890s, or for the Erie Railroad even earlier (Galambos 1975, 14).

Other sectors of the middle class were slower to adopt the corporate culture, but in time came to accept the bureaucratic values. Galambos recounts this long process, replete with fits and starts, as the bulk of the middle class moved toward the new values. The Panic of 1893, for example, left only the engineers still favorable to big business, but others' hostility passed with the bad times and by the turn of the century more favorable views were common. It was the accomplishments of big business more than anything that won over the middle class. The large firms were widely viewed as efficient providers of material goods, jobs, and economic progress.

In the period 1902 to 1914, Galambos finds widespread support for the corporate culture. As bureaucracies spread beyond business to government agencies, labor unions, professional associations, and volunteer groups, more and more people saw the virtues of rationalization and system. An increasing number saw less value in traditional individualism and competition, and more value in cooperative efforts, as exemplified in the large bureaucracies.

The shift in attitudes could be seen in the language employed to describe the large companies. In the 1880s and 1890s, the middle-class writers had often couched their descriptions in emotional terms: the trusts were "extortionate, tyrannical"; they were the "octopus," the "hog," the "outlaw." In the early twentieth century, much more neutral terms were common: "firm," "company," "business." (Galambos 1975, 153). By the 1920s, the shift from the old middle-class values to the new corporate culture was largely complete, according to Galambos's analysis. This explains a puzzle from his data. i.e., the relatively mild reaction to the Great Depression. Galambos saw an expected downturn in support for large corporations in the 1930s, but not nearly as severe as the discontent experienced in the depression of the 1890s. He attributes this mild reaction to the new mentality's hold on a large proportion of the middle class, which was firmly in place by 1930 (Galambos 1975, 236). I believe that the same explanation applies to my findings on the moderate reaction of my cohort 1 subjects to Corporate America's abandoning welfare corporatism. Steeped in the old dispensation—the corporate culture—they have maintained their faith in the bureaucratic values in spite of the pillars of welfare corporatism falling all about them. Their younger colleagues of cohort 2 had a good deal less early socialization to these values, but found them alive in their work culture. They reacted with dismay and disillusionment as the old dispensation passed, while the youngest group, never believing in the values in the first place, shrugged when the masks were torn aside.

As we have seen, the experience of the Great Depression and the Second World War solidified the corporate culture. Large bureaucracies were seen to be efficacious, saving the country from chaos in the Depression, and going on to win the war. After the Second World War, Americans had tremendous faith and confidence in business institutions and in the federal government. The corporate culture, that matrix of bureaucratic values that I have called "the old dispensation," had been a-building since the 1870s and had attained majority support by the 1950s.

Causes of the Modern Transformation of Values

Earlier, we reviewed the dissolution of the old dispensation among the younger generations, the turning away from the old values of corporate loyalty, mutual trust, confidence in institutions, and support for a robust social capital. The declines in trust, loyalty, and confidence are leading us toward Tocqueville's specter: "Each man is forever thrown back on himself alone, and there is danger that he may be shut up in the solitude of his own heart" (Tocqueville 1988, 508). But how did we come to this pass? How in the space of thirty years or so did America turn from a corporate culture that had formed over eighty and more years, that had nurtured generations, that had contributed to a vast expansion of material well-being? The answers are difficult to state definitively, and, while I will make an attempt at explanation, you should note that the following is a good deal more speculative than the material I have presented thus far.

It would seem clear that the formation of the new generation's culture was not "demand driven," as the formation of the new middle-class values rather evidently were. In that earlier phase, American industrialization required large numbers of willing white-collar workers, who would voluntarily give the corporation their loyalty and their best efforts, their hearts as well as their minds. And such a social character emerged. Now the dominant social character is changing, but it is difficult to see what possible demand there could be for people who increasingly eschew organizational ties, who mistrust one another and distrust all their institutions. Corporations and other institutions still need trust, loyalty, and confidence, I would think. So a demand argument must necessarily fall to the ground.

We have reviewed the alternative causation—cognitive shift—in its application to the formation of the old middle class. In that time, before any substantial technological breakthroughs, a new breed of men came into being with new outlooks derived, according to Weber, from a distillation of Calvinist attitudes, largely with the religious content leached out. Perhaps a similar cognitive shift can account for the demise of the corporate culture, the old dispensation. Let us explore that.

I should note that we can see the effect of cognitive change on at least some sectors of the new middle class, a cognitive change that was not demand driven. As Galambos notes, Congregationalist ministers and independent farmers came in time to accept bureaucratic values, and they did so hardly as a result of employment in large organizations. Rather, Galambos asserts, they embraced the corporate culture because big business was seen as efficacious, providing society with necessary goods and services (Galambos 1975, 160–66). It was their exposure to a society comprised of large organizations—organizations which seemed to work—which changed their minds.

Today, without belaboring you further with poll data and statistics, it is manifest that this consensus about the corporate culture is fast fading, especially among the young. That a cognitive shift has occurred, I think, is beyond dispute. But why? Why is a system which produces such great material benefits being rejected? Why do so many no longer trust one another and no longer extend loyalty to institutions? If we look at some theories of social change we can find some tentative answers. There is first the impact of technology. Putnam and others claim that this is a root cause of the growing privatization of American life, the withdrawal from society which Gans has charted (Putnam 1994, 25). Putnam refers to the privatizing of leisure, the availability of home entertainment of all types that lures the citizen from socially oriented leisure to a comfortable, but isolated existence "shut up in the solitude of his own heart." In this view, cable television, stereo sound systems, video cassettes and computer games have made it irresistible to stay home.

We can see the impact of technology and economics as well in the transformation of the retail trade, the disappearance of corner grocery stores and shops and the growth of impersonal shopping centers. And more than that, we see the increase in home shopping, home banking; the replacement of cashiers by ATMs; the neighborhood library by the Internet. All of this is true, but the question of causation is not yet answered. After all, home entertainment has been a reality since Gutenberg. One can stay home and read as easily as use a videocassette, or one can choose to get out and socialize. There *are* stores still open, we are not compelled to shop by phone. There are concerts, plays, neighbors and friends, we are not prisoners in our own homes. I believe that the technological argument has the causal arrow reversed: the availability of all the privatizing technology can be seen just as readily as a *demand* for such things, a demand fueled by people who simply do not want to be engaged in the larger society. Are we so shallow that some new technological toy would overturn the values of an entire culture? Would the patriots of 1776 not have acted if they had had HBO and the Internet? I hardly think so. Something more fundamental is afoot.

There has been a good deal of speculation about the root cause of the modern discontent. Technology itself has been seen as a causative agent, but technology far beyond the new technological leisure-time products. This is the critique of Jacques Ellul, which we have visited before, the idea that modern society is enmeshed in *la technique*. The French term is broader than the English "technique"; it is expressive of an attitude or way of life, an orientation toward efficiency, efficiency in all aspects of life, which creates a bureaucratic imperative to solve all problems with rationally developed technical means—administrative processes as well as physical devices (Stivers 1994, 8). As a result, all progress in human affairs is assumed to be technical progress. We have become infatuated with technical means to address any issue in the name of efficiency. Ellul sees the danger in believing technology the answer to all human concerns, because in the process, true human concerns are disvalued. The more we apply technology the worse we make many problems. Power generation creates pollution; rationally devised bureaucratic procedures create alienation (Ellul 1990, xvi). Jerry Austin of cohort 2 spoke to this dehumanizing trend: "Just generally I think there's a crisis in American business today with the lack of corporations valuing people and their employees."

I noted earlier that exposure to the benefits of bureaucratic organization in time won over a majority in favor of the bureaucratic culture, changing their minds from the old middle-class value set. Perhaps it is now an unremitting and long-prolonged exposure to impersonal bureaucratic institutions that has changed minds again. A number of thinkers have made this basic critique of modern society. Central to this criticism is Raymond Aron's notion of "Advanced Industrial Society," expressed in his book of lectures, *Dix-huit Leçons sur la Société Industrielle* (1962). His is a non-Marxist analysis, since he argues that ownership of the means of production is irrelevant today. Capitalism and state socialism have evolved into remarkably similar systems, with central planning (by either the state or the giant corporation) perforce required to operate the system. In either case, the economy cannot be left to chance; technicians are needed to insure its smooth operation. The myth of the "Invisible Hand" has been exploded in modern times.[4] Rather than the atomistic markets of Adam Smith, we have today the visible hands of Alfred Chandler, the army of corporate and government bureaucrats who monitor and control the economy. Aron's analysis, however, did not offer a critique of advanced industrial society. He took it as a given. His only reservation was his belief that democratic, capitalistic systems were more likely to combat the tyranny of technical elites than socialist societies would.

But others stepped to the fore to find pervasive ills in such advanced industrial societies. We saw the nebulous countercultural attack on modern society, which Ginsberg identified as "Moloch," the god who demanded the sacrifice of children. More systematic thinkers than Ginsberg have followed this line of attack. Karl Polanyi assailed capitalism in *The Great Transformation* (1944), asserting that it was the market system itself that had led to the modern malaise, the myth that the factors of production—land, labor, and capital—were commodities produced for sale (Polanyi 1944, 42). He has some vivid language to express the consequences of this myth, this "commodity fiction":

> labor and land are not other than the human beings themselves of which every society consists and the natural surroundings in which it exists. To include them in the market mechanism means

> to subordinate the substance of society itself to the laws of the market. . . . The alleged commodity 'labor power' cannot be shoved about, used indiscriminately, or even left unused, without affecting the human individual who happened to be the bearer of this peculiar commodity. . . . Nature would be reduced to its elements, neighborhoods and landscapes defiled, rivers polluted . . . the power to produce food and raw materials destroyed. (Polanyi 1944, 71 and 73)

Raymond Aron thought that it was not the market system per se that could be the problem. Rather, he concurs with Ellul in that it is the technological and bureaucratic imperatives that have spawned advanced industrial society. Because in both market and socialistic economies we see the thousands of workers at a single site, the separation of home and workplace, the extreme division of labor, the accumulation and reinvestment of capital (Aron 1962, 97–100). If there is an issue, says Aron, it has less to do with market economies than with advanced industrialism.

And that is the position of Herbert Marcuse who mounted a new-style Marxist attack on industrial society, lumping the bureaucratic socialist states together with the Western democracies. In the American counterculture and the French students' revolt of 1968 Marcuse thought he saw a widespread rejection of the bureaucratic world, a world of repression. Marcuse's argument is new Marxism since he grants capitalism its material successes, but assails it for its spiritual aridity, "its false and immoral comforts, its cruel affluence" (Marcuse 1969, 6). Exploitation is still exploitation; even if the subordinated lead a comfortable life, their human needs are mortgaged to this affluence. And Jürgen Habermas, another humanistic Marxist, failed to see why things had to be that way. After all, the struggle against poverty was over, we no longer needed the discipline of alienated labor. We have institutionalized the struggle for existence and perpetuated a lifestyle and a set of values which were valid only in an economy of poverty, not the present-day world of abundance (Habermas 1968, 25). The critique of advanced industrial society centers on this: we have institutionalized nineteenth-century means to cope with poverty, and in the process have produced a system which devalues human concerns. Stuart Gregory of cohort 2 spoke to that issue in our discussion of Sun Microsystem's "throwaway" personnel policies:

> Well, the society we live in is not a very supportive society. It is a society that is set up to make profits, basically, and those kind of

attitudes would naturally come out of that environment, but they're not human . . .

Marcuse, writing in 1969, thought that the values of the inhuman, repressive system would soon dissipate under the weight of their manifest contradictions, i.e., the promise of fulfilled lives and the reality of anomie and alienation. He thought it likely that a massive social and political change would ensue, when the "belief in one's beliefs" waned, and the society would be marked at first by "a spread of discontent and mental sickness, . . . inefficiency, resistance to work . . . negligence, indifference . . ." (Marcuse 1969, 84). Well, there has been no social revolution since 1969. About that Marcuse was wrong. But although I am far from agreement with Marcuse, it must be said that his projections of social ills to come have been quite prescient. A lessening interest in work, growing anomie, loss of trust in institutions and loyalty to them—all seems to be proceeding according to Marcuse's dark vision.

Marcuse's argument is an orthodox Marxist one: changes in material conditions have brought about cognitive change; advanced industrialism, driven by bureaucratic and technical imperatives, has reached a point where its denizens increasingly cannot stand to live there. This is certainly arguable and suggests the alternate explanation: changes in people's attitudes have occurred, independently of the march of *la technique.* This is the position of Daniel Bell, found in *The Cultural Contradictions of Capitalism* (1976) and also the argument of Bernice Martin in *A Sociology of Contemporary Cultural Change* (1981). First let us look at Bell's argument.

Marx argued that a society's economic basis created a "superstructure," the political and cultural institutions which reflect the underlying economic organization.[5] Without accepting Marx's causation, Bell notes that historically most societies have exhibited a basic unity between their aesthetic cultures and their social and economic structures. Max Weber found this homogeneity in early capitalistic societies; the economic, social, and cultural realms uniformly prized a rationalistic outlook. But, Bell argues, today there is a "radical disjunction" between the social structure, which he terms "techno-economic" order, and the culture. Our political and economic institutions are ruled by the bureaucratic principles of collective effort, order and rationality; our modern culture is antirational, anarchically individualistic. Modern individuals are thus compelled to act in the economic realm like the old middle class, exhibiting self-discipline and delayed gratification. But in the private realm of culture, we are encouraged by media products of all varieties to act entirely freely, to put our own individual stamp on our lives and express ourselves in any way that suits us. Old bourgeois values in the work place, bohemian values in our private lives (Bell 1976, 36–37). This is hardly a stable situation. No one can be that schizophrenic for long; the unresolved tension must in time give way. In the dissolution of the old dispensation, it could be said that the radically individualistic cultural impulse is winning out over the old bourgeois culture.

Bernice Martin makes a similar argument, but puts it in the framework of the sociology of knowledge. She asserts that the profound social change that has occurred in the last thirty years is the inevitable product of new ideas working themselves slowly into mass consciousness. The values and beliefs of a small cultural elite have gradually become majority opinions. Martin points to the early nineteenth-century Romantic movement as the immediate source of 1960's countercultural attitudes, attitudes which, as we have seen, have permeated mass consciousness in our own day. Romanticism is preeminently a form of radical individualism, a celebration of personal expression and the supreme value of the individual (Martin 1981, 1–21). We certainly saw that in the counterculture of the 1960s, but it does require some imagination to translate the ideal of self-expression into the more negative of current day attitudes. I suppose it could be argued that the widespread strategy of withdrawal from society is an individualistic stance, and it could even be argued that lessened trust in others could count as valuation of the self above all others. But those arguments seem to stretch the Romantic point a good deal; my image of Jean-Jacques Rousseau is hardly that of an eighteenth-century couch potato. The argument does, however, have some force regarding organizational loyalty. An extreme focus on the self, in the old Romantic tradition, would certainly be incompatible with the sacrifice and community spirit of robust corporate loyalty.

But, all in all, I think that the emphasis on a raw form of individualism may miss the mark in explaining today's attitudes. I believe that Joseph Schumpeter's insight might have more merit as an explanation. Schumpeter noted, as Weber had, that the transition to capitalism was accompanied by a change in the dominant mentality, a cognitive shift. Weber of course emphasized that the shift was toward a rational approach to the world, ordering men and things into new social and economic configurations. But for Schumpeter, the important shift was to a a "critical frame of mind," a mentality which employed rational procedures to question everything. As I have noted above, Schumpeter summarized this thusly:

> capitalism creates a critical frame of mind which, having destroyed the moral authority of so many other institutions, in the end turns against its own; the bourgeois finds to his amazement that the rationalist attitude does not stop at the credentials of kings and popes but goes on to attack private property and the whole scheme of bourgeois values. (Schumpeter 1950, 143)

Schumpeter also thought that capitalism's material success would lead to its destruction from within, that an educated citizenry with ample leisure would lose the entrepreneurial spirit and in time question the moral basis of the economic system. Keynes had another prescription. He agreed that the entrepreneurial spirit would fade, but saw that as a social benefit, since grasping entrepreneurs were unpleasant people and in a hundred years time (he wrote this in 1930) we would no longer need such people anyhow. The accumulated wealth built up since the Industrial Revolution would be sufficient to sustain us; we could live off our capital. (Keynes 1963, 365–68).

I think neither Keynes' nor Schumpeter were right in their prognoses. Neither Schumpeter's view that we would fall into socialism, nor Keynes' view that we will shortly have effortless affluence—neither seems realistic at the end of the twentieth century. But the insight that the rise of capitalism was accompanied by an all-consuming skepticism is, I believe, valid. More and more, people can be seen to adopt the rational-choice stance of capitalism: thinking a situation through, weighing their self-interest, and acting on it.

It is possible, therefore, to see that the root cause of the old dispensation's end—including loyalty lost—is to be found in a cognitive shift, a shift caused by an increasing acceptance of the rationality behind the capitalistic mindset. This assertion is difficult to prove from my data, since I am listening to people at a point in time, and do not have access to their thinking over the years. But, the poll data does unequivocally show evidence of a cognitive shift in the direction Schumpeter proposes, a shift away from confidence in institutions, which could be related to a more reasoned assessment of these institutions. And loyalty itself, with its irrational psychological roots, could as well be seen to have disappeared under the weight of more rational assessment of the true situation. Some hints of this appear in my cohort 2 interviews, as the subjects recount their changed views on society and corporations. For example, recall Jane Light of cohort 2's words when she explained her loss of loyalty:

> Well I think for me it's several things, one of which is experience. I mean . . . I have watched myself and other people get booted out the door so many times that after a while you say, "Well OK, I got to look out for number one . . . They're not looking out for me, so I got to look out for myself." But part of it I think is almost a societal thing. Sort of "everybody for themselves" kind of attitude and I think companies used to be more loyal to their employees. Especially in the last few years I think it's gotten even worse in the last several years with this whole American business, "lean and mean" attitude and "produce or you're out the door" and you know that kind of thing. . . . I've seen a lot of incidents . . . of people who are older that have lost their jobs and you know they can't prove it, but it's like they know that their employers can pay someone 28 years old . . . to do the same thing that they do for half as much and you know that undermines your trust in them you know and I've seen a lot of that . . .

If we examine this, we can glimpse Jane's revelation that capitalism, with its extremely rational approach, takes no account of human values, it becomes "lean and mean." She sees people—herself and others—"booted out the door," sometimes just to make room for a lower-paid replacement. And, just as Schumpeter posits, she accepts the capitalistic premises, she comes around to their way of thinking: "I got to look out for number one . . . They're not looking out for me, so I got to look out for myself."

Jerry Austin of cohort 2 describes a similar revelation, and a similar shift in his thinking.

> I think I was much more "anything to help out." Anything, always, always going the extra mile. . . . But I've seen too many instances of individuals who have been with the company a number of years, they're three years from retirement . . . and like fire you

and hire two college students . . . and still have a net savings. Now what's that? . . . Should those people be loyal?

Jerry, like Jane Light, has an organizational commitment score more than one standard deviation below the Softmatics mean. I asked him what had caused his loss of loyalty, and he pointed to the company's "rationalistic" practices, and his own decision to act in the same way, to eschew loyalty and behave less naively. What changed him?

> Just my witnessing, my personal experience and my witnessing within the corporate world where management . . . has not gone the extra mile for employees, . . . not tried everything possible to keep these people employed, but just callously (fired them).

He now sees the world differently. He sees it differently, as Schumpeter would argue, because the corrosive effects of rational, capitalistic thinking make loyalty simple naive:

> I've been laid-off twice, you know. It's hard. Seeing where if it behooves the company . . . I'm out the door tomorrow . . . Therefore, if it behooves me to take another job, for example, even though I might be in the middle of a critical project. At one point in my career I would not have left in the middle of a project. Now I think I would.

Jane's and Jerry's stories, their epiphanies, appeared to have occurred at points in time when their older views of reality became inadequate for them, when they saw that loyalty and confidence no longer made much sense. How do these individual stories relate to the long slide in trust, loyalty, and confidence that we have seen from the poll data, which portray a gradual decline beginning in the late 1960s? We must be aware of what sociologists term the "ecological fallacy," the error of attributing data from aggregates to single individuals who are part of a group. Rather than individuals experiencing gradual shifts in attitudes, the poll data are telling us of the aggregation of many individual attitude changes which themselves most likely occurred over a short space of time, as we saw with Jane and Jerry.

If we listen to the stories of the younger people, those of cohort 3, we find no such sudden attitude changes. Rather, they seem to have always accepted the capitalistic attitudes of extreme rational self-seeking. I asked thirty-two-year-old Sue

Mineo what she thought of Mattel Toy's layoff accompanying their announcement of record profits. She expressed a view characteristic of cohort 3, the notion of separate spheres of morality, a return to the old middle class's split between business and private morality:

> Well I think it's terrible when people get laid off, but maybe it sounds like they re-engineered their company . . . and found out that they can do a lot more with a lot less people . . . and maybe it's just a cold, hard fact that they found out that there's some capabilities that are out there that it helped them to increase their productivity with a fewer . . . people and that happens. I mean if they can be profitable . . . I don't think it's great when people get laid off, but I do think if a company finds new ways to do business that are profitable for them, you know, it does benefit the economy in the long run.

Hal Richards, a thirty-three-year-old whom we met before, expressed the same idea of two spheres of morality, with his metaphor of the "two hats" which must be worn when ethical questions are addressed:

> I'll put my business hat on, OK, and my people hat and I've put my business hat on and (it) says "OK, where am I in relationship to the rest of my competitors in this industry? . . . Maybe there's a slump coming . . ." You know your people hat . . . I feel that's probably unethical. My business hat says there were probably some good reasons for it.

And thirty-one-year-old Ernie Travis had much the same approach, the bifurcation of morality characteristic of the old middle class:

> I could look at that in two aspects. A human aspect and a business aspect. . . . At first impression the human aspect answers first only in the fact that they're men and women without jobs now . . . When you . . . automate your processes and eliminate jobs, (the) human factor is factored out . . . But if you're looking at the business aspect we can produce more, productivity will increase . . . It's cruel. It's hard, but it's done. . . . I could answer emotionally, but that wouldn't be the intelligent thing to do.

"The intelligent thing to do." Who could argue with that? I certainly have no intention of arguing with Ernie and his cohort 3 colleagues. My point is that they have taken for granted a view of business and the economy that is highly rationalistic, that sets aside the human question in discussing business, that sees the business arena as solely ruled by the principles of economics, particularly its pole star principle: self-maximizing individuals making rational choices of the means to maximize their self-interest.

Let me try to summarize the natural history of loyalty, a history indivisible from the rise and fall of a corporate culture, a set of bureaucratic values. The old middle-class values came into being from a cognitive change, a change that Weber attributes to the spread of Calvinist ideas that in time metamorphosized into a secular faith in individual effort and into the belief in material success. It is this mentality which was responsible for the growth of merchant capitalism in early nineteenth-century America. But as the enormous vertically integrated corporations came to the fore after the Civil War, a demand arose for a new social character, for people who valued collective effort and organizational loyalties. This new corporate culture, which I have called "the old dispensation," built itself into a majority view between 1870 and 1920 and was strengthened by the successes of bureaucracies in the Great Depression and the Second World War.

Beginning in the 1960s, a cognitive shift occurred in our time, a shift toward radical and asocial individualism, which has put in question all the values of the old dispensation, including corporate loyalty. This shift can be attributed to the slow acceptance of Romantic ideas of the self, to the corrosive influence of a highly individualistic artistic tradition, or to the logical extension of the skeptical, hyper-rational habit of mind which produced capitalism in the first place. The shift is slow in the aggregate, as individuals make their own way through their thinking, arriving at new conclusions at different points in time.

None of these views is incompatible with the critiques of Ellul or Marcuse, the idea that prolonged exposure to massive bureaucracies and their technological imperatives have, in the end, turned people away from these institutions. The bureaucratic mentality served well to organize society in order to deal with real and compelling social and economic problems. But the piper now must be paid. The very same institutions, by their internal logic, can be dehumanizing, or at the very least, insufficiently attentive to human concerns, as Stuart Gregory showed us. ("Those kind of attitudes would naturally come out of that environment, but they're not human.") With an alternative clamorously announced in high and popular culture—an alternative of extreme individualism—increasing numbers of people have turned away from the values of collective effort and corporate loyalty. And, that may be the rational course.

So in the fullness of time, the old dispensation is passing away. In the next chapter, the last, we will try to see what lies before us in the death of the old dispensation.

13
Consequences: The Old Dispensation's Demise

civic privatism—that is, political abstinence combined with an orientation to career, leisure, and consumption . . .

—*Habermas, Legitimation Crisis*

There are now many voices decrying the direction that unfettered individualism is taking our civilization—taking us to the point where a raw individualism will have eradicated our common heritage. We can see disturbing symptoms in today's society that suggest we should not brush these critiques aside too readily. First, we must be concerned with the corrosive and all-pervasive cynicism of our times, which I will address in the next section. We must also worry about loss of trust, confidence, and loyalty, and where those losses might lead. In particular, they could lead to a destabilizing *ressentiment.* Further, the passing of the old dispensation, the loss of loyalty, could have lasting and damaging effects on companies and the economy. I will address these issues in turn: cynicism, *ressentiment,* and loyalty lost. I shall conclude with a possibility that there is a road out of this impasse we appear to be in.

Cynicism

In the last chapter we saw Schumpeter's insight that capitalism has formed an essentially skeptical social character. But skepticism is not cynicism. Skepticism is rather a doubting, critical cast of mind. Cynicism has no doubts. Cynicism assumes everyone is motivated solely by self-interest, that people are "selfish, hypocritical, insincere" (Angeles 1981, 52). Ironically, the fourth century B.C.E. Cynic philosophers, who gave us the word, had no such view of human nature. Their critique was rather a moral one, a reaction against a materialistic society which stunted the virtues of independence and mastery of material desires. Their method was what now would be called "street theater," outrageous public acts of antisocial mockery intended to illuminate the vacuity of civilized conventions—very much like the Diggers of the 1960s (Blackburn 1994, 91). So, unlike modern cynicism, the Cynics had an underlying concern for virtue and the overall good of society. After all, it was the Cynics' founder, Diogenes of Sinope who, legend has it, walked about with a lantern in search of an honest man.

But our modern meaning of the term "cynic" has no room for virtue, in fact it has only retained the old Cynics' caustic mocking of everyone and everything—including purported virtues. Here is an example from John Francisco of cohort 2, who compares the fine words of management in the company's "Vision Statement" to their actions: lining their pockets at the expense of furloughed employees. John refers to Wall Street's favorable—and now automatic—reaction to staff cutbacks:

> The stock price had dwindled. I know who owns bunches of the stock and those are the people that make these kinds of decisions. And I guess having that demonstrated here and having to go out there on the sixth floor and read that Vision Statement (and see) that it's (not) too difficult (for management) to pick and choose. (The management) made those "hard" decisions on (their) assets . . ."[1]

What does cynicism have to do with our study of corporate loyalty? I believe it has everything to do with it. The inverse of loyalty is not disloyalty, it is cynicism. Disloyalty implies that one knows he has a duty and deliberately rejects it, just as adultery is possible only if one believes in the vows he has taken. Cynicism is the antithesis of loyalty because it denies the existence of such a bond, it considers loyalty merely a word. As John Francisco said, loyalty was an "implied myth," a term that managers employed only to gain workers' compliance.

> Is it a thing that really doesn't have any value? Is it one of those religious things that never really had a foundation? . . . Loyalty

can be purchased, you know. I've been seduced. I suppose I could become cynical enough now that I don't trust the seducer.

John's attitude recalls the antinomianism of the old Cynics who disputed conventional mores, claiming that they were merely words, words which did not benefit individuals, but rather enslaved them to false obligations, to duties towards the ruling class (Angeles 1981, 52). Recall Gene Evans of cohort 3 in his definition of "loyalty": "not steal, or you know, try to take advantage of the company." Clearly the very foundation of loyalty—the setting aside of self-interest for some higher goal—is missing from this definition and missing from this consciousness. He, and many his age, are in the predicament of Scott Fitzgerald's protagonist," a new generation . . . grown up to find all Gods dead, all wars fought, all faiths in man shaken . . ." (F. S. Fitzgerald 1951, 304)

That we live in a cynical age is evident. Richard Stivers believes that it is not simply a matter of social problems which conventional morality can no longer control. Rather, our predicament is caused by "the very morality itself, a morality that encourages, even promotes, cynical and self-serving behavior" (Stivers, 1994, vii). Stivers may be right. It certainly appears that our culture tolerates cynicism, perhaps even endorses that stance. We hear it all around us. Pronouncements of government officials and corporate executives are routinely discounted as self-serving. The opinion polls' vote of no confidence in institutional leadership is just one manifestation of that phenomenon. Motives are always suspect. Expressions of ideals and self-sacrifice are widely assumed to be either mendacious or naive, almost always the former. As only one example, look at the career of Bill Clinton. With his intelligence, energy, and education he could certainly have made a fortune in a law practice, but chose politics, he said, because of the inspiration of John Kennedy and a belief in service. Most people scoff at Clinton's explanation. Rather, he is widely rated as a power-hungry politician who will do or say anything to be elected.

Our popular culture has a sharp and mocking edge, whether it be *Saturday Night Live*, or more serious works such as Joseph Heller's *Catch-22*. All is held up to ridicule, but with a cynical slant—cynical because you can ridicule someone for being either a knave or a fool, but cynicism sees only the knave, the self-serving one. Ironically, this cynicism can be seen to be a by-product of capitalistic thought, as Schumpeter asserted. From de Mandeville to von Hayek, with intermediate stops at Smith and Friedman, market economists have insisted that the primary human motivation is self-interest. Adam Smith also wrote of the human impulse for sympathy and solidarity, but that strain of his thought did not carry forward to his successors. Milton Friedman and others have decried the public's lack of economic sophistication, but the public—I say it ruefully—has at least now grasped and accepted that one basic economic maxim: everyone is in it for the main chance.

Just as the certain defense against libel is the truth, the justification for cynicism is that it is not a misguided belief in the venality of others. Rather, it is an accurate view of human nature. This can be seen to be a question of power relations. Any society requires some sort of power to function, and most often it is "conditioned" power, the beliefs to which we are socialized, beliefs that imbue society's powers with legitimacy. When these beliefs are definitively shown to be false, the reaction is at first indignation, but then it settles into a pervasive and corrosive cynicism about all forms of authority (Galbraith 1983, 13). Everyone has feet of clay. (We saw this earlier with the 1950's quiz show scandal.) And, when government officials espouse ideals and are then definitively exposed as liars and thieves, when corporate executives pontificate about people being their most important asset as they are throwing them into the street, what result, then, but "cynicism" could we expect? What is the sense in a trusting and loyal attitude in such circumstances? What else is there to believe but Ambrose Bierce's dictum that loyalty is "a virtue peculiar to those about to be betrayed"? (Bierce 1958, 42). Is that cynicism, or is it a firm grasp on reality?

A number of my subjects addressed cynicism, some openly, some betraying the attitude in our conversations. Joe Weston of cohort 2 described earlier days at Softmatics when a mocking attitude prevailed, yet he thought healthily so. But that changed:

> the Softmatics organization always had a bit of an edge to it. . . . it wasn't necessarily bad. I didn't dislike it, but it always had that little edge. . . . the way we teased each other and there was always that little edge of cynicism. It was healthy. I didn't have a problem with it. When we came (to DRI) some people took . . . that cyni-

cism and now it has just become—it looks like it's eating them alive.

Milt Sherrard of cohort 2 seemed to think that a cynical attitude was engendered necessarily by life in a bureaucracy, in which, at the end of the day, management must choose between complete candor and the needs of the organization. Milt shows the limitations that employees' pervasive cynicism has placed on management's ability to rally people:

> It's . . . cynicism towards bureaucracy that happens, in I would guess most large companies. . . . Why do I think it's that way? . . . I don't have any question that there's cynicism when there's a big "rah rah" rollout of something new . . . (like) the reorganization that took place . . . The best one was the one that took place a year ago because of the way they did it, where they had a group of people for four months or so looking at making recommendations on how to re-engineer the organization . . . That was the first thing that came up in a long time that made me feel very positive about the future because things were being looked at the right way. It wound up getting implemented only 60 percent of what they said and in fact, the other thing was just like TQM, I remember they said everybody's fired and then we're going to have to re-interview for the jobs, the idea being there it's not going to be the good-old-boy network and so and what happened was everybody was interviewed and the good old boys got the jobs, that kind of thing. . . . You know, it's just a cynical attitude.

Another thirty-nine-year old from cohort 2 attributes his cynicism to management's repeated demands for more work, without any letup in sight. Again, we see the narrowing of management's persuasive powers:

> the work load never seems to let up. . . . You're being told constantly that you're going to have to do more with less . . . After a while you just say: "Why?' Because whether I do or whether I don't, they're going to ask me to do the same thing in six months anyway and it isn't going to make one bit of difference. . . . After a while you say: "OK, I've heard this before" and they tell you something like: "We have to do this or else, we'll be going out of business in a year" . . . How many times do they cry wolf? . . . You get to a point where you sort of say: "OK, I've heard it before. I'm not going to do anything differently than what I've been doing because what I do personally isn't going to make that big a difference."

Opposed to these attitudes we find the authentic voice of the old dispensation, the values of cohesive and cooperative efforts to accomplish important purposes. Here is Ralph Simmons of cohort 1, whom we met earlier:

> I like my job. I like the people I work with. . . . I am convinced that . . . to get through life . . . you need within you some kind of a mean for your life. . . . Some kind of a code . . . that enables you to accept some of the bad things that happen. . . . You start thinking about what is your legacy in this life. . . . When they remember you . . . are they going to say—which is important to me—that guy was a nice guy. He was nice to be around. He had good values. He worked hard. He got results. He was easy on people. He made a contribution. . . . In general I think I'm OK and I try to be nice to people and not cut anybody's throat and we have that in business . . . Try to be on the ideal, even though you don't attain the ideal. That's my philosophy of life and that's important.

We see in Ralph a complete lack of cynicism, rather a set of values that enables him to weather the vicissitudes of life, to accept that bad things can happen. We see also how he values the social ideal, the value of other people and the imperative to make some contribution in life. This is as far from a corrosive cynicism as one could imagine. But these are the old dispensation values, alive it would seem only in such aging people as Ralph. For far too many, ideals of duty and solidarity have become mere words and—worse—words employed by self-serving leaders who use them to entice people to do their will, as the old Cynics maintained. And what are we left with? We are left with, in Henry James' phrase, just "the faint, flat emanations of things, the failure of fortune and of honor" (James, 1965, 5).

Ressentiment?

It is twenty years now since Daniel Yankelovich raised the specter of American society experiencing widespread *ressentiment*, as has happened from time to time in Europe and Latin America (Yankelovich 1975). The trends in public attitudes—confidence, trust, anomie—that I have charted here were apparent to Yankelovich in 1975, and he asked if those trends would lead to something worse than passive withdrawal. The French term *ressentiment* is roughly equivalent to the English "resentment," but with a crucial additional sense. Whereas in English we intend by the word a feeling of ill will and indignation stemming from some injury, the French term further conveys the sense that the injured party intends to wreak vengeance, to take action against the injuring party.[2] Joseph Conrad gives us an exemplar of *ressentiment* in his novel *Chance.* The governess, a ruthless and grasping woman, has for years hidden her rancor for a thousand slights, but finally lashes out at her helpless charge, and it is the furious outburst against a system which has thwarted her so long that encapsulates the idea of *ressentiment.*

> (the governess) went on pouring all the accumulated dislike for all her pupils, her scorn of all her employers . . . the accumulated resentment, the infinite hatred of all these unrelieved years . . . the years, the passionate, bitter years, of restraint, the iron, admirably mannered restraint at every moment, in a never-failing correctness of speech, glances, movements, smiles, gestures, establishing for her a high reputation, an impressive record of success in her sphere. It had been like living half strangled for years. (Conrad, 1988, 119–20)

When such emotions are increasingly aimed at the institutions of society, we have the potential for calamitous events. The *ressentiment* of the lower middle class in the Weimar Republic was one cause of the rise of Nazism; the accumulated *ressentiment* of the lower classes can be seen to have brought on the Terror in revolutionary France. The ghetto burnings in Watts and Detroit in the 1960s have been explained in the same manner. Clearly, we are hardly near a violent collapse of society in the United States, but the question that Yankelovich asked in 1975 is still valid: Why not? Why has the pervasive loss of confidence, why have cynicism and mistrust not boiled over into a radical overturn of institutions? Yankelovich offered one explanation in 1975. He had carefully read the poll data for the 1970s and noted that, while anomie and mistrust were rampant, attitudes about personal situations were healthy, and stable. Most people were happy in their personal lives and also satisfied financially. Yankelovich concluded: "As long as people feel reasonably comfortable in their personal lives . . . *ressentiment* will be kept at bay" (Yankelovich 1975, 77). Unfortunately, in the last twenty years, personal satisfaction has declined. From 1970 to the present day, the General Social Survey data reveal a definite downtrend in the proportion of those claiming they are "very happy" and of those saying they are "satisfied with their present financial condition."[3] (Davis and Smith 1994).

Another way to explain the lack of *ressentiment* is to deny that there is any real threat to our institutions, that Americans have few doubts about the legitimacy of their system. Lehman makes the very valid point that there is a distinct difference between confidence and legitimation (Lehman 1987, 204). To understand the implications of this, it is important to note that the public-opinion polls ask about confidence in institutional *leadership*, and it is from those responses that we see the dreary decline in the polls. Faith in the institutions themselves remains high. There has been no discernible drop over the years in support for democratic institutions, nor for free enterprise, despite the enormous loss of confidence in the people who lead those institutions. American beliefs in democracy and capitalism were formed in our earliest times and have stubbornly resisted becoming tarred with the same brush as institutional leaders. This is a puzzle: great confidence in the institution and almost none in its leadership. Lehman asserts that the disjunction is due to the public's faith that the institutions are sound, but more than that, that poor leadership is easily replaceable in a democratic society (Lehman 1987, 209). Lipset and Schneider, who did a massive study of the American "confidence gap," concluded that "The problem . . . lies in inadequate, inept, and even corrupt leadership . . ." (Lipset and Schneider 1987, 351). That explanation—it is just bad leadership, which can and will be replaced—is plausible, but plausible, it seems to me, only for a time. Recall that the declines in confidence in leadership began *thirty years ago*. We have had seven presidents in that period, thousands of new congressmen and legions of new CEOs. After a while, it would seem that common sense would conclude that those are "widowmaker" jobs, jobs that no matter how accomplished and well-meaning the occupant, everyone seems to fail at them. In business such situations are rather common, putting good people into positions in which one after another fails. A manager does not have to be especially astute to conclude, after two or three good people fail, that there is probably something wrong with the job's scope of responsibility and authority. But with respect to our institutions, no such conclusion has been drawn in the society at large. Time and again, leaders are exposed as knaves or fools who must be replaced, and—shockingly—they are replaced by new knaves and fools. This has been going on for thirty years. Can we expect it to continue for long before either leaders are given more credit, or the institutions are changed?

Perhaps nothing will change. Perhaps Americans have reached a stable state of privatism to deal with anomie and cynicism. As we saw earlier, Americans have dealt with distrust and lack of confidence not with active resistance but with the strategy Merton termed "retreatism," the avoidance, if at all possible, of large organizations. The unavoidable organization for most people is the workplace, and there the increasingly dominant strategy is that of emotional distancing, and attitudes of suspicion and cynicism. Herbert Gans claims that the poll data on lack of confidence do not reflect the intensity of the feelings people hold toward institutional leaders, that many employees believe their managers to be ruthless and amoral (Gans 1988, 52). We have already seen much of that sentiment from my subjects, especially from cohorts 2 and 3. Jane Light of cohort 2, whom we met earlier, expressed her concern for the trends in society, and how people like her were helpless in confronting a large organization.

> I have watched myself and other people get booted out the door so many times that after a while you say: "Well OK, I got to look out for number one, you know. They're not looking out for me, so I got to look out for myself." But part of it I think is almost a societal thing. Sort of everybody for themselves kind of attitude and I think companies used to be more loyal to their employees. . . . I think it's gotten even worse in the last several years with this whole American business, lean and mean attitude and produce or you're out the door. . .

Jane links the management's ruthlessness to a more general attitude in society "of everyone for themselves." As a result, she goes on to lament that all are on their own, there is no solidarity, no bulwark against ruthlessness.

> I think of people who are older that have lost their jobs . . . they know that their employers can pay someone 28 years old . . . to do the same thing that they do for half as much . . . In some ways it's even worse in professional positions like ours because there's less protection. There's no union to say: "No, you can't do that" and (with) exempt employees in this state (management) can do darn near anything they want.

A union, or other collective action, would seem to be a logical response to the resentment so many express. But it seems very unlikely that withdrawn individuals will ever take that step. Thirty-five-year-old Mitch Blanchard of cohort 3 first noted that many modern "professional" knowledge workers and software developers are in reality today's production workers—they make the product, just like blue-collar assembly line workers. But they will never organize, in his opinion:

> I produce software the way I look at it. . . . Software developers are a new labor force. I think technical people in general are. They're not going to be protected by a union because (they have) too much education and they're too arrogant to be that way it seems like. So they're really caught in the middle I think . . . to where I see management really takes advantage from technical labor which is almost the same kind of labor (as manual labor).

Mitch could see the need for something like a union of the new production workers, but doubted it would ever come to pass.

> I wouldn't want it to be . . . like a traditional labor union where you stand outside with a sign . . . It wouldn't fit right away because I think people with . . . a pretty varied educational background like we have would have a hard time doing some of that kind of stuff. It is kind of demeaning . . .

Mitch returned to the union idea in response to my question about Sun Microsystem's stark "employment contract":

> They might need a union of some kind . . . (management says): "As long as we're making the widget that you make, you have a job and if we stop making it tomorrow, oh well you know." And meanwhile they're probably making money hand over fist . . .

As Jane Light put it: "No union to say 'no'." No collective effort to right a wrong, and no apparent intention to band together. Resentment but not *ressentiment.* Retreatism rather than activism. But what else can we expect from a society that is rapidly depreciating its social capital? To do something about society's ills requires organization and collective action, and those are precisely the things that people more and more are avoiding. The nature of the disease itself prevents its only cure.[4] Rampant self-absorbed individualism is responsible for both the ruthless leadership that exploits and the passivity of those exploited. Neither the leader nor the led any longer have the sense of common purpose and the efficacy of collective effort which might turn us toward some solutions. It is this issue which is so troublesome for the fate of the corporation and the economy. Let us turn to that now.

The Tragedy of the Commons

I wish to argue that we run the danger that our corporations will suffer the tragic fate of the commons, i.e., since no one cares sufficiently for the corporation per se, all will lose if and when it fails. Hume first exposed the problem of self-interest in his parable of the two farmers considering cooperation:

> Your corn is ripe today; mine will be so tomorrow. 'Tis profitable for us both, that I shou'd labour with you today, and that you shou'd aid me tomorrow. I have no kindness for you, and know you have as little for me . . . I know that I shou'd in vain depend upon your gratitude. Here then I leave you to labour alone: You treat me in the same manner. . . . and both of us lose our harvests for want of mutual confidence . . . (Hume, quoted in Putnam)

This is the old dilemma posed by the prisoners' dilemma game: the rational strategy of both players is to be uncooperative, and both suffer for it. It is the "tragedy of the commons," in which no herder can limit others' grazing, so each overgrazes, since moderation harms only the moderate if everyone else overgrazes. Inevitably, the commons is destroyed, and all—who would benefit by cooperation—lose everything.

The commons is a public good, a facility all can benefit from without contributing to it. A public good is always subject to the "free rider," who benefits but does not pay, and since the rational strategy is to be a free rider, none contribute and tragedy ensues. I would argue that a corporation is in a sense also a public good. Legally and by conventional economic thinking, it is of course nothing of the sort, it is private property, owned by the shareholders. But a corporation, especially a large, complex organization, is far more than a piece of property, a commodity as conventionally viewed on Wall Street. John Francisco understood this perfectly:

> Companies are part of the country's infrastructure . . . and if they're all in for the short haul, then the country's is in for the short haul because the country is only as good as its business. If it doesn't have the business, it doesn't have anything else and so if the people aren't woven into that just like they are supposed to be woven into the government, then (it's) a commodity . . . Then it's the lottery. It's a crap shoot. You're wealthy one day and dead the next but there's no progress in that.

Old Henry Ford said "There is something sacred about a big business . . . Its continuance is a holy trust" (Ford 1923, 264). Ford was hardly a mystic, he was an intensely practical man. But he sensed that a great organization had something inviolable about it, qualities that demanded its preservation and required careful tending. A corporation affects all of society; as John Francisco said, it is part of the infrastructure. And like the physical infrastructure, a corporation is in that way a public good. Successful companies pay taxes; they provide useful products and services; they are the engines of technological and economic progress; they increase the wealth of their shareholders; they provide employment, and thereby both a livelihood and the opportunity for meaningful work. A corporation is a great deal more than an assemblage of economic abstractions like labor, capital, and technology. "Capital" is embedded in firm-specific productive capacity. It is not fungible, readily auctioned off to the highest bidder. "Technology" is much more than transferable intellectual property, it is knowledge in the minds of skilled people, much of it judgment born of experience. "Labor" is people who not only know intimately the company's products and services, but work with a will, with a commitment, in short, with loyalty.

The question comes down to: who cares about the fate of the corporation? Someone will have to care, for I cannot believe that there is an "Invisible Hand" that ensures that all can operate selfishly yet the corporation will prosper. But who cares? Is it the shareholders, the management, the employees? Is it any of them?

Is it the shareholders, the legal owners of the corporation? That is a highly dubious proposition. Corporations have been "commodified" by Wall Street, reduced to the status of mere items of exchange, indistinguishable from a barrel of oil or a hundredweight of pork bellies. Shares are daily bought and sold in enormous volumes with no concern for the underlying social value of the entity. Investors consider corporations to be commodities and corporate management, willing or not, comes to think the same way. As one observer said: "Firms once committed to long term thinking now faced money managers and speculators little concerned about their existence beyond the life of a futures contract" (Fallows 1995, 6).

To suggest nowadays that an investor "cares" about the future of a corporation is to be guilty of an absurdity. The investor certainly cares about the corporation's stock price, but hardly about its potential as a public good. To suggest otherwise is to suggest that the speculator in pork bellies cares about the pigs.

And what of the management, do they care? It is questionable. There was a time, not that long ago, when top managers saw themselves as stewards of organizations, organizations that should go on indefinitely serving their constituents—their customers, shareholders, employees, and the society at large. This indefinite extension in time is at the heart of Henry Ford's feeling that a big business was sacred, and managing it a holy trust. The notion of stewardship was common in the heyday of welfare corporatism, the 1950s through the 1970s. Reg Jones, chairman of General Electric in the 1970s said it explicitly: "This is an institution, and I'm steward here. I have it for a while, and then I move on" (Levinson and Rosenthal 1984, 49). Welfare corporatist managers like Jones believed that their role was to extend the corporation's scope, but more importantly, to preserve its unique potential for contributing to the welfare of all the stakeholders—including society at large.

It is difficult to find that point of view any longer in top management. We are more likely to hear something like Lee Iaccoca's remark, although few would be as crudely candid as he: "It wasn't prestige or power I wanted, it was money" (Iaccoca 1986, 42). Josiah Royce warned long ago of management's shirking their duty to the common welfare: "What we want . . . from some of the managers of great corporate interests is more loyalty, and less of the individualism of those who seek power" (Royce 1908, 230–31). Royce wrote that in 1908, at a time when most managers were men like Rockefeller and Carnegie, men who had large stakes in the businesses they ran. By the 1930s, as Berle and Means showed, corporations were mainly in the hands of salaried managers who had little ownership of the firm. This posed a dilemma: were the passive owners still, as traditionally, due the full profits from the firm? Or should the controlling management simply give the legal owners a fair return for their capital and keep the rest for themselves? Neither approach seemed right, so Berle and Means suggested that the new situation—management control without ownership—required a new solution. They proposed:

> that the modern corporation serve not alone the owners or the (management) but all society. . . . Should corporate leaders, for example, set forth a program comprising fair wages, security to employees, reasonable service to the public, and stabilization of business, all of which would divert a portion of the profits from the owners of passive property, and should the community generally accept such a scheme as a logical and human solution of industrial difficulties, the interests of passive property owners would have to give way. (Berle and Means 1932, 356)

In other words, they suggested that the corporation should operate as a public good. That position could be dismissed as quasi-socialist New Deal thinking, but a true Socialist, the British politician Anthony Crosland, asserted that what Berle and Means proposed as a radical idea was actually happening. During the Socialist Party debate in the 1950s over the party plank on nationalization of industry, Crosland was on the right wing, arguing that the party should drop this position, since the days of the exploitative capitalist were past. Crosland noted, as Berle and Means had, that corporations were now controlled by salaried managers with little ownership in the firm. As a consequence, he thought he saw a shift in the motivation of management—away from money and toward prestige. Since the manager does not own the company, profits are not generated for personal consumption, nor for the shareholders' benefit, but mainly as a source of social status, power, and prestige. Prestige can be won also from a reputation as a progressive, caring employer, or by being involved in civic affairs and being heard in the councils of government (Crosland 1956, 35). Lest this seem merely very British and very Socialist, we need only consider the career of Reg Jones, CEO of General Electric in the 1970s, an archetypal welfare corporatist executive. Jones minded the store, increasing GE's earnings, revenues, and return on capital in his tenure. He accomplished those things while bringing labor peace to GE with a fair union contract, and by establishing himself and his company as reliable partners with government. Jones served on Presidents Ford's and Carter's Labor-Management Group and participated actively in formulating other public policy. He became a respected spokesman for the business community to the general public as chairman of the Business Roundtable. Art Merrill of cohort 1 also expressed the notion of stewardship in his conversation with me, saying:

> I've made so many promises to the people and to the customers. I ask myself the question often myself, why do I put up with this, but because at times it's very difficult. But I think I want to see it work. I've made so many commitments, sincere commitments to customers to help them get their job done, I'd like to see the thing done and I'd like to see what we've been working on so long be successful.

But Art is nearing the end of his stewardship, Reg Jones has left the scene, and Berle's and Means's notion of management now seems as quaint as Aristotle's physics. We have quite a different situation in corporate governance today. Top managers are now paid, in stock and stock options, on the financial performance of their firms. But that statement needs amplification and even correction. It is not the performance of their firms that counts—performance in terms of increased market share and new product introduction—what counts exclusively is the firm's stock price, Wall Street's valuation of the company. And top managers are not just paid, they are paid enormous sums if they can increase the stock price in the relatively short term. Now corporate CEOs have always done well and have always had some stock incentive. In days past, any successful CEO could look forward to a comfortable retirement in Florida or Arizona and a nice nest egg for his children. Today, a CEO can become greatly rich, so rich that his grandchildren will be rich, and their grandchildren too. Today he or she can become as rich as Rockefeller or Carnegie, and the route is clear: move the stock price up. Is there any mystery that today's CEOs are as ruthless as the old robber barons? The motivation is precisely the same: riches beggaring description. Crosland's felicitous days when management and the public's interest coincided are gone. We have made a long circle back to the state Royce deplored, the state of "the individualism of those who seek power."

So, does the CEO care about the corporation, about its long-term survival, its constituents? It would be to disregard human nature to think so. They may be decent men, but Saint Francis of Assisi, the Apostle of Holy Poverty, died more than 700 years ago. And the managers' motivation is not lost on their employees. As we saw, employees now see clearly that the "hard" decisions about layoffs are often made to enhance the managers' own portfolios, since layoffs nowadays are mindlessly translated into higher stock prices. Just one example: the chairman of Firestone cut his workforce from 110,000 to 53,000 and was rewarded with a $5.6 million bonus (Bennett 1990, 165). Just as Wall Street views the corporation as a commodity, the employees fear they are being seen in the same light. The columnist Bob Herbert assailed the leaders of corporate America for amassing riches at the expense of their discarded workers who, more and more, were being treated not as human beings, but as items on a financial statement (Herbert 1995, A-9).

My cohort 2 subject, John Francisco, thought this attitude was not just inhuman, it was a threat to the corporation itself, to the commons:

> I still think of people as valuable assets and not commodities. They are not things to be traded. And I guess my cynicism is from evidence that I see. It seems to be a management attitude that they are (commodities). "Gee, these are (commodities); pay them (and the) problem goes away. . . ." So that solved that six-month problem, but it didn't do anything for . . . the three-year problem. And (as far as) competition: . . . it's not what (it) was doing to you today but (what) is about to do to you. . . . (so) that you don't see and (it is) those kind of things that we don't pay attention to . . . What are we going to make three years from now?

Another cohort 2 member, Bill Anderson, expressed his doubts that the company cared anything about him. We were talking about layoffs, and like so many in cohort 2, it took harsh management actions for Bill to change his attitude toward the company. The layoffs fractured his brittle sense of loyalty.[5]

> It does tend to make you a little bit more cynical . . . I don't know if that's really the right term, but you come to realize that . . .

> within my own group I may be recognized as somebody of moderate importance, but the company doesn't really know or necessarily care. You get up to some point above you in the chain of command and basically the people down there are numbers. . . . and under the right circumstances they would have no real reservations necessarily about laying me off as well. DRI, I don't think, cares about me at all. . . . Once the layoffs start, that sort of really opens your eyes.

In fairness to today's CEOs, it will be said that they run enormous risks of dismissal if they do not perform. The investment community has lost all patience with managers who do not rapidly run up the stock price. And since financial theory specifies that risk and reward must be matched, it is no wonder that CEOs are handsomely rewarded for their risk. Would it be so. In fact, their financial risk is minimal. Examples abound of top executives forced out for poor performance and then receiving enormous sums from their complaisant boards: $20 million to the ousted head of W. R. Grace ($5 million more than his contract stipulated); $3 million for K-Mart's ex-CEO; $50 to $75 million to the head of Warner Music Group when he was dismissed. (Deutsch 1995, F-10).

Do the top managers care about the fate of their corporations? With those sums dangled before them, even for nonperformance, it hardly seems likely. A rational strategy would seem to be to drive up the stock price through layoffs and reductions in R&D; to not invest in long-term projects that will pay off only after you are long gone; to take the huge bonuses for these actions, and if they fail, leave happily with a golden parachute. Am I being cynical, or just reporting the obvious?

What of the employees themselves, my real subjects in this work, do they care about the corporation? Evidently they do not. The statistics on organizational commitment, if nothing else, bear that out. What loyalty that exists is largely confined to older people, cohort 1, who have retained the bureaucratic values of their youth. The loyalty of cohort 2 people was washed away in the shipwreck of welfare corporatism. The loyalty of cohort 3 members, in my view, never existed at all.

In strictly financial terms, there is less reason for workers to care about the corporation, or for the economy in general, for that matter. The reason is that the middle class is receiving a smaller and smaller share of the gains from economic growth. The golden promise of Adam Smith, that economic progress would benefit all, is a fading dream in today's America. The Wealth of Nations has become the wealth of the wealthy. For the first time since the 1920s, an era of weak unions, wage increases have not kept pace with productivity gains. Worse, real incomes, adjusted for inflation, have not increased in more than twenty years. Actually, between 1979 and 1990, the real incomes of male college graduates fell about 1 percent, while male high-school graduates' incomes fell 21 percent and high school dropouts did much worse (*Economic Report of the President.* 1994, 25). The trend continues. From November 1994 to November 1995, at a time of economic expansion and rising stock prices, wages and benefits rose the smallest amount on record, 2.7 percent. Inflation for that period was 2.5 percent and economic growth was 3.5 percent. Even a conservative economist, Federal Reserve Board chairman Alan Greenspan, admitted there was a connection between the threat of layoffs and the modest pay increases (Hershey 1995, A-10).

As a result of this rupture of the historic connection between growth and wages, and the impact of American tax policies, the United States now has the highest income gap between rich and poor of any large industrialized nation. Income disparities began to rise in the 1970s, then accelerated in the 1980s. Today an American in the top ten percent earns 5.9 times one in the bottom ten percent. In Finland, the country with the least inequality, the ratio is 2.6 (Bradsher 1995, p. C-2). And this gap has grown in an era of strong economic growth. The American economy has roughly doubled since the early 1970s, but the benefits have gone almost exclusively to the richest Americans, the owners and mangers of capital. The median income, adjusted for inflation, has actually fallen in that time (Fallows 1995, 6).

In light of the shrinking economic rewards, the constant threat of layoffs, would we expect that employees care about the fate of the corporation? I believe not. I believe that many share the sentiments of 43-year-old Charles Pearson of cohort 2:

> I've had numerous jobs over the last 22 or 23 years. . . . I think we put too much emphasis, anymore, that people should put their number-one priority as being their job which I don't think is quite correct. I think our family values have slipped. . . . I don't know

> if a lot of people think the way I do or not, but there's more to life than coming to work and working 10 or 12 hours and going home dead tired and not be able to enjoy your family or do anything else because you are too tired to do anything . . .

Charles's organizational commitment (loyalty) is substantially below the mean, as is his job satisfaction. His loyalty trend is down. The company to him is a means to make a living, a vehicle for fulfilling other aspirations.

> I'm loyal to my job in the respect (that) my family needs my income. . . . To me more companies look at people not as individuals, but as numbers and I think a lot of people look at companies as a place to go work, you get a paycheck, you go home. . . . To me there's a lot more in life than a dollar bill. To me, as long as I got a nice roof over my head, I can put food on the table, I can watch my television, I can go play golf, I don't bother anybody . . .

Gone is the sense of solidarity and common purpose, the old welfare corporatist ideal that the corporation was a special place, an arena for achieving worthwhile objectives. Charles said:

> I think a lot of companies have lost the trust of their people or the people lost trust in the company they worked for. . . . If you don't have trust, if you don't have loyalty, then what is there left?

Indeed, what is there left? If no one cares any longer about the corporation and its fate, what is there left? And that will be the corporation gone, that marvelous combination of skills, technology, embedded capital, that engine of social progress for so many generations. The commons will be destroyed if all take from it—investors, managers, and employees—and none are bound to it by the ties of loyalty.

The Road Out

We risk the tragedy of the commons, the destruction of the public good that our corporations represent. There are of course those who believe there is not a problem here, that loyalty lost is even beneficial, that loyalty and trust can be replaced by technological marvels and the corporation in some form survive. Alvin Toffler and Charles Handy subscribe to the view that communications and computer technology have emerged that can lower the transaction costs in business such that the old corporate forms can disappear. The corporation can become a very small shell which contracts out most of its work to independent people. Presumably, economic activity will proceed with new efficiency, and further, we will see the rebirth of an independent citizenry, some latter-day Jeffersonian yeomen (Rapoport 1994, 155–68). This vision, in essence, is a return to the market, a repudiation of the corporate form of economic organization. Is this feasible?

You will recall from the theory of the firm that the corporation exists only because there are costs to using the market for materials and labor services, the costs of negotiating, monitoring and enforcing supplier and labor contracts. Now, it is thought, with the Internet and personal computers, armies of scattered independent individuals can be amassed to carry out tasks once performed by long-term employees, individuals paid by the task as in the days of the old putting-out system. Management's job is then just setting the tasks and enforcing the contracts. As Alchian and Demsetz said in another context: "This is delusion" (Alchian and Demsetz 1972, 777). Without a modicum of mutual trust and loyalty, such a system will never work. Independent contractors have no interest in the firm nor its products and cannot be expected to sacrifice their own interests for the company's. Much more likely, the company will be vexed by opportunistic contractors, whose interests lie only in fees and enhanced reputation, contractors who will act, as Oliver Williamson said, with "a lack of candor or honesty . . . to include self-interest seeking with guile" (Williamson 1975, 9). This is recognized even on Wall Street, the epicenter of individual self-interest, where it was long believed that the firm would survive and prosper, regardless of the sojourning of self-seeking transients, since its name constituted a franchise which would always attract business. A Morgan Stanley executive recently disputed this conventional wisdom:

> The tragedy is that any great franchise is built on the loyalty and hard work of its people. When that loyalty is lost or abused, the franchise can't survive. . . . You can walk around all day saying it's a great name, it's a great franchise. But the fracturing of the culture will ruin any great franchise. (J. B. Stewart 1993, 39)

The effects of loyalty lost and trust lost are real, and they can be disastrous, and they cannot be shrugged off by some technological magic. I have already specified the costs of loyalty lost, but a brief summary will be useful. There is first the issue of lower performance, lowered productivity. I noted an AMA survey of some 830 firms which have reduced staff since 1987. Only 43 percent reported profit improvement and only 31 percent higher productivity (Yates 1993, 20). Empirical research has shown that survivors of cutbacks will not only show less commitment, they will perform at lower levels (Brockner et al. 1987). And it is not just individual performance that suffers, it is overall organizational performance, because networks of trusting relationships are disrupted by indiscriminate downsizing. In the rush to cut costs, many companies not only wrote off their human capital but their social capital as well, overlooking the true value of social capital, the informal relationships which aided productive effort.

I also noted that loyalty lost deprives management of the essential contribution of "voice," in the sense that Hirschman uses the term. The loyal employee does not leave, at least immediately, when things have gone awry in the company. Rather, he voices his discontent, and thereby sends management an invaluable signal that the business is drifting off course. But the un-loyal do not bother; they just leave, and management loses the information essential to putting the company aright.

We saw that those without loyalty are very much less likely to take risks on the company's behalf. This is a particularly acute issue for management employees and lies at the heart of Chester Barnard's dictum that, for executives, "The most important . . . qualification is loyalty. . . ." (Barnard 1950, 220). A manager who thinks only of his own career, who serves only himself, is very unlikely to take risks which may benefit the company. And without devoted risk-takers, no company can survive for long, because the lifeblood of a company is new markets, new products, and new production processes—all risky undertakings.

Finally, we saw that the increased cynicism, the "un-loyalty" of the employees, has severely limited management's ability to motivate people and marshal their efforts towards company goals. Without a reservoir of trust and loyalty, management must resort to the crudest and least efficient forms of motivation: threats and bribery. This is the culmination of, in effect, a return to a free-labor market. As the theory of the firm illuminates, a company can employ people in an open-ended contract and rely upon mutual goodwill and loyalty to motivate right action. Or, the company can make arms-length labor agreements, paying for output and able to break the contract at will. Although most people are still nominally employed in the old open-ended form, in reality they are in a free-labor market, constantly at risk of dismissal and paid only so long as they perform to increasingly higher standards. To say that management was easier and more effective with a loyal workforce would be to restate the obvious.

Those are the consequences of loyalty lost. But it does little good to lament loyalty's passing, because social character has changed and it seems very unlikely we will see a return to the old dispensation in the foreseeable future. The question must be what the future holds for us, is there a road out of this thicket, the looming destruction of the commons? Let us explore some thinking about how a stable economy and healthy companies might yet be built on the ruins of corporate loyalty. Let us first look at the theories of Michael Maccoby and Charles Heckscher.

Both Maccoby and Heckscher see a dominant new type of employee forming, a person with attitudes that we have seen especially in the young, the cohort 3 people. Maccoby calls them "self-developers," people whose loyalty is entirely to themselves, who see the corporation only as a vehicle for skill development and self-advancement. They are not *dis*loyal, nor are they idle. They have come to terms with the corporation and will make substantial efforts on the job (Maccoby 1990). Maccoby has nothing but praise for this new type, especially for their fierce independence and their desire to develop themselves at work both intellectually and emotionally (Maccoby 1988, 230). He finds no issue with the fact that when push comes to shove—in the crisis when the company needs Royces's "thoroughgoing devotion"—these people are unlikely to respond.

Charles Heckscher as well salutes the independent spirit of the new employee type, people he calls "professionals." The old "loyalists" for Heckscher have lost their usefulness in today's economy. And he thinks that is not such a bad thing: "I for one . . . will not mourn the loss of the paternalistic ethic of dependence and protection." Heckscher does recognize that loyalty loss could result in asocial cynicism, but he believes that the ethic of loyalty can be replaced by a new ethic of professionalism, an ethic which specifies obligations among people pursuing something beyond individual interest (Heckscher 1995, 175). He believes—or hopes—that the professional ethic stresses working to the common purpose and in that lies morality.

> This leaves the obligation to develop the person not on the company, but on the individual. The employee is seen as an independent moral being with multiple commitments, of which the job is only one: "private" claims can be publicly brought forward, criticisms can be voiced, without the stigma of disloyalty. For my money, that is morally better than the dependent ethic of loyalty. (Heckscher 1995, 177)

Heckscher, like Maccoby, is making a virtue of necessity. In the fading of loyalty, some new moral center must be found. They both take up the critique of William H. Whyte, Jr., the critique of the the Organization Man, who has mortgaged his independence to the "magic helper" of the Organization. But while Maccoby seems to think that loyalty can be replaced by some ethic of self-development, I believe that Heckscher is closer to the mark in noting that there is still a need for some "common purpose." For the human need for loyalty did not disappear with the end of welfare corporatism. People in their deepest being have a need for loyalty, attachment to a cause larger than themselves, as Royce and Fromm have explained to us. But loyalty to what? To a corporation that bullies and discards them? That seems folly. To themselves and their careers? That seems too narrow, and ultimately unsatisfying.

In my own experience of managing high-technology organizations, I found that people, curiously perhaps, become loyal to the *product*. The most "cynical" of people who would scoff at anyone's expression of corporate loyalty, nonetheless, in word and deed, express their loyalty to the product they helped form. Here is Henry Archer, a forty-four-year-old cohort 2 software development manager:

> My loyalty to the companies, the corporations I've worked for, has never been particularly high. I mean it never entered my mind that when the Softmatics unit was sold to DRI (that) I would continue to work for RLX (the former parent) instead of DRI. I don't think that entered anybody's mind (in the R&D organization), so my loyalty's to the product really.

Another from cohort 2 also framed the issue of loyalty in terms of the company's product: "I'm more oriented towards the product than the company. I mean it's the product that brought me here. It's the product why I'm still here." Pat Flaherty, a cohort 3 manager expressed best the bonding of the individual to the product, the identification with the product's success:

> So what am I working hard for? I mean there's a certain amount of personal pride and a certain amount of loyalty to—it's almost more to the product than it is to the (company). The product's almost like our child. We're putting effort into it because we want it to grow up well.

This is the bonding that I observed in my time in management, the motivation for many, many talented people to sacrifice their narrow interests for the sake of a product's success. To an unusual extent, I have found that software developers care little about the company or its management. As Henry Archer observed, it did not matter to him who owned the product, his allegiance was to the product alone. And while these people may be cynical about the company and scoff at the management, they are never cynical about the product. They are fiercely proud and protective of their handiwork and will not abide criticism. It is their "child." And there is more. A palpable bond exists among the people who have put their best efforts in bringing a product to market and seeing it succeed. I could see it time and time again in their eyes when their new product was first demonstrated at a trade show, see it in the loyalty and trust they had one with one another when outsiders—including management—seemed to attack their "child." I could see, in short, the old solidarity which once existed under welfare corporatism. They have a "cause," in the strict sense of Royce's term, something that binds people together. "Loyalty is social. . . . Since a cause, in general, tends to unite the many fellow-servants in one service . . ." (Royce 1908, 20). Through their devotion to the product they have escaped the abyss of cynicism, they have satisfied the human need for loyalty, and they have achieved a necessary solidarity with other "fellow-servants."

The task ahead for corporate managers, then, is to rally people to this cause. I believe it is pointless to try to motivate people by "vision statements" and appeals to corporate traditions. Those days are past, if for no other reason that in our cynical times, such appeals are laughable. But there is an untapped reservoir of loyalty to the work of people's own hands, the products or services they produce, and of which they can and should feel proud. The actions and words of management must be aimed at this natural pride in handiwork, and organization and reward systems must capitalize on that. The current conventional wisdom is that shareholder value is supreme, and the route to that is satisfying customers. That may all be true, but it is hardly a message to rally people. I never saw anyone come to work on her wedding anniversary to "maximize shareholder value." I saw many sacrifice an anniversary to fix a product problem or meet a release schedule. Management themselves must attend to shareholder value, but exhorting employees in that fashion is bootless. They do not care. But they do, or can be made to, care for the product, since that is a natural expression of the need for loyalty.

Management must try to capitalize on that natural need. Organizational design is one factor. A "re-engineered" organization may be more efficient in objective terms, but often the result fails because of the old fault of Scientific Management: it does not satisfy people's basic aspirations. An organizational form that may not look as efficient, but maximizes people's identification with a product, is much more likely to release the creative energies and commitment of employees. Reward systems as well must be attended to. Although gain sharing, profit sharing, and stock options are very popular nowadays, there is little evidence that the increased productivity obtained thereby even pays for the incentive systems' costs (Blinder 1990, vii–7). And I believe the reason for that finding is that, at bottom, most nonmanagement people care little about abstractions such as return on investment and shareholder wealth. But, if incentive systems can be devised which tap into true interests—the health of the product—I believe these can be more successful in marshaling effort. Perhaps incentives for meeting schedules, for market share or numbers of customers, for improved quality and the like will be more effective than trying to tie effort and commitment to financial performance, which is really management's province, not employees'. A new attention to product loyalty may be the road out of the thicket of cynicism and mistrust that is so apparent today. I recognize that this is not a complete solution. After all, a minority of people actually help produce a firm's products; many are in administrative jobs and find it difficult to relate their work to the product or service the firm produces. But the attempt must be made. Without some locus for loyalty, I fear the inevitable destruction of the commons, and an attendant social and economic tragedy.

And so, at the end we can only place our hopes in the new generation. The old dispensation dies with the passing of our cohort 1 friends; Matthew Arnold's Sea of Faith will never again be at the full. The future conceals from us the fate of the younger people, and whether they will look back with Arnold's sense of loss.

Appendix A: The Survey

The Research Site

The research was conducted at Softmatics, a Strategic Business Unit (profit center) of a multi-billion-dollar information services company (DRI), which itself is a unit of a much larger diversified corporation (ACC).[1] Softmatics provided a number of advantages for the research project:

1. The employees are virtually all college graduates and professionals, and thus representatives of a key sector of the late-twentieth-century knowledge industry workforce.

2. Softmatics is equally divided in employee population between a midwestern headquarters location, a California R&D site, and sales and service locations scattered throughout the United States. Thus, the attitudinal effects (if any) of regional location, headquarters location, and remote office location could be studied. Further, since the remote offices are comprised mostly of sales and sales support people, the differences (if any) in attitudes of sales-related people can be studied.

3. Softmatics employees have experienced a prototypical round of mergers, acquisitions, and substantial reorganizations. Within the recent memories of most employees, Softmatics had been a division of another diversified corporation, RLX.

4. Softmatics has also experienced a number of "downsizings" in the recent past, both as part of DRI and before that, as a unit of RLX.

5. As a result of changes in ownership as well as new management thinking, Softmatics management practices and personnel policies have changed markedly in the recent past.

The Survey

After pretesting and minor revisions, a self-administered questionnaire was mailed to all Softmatics employees based in the United States, a total of 791 people. The questionnaires were mailed at the end of October 1994. The Softmatics human resources staff sent reminder e-mail messages to all employees after one week and again after two weeks. Further, for four weeks posters were set up in hallways and elevators urging people to complete the questionnaire. Although responses were requested no later than 12/1/94, some came in as late as 1/17/95. In total, 313 questionnaires were returned, 307 of which were usable.

The return rate is thus seen to be 39.6 percent, which is relatively low. Softmatics human resources people opined that the employees were "surveyed out," that is, they had been surveyed regularly for the last several years (including earlier in 1994) and apparently had seen no benefits accruing to them. (Softmatics own surveys, conducted electronically, had seen a fall off in response from 80 percent in 1993 to 61 percent in 1994.) Regardless of the reasons, a return rate under 40 percent raises some concerns.

Although 40 percent is a substantial proportion of the total population, the respondents are clearly "self-selected," and thus suspect as representatives of the overall population. Social scientists are divided on the possible effects of nonresponse, because some assumption must be made on the nature and motives of the nonrespondents. There is no formal, explicit theory of response behavior available to us, but some empirical studies are informed by implicit theories. Some studies have researched the personal and socioeconomic status of nonrespondents and have concluded that they tend to be in effect socially isolated: typically less educated, lower occupational status, and low income, elderly, and unemployed (Filion 1976, 483). It should be stressed that much of the sociological information on nonrespondents is based on these sociodemographic profiles. But, these characteristics are unlikely to hold for this study, since the population is quite uniform in education and in income, and all are manifestly of working age and, indeed, employed.

More seriously, some studies have indicated that nonrespondents are a class of "resisters," who are prone to nonparticipation in social groups, such as neighborhood associations. And, they can characteristically have low morale, and be dissatisfied with their work (Goyder 1987, 15). Results from Softmatics' own surveys provide some evidence that the nonresponse issue is less serious than might be thought. A measurement of job satisfaction, using wording close to that used in the present study, indicated that in 1993 and 1994 the mean of this variable was 5.12 and 5.09, respectively. (Their 1994 response rate was 61 percent). This is on a seven-point Likert scale; I, using a five-point scale, determined a mean of 3.69. Interpolating between these scales shows that these means are quite close, indicating that, at least for that one variable, job satisfaction, the populations surveyed have at least the same mean.

As noted, we do not have very good theories of nonresponse. What does seem clear, in light of continuous decline in response to surveys since the end of the 1960s, is that many people simply do not like surveys (Goyder 1987, 61). And, conversely, some do enjoy being surveyed, and make a conscious decision to respond (Goyder 1987, 28). One study followed up on those who did not respond and found their motives to be: invasion of privacy (23 percent cited this); concern over confidentiality (21 percent); expense (3 percent); and, length of the survey (2 percent) (Goyder 1987, 69).

To put this issue in perspective, it is important to understand the purpose of the current study. I was not trying to predict something like the outcome of an election, that is, ascertain within a confidence level of five percent the *actual* levels of the variables from a disparate population of highly varied socioeconomic and sociodemographic levels. I was dealing with a relatively homogeneous population, insofar as socio-economic status, and I was also unconcerned if the true population mean of job satisfaction, e.g., was 3.69 or 3.54 or even 4.2. My concern was with the *correlations* of the variables one with another and with personal characteristics, particularly age. I am not convinced that the phenomenon of self-selection would have a major impact on the validity of the reported correlations. While it can be argued that the self-selectors would have different levels of job satisfaction or organizational commitment than their more reticent colleagues, it seems not to follow that they would therefore exhibit different correlations with other variables. This conviction is supported by the fact, as shown below, that the correlations obtained closely track with those of other researchers.

Let us now turn to the data collected from the survey. Personal data on respondents included: age, sex, tenure, and management or nonmanagement position. The intent of the questionnaire was to study a variety of attitudes, most importantly "normative organizational commitment," a construct that is probably the best available surrogate for loyalty to an organization.[2] Data were collected to determine the correlations of various attitudes with one another, and with the personal data. Attitude measurements were constructed from the questionnaire responses in the following manner:

Organizational Commitment (ORGCOM)

The literature of empirical studies of commitment is vast; Mathieu & Zajac's (1990) recent survey uncovered over 200 articles bearing on the subject. By far the most popular instrument to measure commitment has been the scale developed by Mowday, Porter and Steers (Mowday et al. 1982). Their "Organizational Commitment Questionnaire" (QCV) has been used in numerous studies and has almost become a standard. In recent research it is common to remove from the questionnaire items related to "desire to retain membership" (Shore and Martin 1989) or at least to differentiate carefully those items measuring normative commitment from those measuring instrumental (Angle & Perry 1981). In my own research I have eliminated the "membership" questions, as Shore and Martin recommend.

The Protestant Work Ethic (PE)

PE was measured from responses to nineteen questions taken from the work of Mirels and Garret (1972), which has been used by a number of other researchers.

Expressive Individualism (EI)

The questions for expressive individualism were derived from Bellah et al.'s definition of this trait, and their contrast with what they consider to be an earlier form, utilitarian individualism. Their definition follows:

> A form of individualism that arose in opposition to Utilitarian Individualism. Expressive Individualism holds that each person has a unique core of feeling and intuition that should unfold or be expressed if individuality is to be realized. This core, though unique, is not necessarily alien to other persons or to nature.

> Under certain conditions, the expressive individualist may find it possible through intuitive feeling to "merge" with other persons, with nature or with the cosmos as a whole. Expressive Individualism is related to the phenomenon of romanticism in eighteenth- and nineteenth-century European and American culture. In the twentieth century, it shows affinities with the culture of psychotherapy. (Bellah et al. 1985, 333–34)

In contrast, Utilitarian Individualism is defined as "a form of individualism that . . . sees human life as an effort . . . to maximize their self-interest . . ." (Bellah et al. 1985, 336).

Job Satisfaction (JOBSAT)

JOBSAT was measured by the single question: "On the whole, how satisfied are you with your work?" This is the wording used by the Gallup organization since the 1940s, and adopted by the National Opinion Research Corporation's (NORC) General Social Survey (GSS) for their surveys from the early 1970s to the present day. (Flanagan et al. 1974, 107).[3]

Work Values

The technique used to measure work values follows Mottaz, who posited that organizational commitment is largely a function of work rewards and investments (Mottaz 1989). Mottaz classified work rewards as those intrinsic to the task (e.g., autonomy), extrinsic social rewards from the job (e.g., a friendly environment), and extrinsic organizational rewards (e.g., pay). Measurements were made of both respondents' *desire* for a particular reward and their *perception* of how well the company was meeting that need. The difference between the two was also used as a variable in correlations with other variables.

A detailed report on the statistical findings follows, but it can be said that in general, the population has the characteristics predicted by the literature with regard to correlations of organizational commitment with such variables as work values, age, sex, tenure and organizational position. Also, a cohort analysis found that there are quite different levels of many variables in three different age cohorts.

Statistics

The data from 307 usable questionnaires was analyzed using "SPSS for the Macintosh 4.0" (Norusis 1990). The correlations and conclusions follow, starting with correlations with personal characteristics.

Personal Characteristics

Generally, as reported in the literature, personal characteristics do not seem to have a major impact on attitudes. The following results are reports on t-tests indicating differences that are significant at the five percent level or less.

Gender

Age is significantly different at .023 level. Women are younger; more that two years on the average. The means are: men: 40.8095. Women: 38.1655.

INTRS-S is significantly different. Men have higher intrinsic work values. The means are men: 4.2886. Women: 4.1667.

All other variables, including of course organizational commitment are *not* significantly different. This finding is consistent with Mathieu & Zajac's (1990) exhaustive meta analysis of organizational commitment studies which concluded that gender was not significantly correlated with commitment.

Job Code

Age is significantly different. Managers are more than five years older. The means are: mangers: 44.6848; nonmanagers: 39.1663.

Gender is significantly different. Fewer women are in management.

ORGCOM is significantly different. Managers have higher commitment. The means are: managers: 3.8027; nonmanagers: 3.5157.

Tenure is significantly different. Managers have almost eight years more tenure, almost twice that of nonmanagers. The means are: managers: 16.2712; nonmanagers: 8.8737.

All other variables are not significantly different, including JOBSAT. So, most values of managers and non-managers seem to be the same but the experience of management makes a difference in organizational commitment, irrespective of other values.

Location

Respondents were categorized by three locations: the headquarters site in the Midwest (HQ); an R&D and product support site in California (CA); and, various sales and services locations throughout the continental United States (REMOTE).

Age: Significant difference between HQ and CA. HQ respondents are older by more than three years on the average.

EXREW-C: Significant difference between HQ and CA and between HQ and REMOTE. HQ respondents had a higher rating of the organization's performance on wages and benefits than the other two locations.

EXREW-DEL: Significant difference between HQ and REMOTE. This variable is the difference between the expressed need for extrinsic rewards (pay and benefits) and the perception of the organization's meeting these needs. In all locations the mean of this variable was negative, but the REMOTE mean was more negative. Recall that the REMOTE category included a very large percentage of sales people, who are legendary for their interest in compensation, as well as their proverbial belief that they are underpaid.

EXSOC-C: Significant difference between HQ and REMOTE and between CA and REMOTE. This variable is the perception of the organization's performance in meeting the need for social rewards in the workplace (a friendly and helpful environment). The highest rating was for HQ and the lowest for REMOTE. The lower finding for REMOTE could be related to the relatively small numbers of people in the remote offices or to the fact that the jobs are typically higher in stress.

EXSOC-DEL: Significant difference between HQ and REMOTE. This variable is the difference between the respondent's expressed need for social rewards and the perception of the organization's delivery of them.

JOB SAT: Significant difference between HQ and CA. Job satisfaction is higher among the HQ respondents.

Tenure: Significant difference between HQ and CA and HQ and REMOTE. HQ respondents have longer tenure.

Cohort

Three age cohorts were examined, based upon different birthrates in the year of the respondent's birth. The intent was to test Easterlin's assertion that the size of one's birth cohort will have lasting effects on attitudes, as we discussed in chapter 2. The following information is taken from Easterlin (Easterlin 1987, Appendix Table 1.1).

TABLE A-1
United States Birth Rates, 1930 to 1966

Year of Birth	*U.S. Birth Rate in Those Years (Per Thousands of Population)*
1930 to 1940	18.3
1941 to 1945	21.2
1946 to 1955	24.6
1956 to 1965	23.4
1966 and later	17.0

From this data, and an analysis of my interviews with 91 Softmatics people, I decided to divide the population into three age cohorts, as shown in Table A-2, below:

TABLE A-2
Age Cohort Definitions

BIRTH YEARS	COHORT
1930 to 1940	1
1941 to 1955	2
1956 and later	3

Easterlin contends that respondents from the different cohorts will exhibit different levels of values, including normative organizational commitment. As I have argued in detail in the body of this work, it is also notable that the three different cohorts have substantially different formative experiences, growing up in quite different times. The SPSS "ONEWAY" analysis with the Duncan procedure was used to compare cohorts for significant differences (Norusis 1990). The results are shown in Table A-3 below.

TABLE A-3
Survey Variables by Cohort

VARIABLE	*COHORT* 1	2	3	*STATISTICAL SIGNIFICANCE*
EI	3.92	3.72	3.74	Cohort 1 is different from 2 and 3 @ 6.4% level. Cohorts 2 and 3 are not significantly different.
EXREW-C	3.04	2.62	2.67	Cohort 1 is different from 2 @ 2.3% level and from 3 @ 3.7% level. Cohorts 2 and 3 are not significantly different.
EXREW-S	3.96	4.14	4.27	Cohort 1 is different from 2 but only @ 11.6% level. Cohort 1 is different from 3 @ 0.6% level. Cohorts 2 and 3 differ @ 4.9% level.
EXREW-DEL	−0.92	−1.51	−1.59	Cohort 1 is different from 2 @ 1.1% level and from 3 @ 0.2% level. Cohorts 2 and 3 are not significantly different.
EXSOC-C	3.96	3.71	3.79	No significant differences among the cohorts.
EXSOC-S	4.18	4.01	4.12	No significant differences between 1 and 2 or between 1 and 3. Cohorts 2 and 3 are different @ 7.1% level.
EXSOC-DEL	−0.22	−0.29	−0.33	No significant differences among the cohorts.
INTRS-C	4.083	3.82	3.74	Cohort 1 is different from 2 @ 6.9% level and different from Cohort 3 @ 1.9% level. No significant difference between Cohorts 2 and 3.
INTRS-S	4.25	4.25	4.27	No significant differences among the cohorts.
INTR-DEL	−0.17	−0.42	−0.52	Cohort 1 is different from 2 @ 7.2% level and from 3 @ 1.5% level. No significant difference between Cohorts 2 and 3.

TABLE A-3 (*continued*)
Survey Variables by Cohort

VARIABLE	*COHORT* 1	2	3	*STATISTICAL SIGNIFICANCE*
JOBSAT	4.25	3.71	3.59	Cohort 1 is different from 2 @ 1.5% level and from 3 @ 0.4% level. No significant difference between Cohorts 2 and 3.
ORGCOM	3.89	3.57	3.52	Cohort 1 is different from 2 @ 1.8% level and from 3 @ 0.5% level. No significant difference between Cohorts 2 and 3.
PE	3.21	3.09	3.05	Cohort 1 is different from 2 @ 12% level and from 3 @ 3.7% level. No significant difference between Cohorts 2 and 3.

Figures A-1 through A-4 on the following pages show the differences among the cohorts on work values and other attitudes. For work values, Figure A-1 shows the cohort means for the expression of the importance of extrinsic rewards, social rewards, and intrinsic rewards. Figure A-2 shows the means for the perception of how well the company fulfills these needs, and Figure A-3 shows the distance between expressed need and perceived fulfillment. Finally, Figure A-4 shows the cohort means for organizational commitment, Protestant Ethic, expressive individualism, and job satisfaction.

Clearly there are differences among the cohorts in both work values and in attitudes toward the job, toward the company and toward the world in general. Not all the differences shown on the graphs are statistically significant, as noted on the graph legends, but the general monotonic trends from the oldest cohort to the youngest are quite compelling hints that the cohorts differ in ways that suggest an historical explanation.

TABLE A-4
The Correlates of Organizational Commitment[4]

VARIABLE	*CORRELATION COEFFICIENT*
COHORT	−.1295
EI	.1662
EXREW-C	.5257
EXREW-DEL	.3942
EXSOC-C	.3540
EXSOC-S	.2937
INTRS-C	.5271
INTRS-S	.3019
INTR-DEL	.3241
JOBCODE	−.1805[5]
JOBSAT	.5984
PE	.2101
TENURE	.1905

There are a number of noteworthy results from Table A-2. First, it can be seen that organizational commitment is *not* correlated with age; there is not a uniformly increasing (or decreasing) trend of commitment as people proceed through the life cycle. Rather, there is a correlation with cohort, indicating that the age groups have more or less sharp distinctions in organizational commitment. This conclusion in part substantiates Easterlin's thesis that different generations and different generation sizes had different historical experiences and/or received different socialization which persisted through life.

The only other correlations with personal characteristics are consistent with the literature: commitment increases with tenure (Cohen 1993), and commitment is higher among managers. (See Mathieu & Zajac (1990) and Luthans et al. (1987) for excellent summaries of this literature.) The correlations of organizational commitment with two other general attitudes, expressive individualism (EI) and the Protestant work ethic (PE), are significant, but rather weak. As expected, PE is correlated with ORGCOM; those with an inherent need to work would seem to naturally attach themselves to organi-

FIGURE A-1
Need for Work Rewards, by Cohort

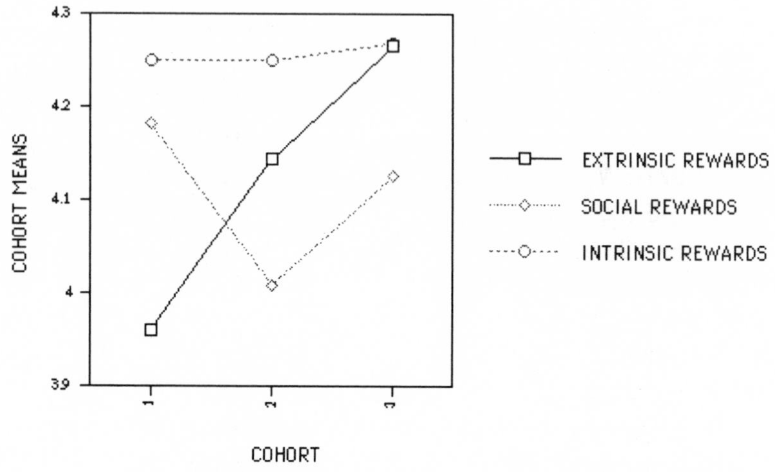

EXTRINSIC REWARDS: All Cohorts are significantly different.

SOCIAL REWARDS: Cohorts 2 and 3 are different.

INTRINSIC REWARDS: No differences among the cohorts.

zations that fulfill that need. This is confirmed by the correlates of PE itself: there are moderate associations between PE and job satisfaction; perception of company-provided extrinsic rewards; the need for intrinsic rewards; and the need for and perception of extrinsic social rewards. This latter may seem counterintuitive, but it would not be surprising to learn that people who want to work also value a cooperative workplace.

Perhaps more surprising is the correlation between PE and expressive individualism, which latter is also moderately correlated with organizational commitment. This may be an artifact of the measurement of EI, but if true it would deny Bellah et al.'s (1985) assertion that expressive individualism is the polar opposite of utilitarian individualism—a form of individualism quite consonant, in their view, with the Protestant Ethic. Again, this may be an artifact, but one possible explanation is that people who are concerned with the development

FIGURE A-2
Perception of Company's Ability to Satisfy Need for Work Rewards, By Cohort

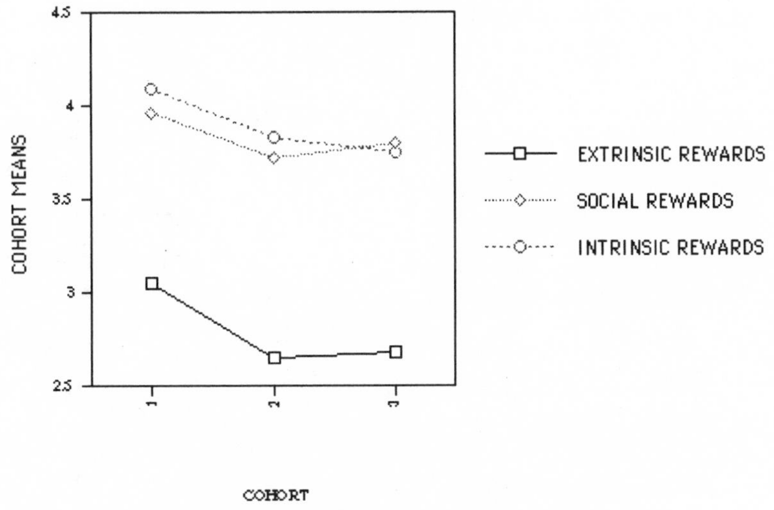

Extrinsic Rewards: Cohort 1 is significantly different from 2 and 3

Intrinsic Rewards: Cohort 1 is significantly different from 2 and 3

Social Rewards: No significant differnces among cohorts

of their own personalities could well seek that development in the world of work. The fact that EI is positively correlated with ORGCOM could be explained through the same reasoning.

Against the view that the findings on expressive individualism are purely artifactual, it should also be noted that whereas EI is mostly highly correlated with the expression of work needs, PE is correlated with the *perception* of the company's fulfillment of those needs; EI is not correlated at all with those perceptions. This can be read as an indication that those with high expressive individualism have a distinct set of personal needs that they bring to the work place, whereas those with high PE are more concerned that their needs are satisfied.

In any event, organizational commitment is most strongly correlated with the various measurements of work values, as

FIGURE A-3
Differences Between Needs for Work Rewards and Company's Ability to Satisfy, by Cohort

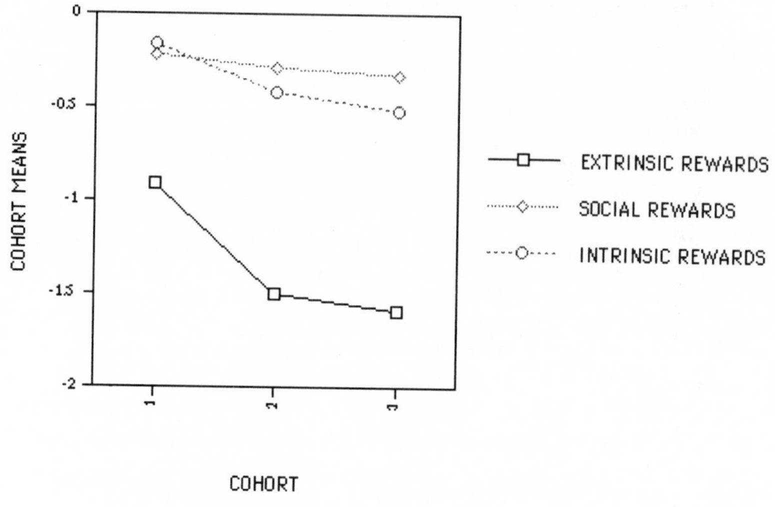

Extrinsic Rewards: Cohort 1 is significantly different from 2 and 3

Intrinsic Rewards: Cohort 1 is significantly different from 2 and 3

Social Rewards: No significant differnces among cohorts

well as job satisfaction, a construct similar, but not identical with, ORGCOM. This finding on work values explicitly confirms the work of Mottaz (1987, 1988, and 1989) as well as that of Butler and Vodanovich (1992). Mottaz found that personal characteristics, including gender and tenure, have little or no effect on normative commitment, whereas work values are the key determinants. But Mottaz's findings were that intrinsic rewards were the strongest determinants, followed next by extrinsic social and last by extrinsic organizational rewards (pay, promotions, etc.). My results are the reverse; the order of importance of determinants is: perception of external rewards, perception of intrinsic rewards (these two are of almost identical importance), and far behind those, the social rewards. One possible explanation for this is that Softmatics had imposed a salary freeze and, with periodic downsizings, promotions have been relatively rare. Hence, the paucity of

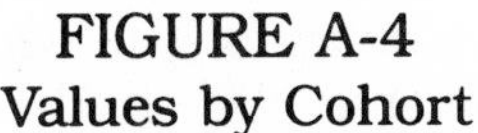

FIGURE A-4
Values by Cohort

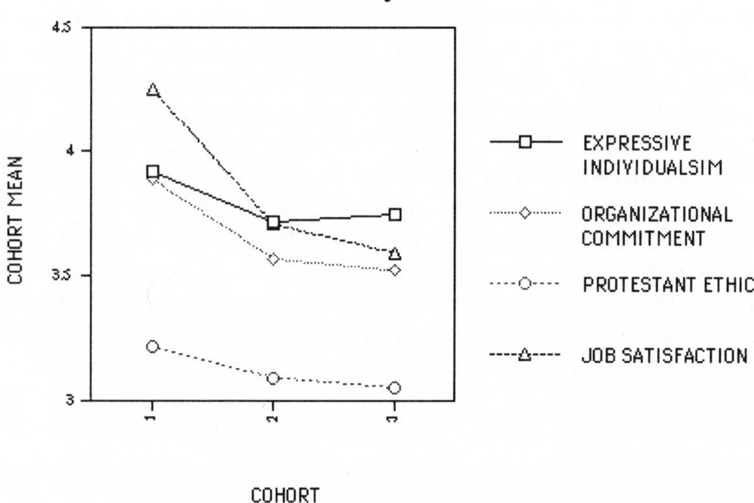

For all variables, Cohort 1 is significantly different from Cohorts 2 and 3.

external rewards may have brought this determinant to the fore in many people's minds. Still, as Mottaz found, the correlation with intrinsic rewards is quite strong in this study.

Finally, I should point out that partial correlations, controlling for a variety of variables including personal characteristics, had no appreciable effect on the findings presented above.

Conclusions

We can conclude from the statistical analysis that the findings are consistent with the literature in important ways. The results from Softmatics match both the empirical work of Mottaz (1987, 1988, and 1989) and Wiener (1982) and the psychological model of Ajzen and Fishbein (1977), presented in chapter 5. The literature is confirmed in that organizational commitment—loyalty if you will—is principally a product of two things: the needs for certain intrinsic and extrinsic rewards which people bring to the workplace, and the actual rewards they perceive that they find there. The perception of rewards is determined by both management practices and by the employee's perception of those practices. Both that perception and the needs brought to the workplace are determined by a person's ideology—his values and beliefs. It is a strong finding of this study that the ideology of the oldest cohort is substantially different from the younger ones, that the younger cohorts have an ideology much less conducive to loyalty. The conclusion seems inescapable: the natural succession of the younger cohorts in the working population, along with different management practices springing from a new management ideology, account for the overall waning of loyalty in present-day America.

Appendix B: The Interviews

Selection

THE survey questionnaire included the request for a yes or no answer to "I would be willing to be interviewed," and the request for a name and contact telephone number. Of the 313 people who responded to the survey, 111 agreed to an interview, an agreement rate of over 35 percent. Attempts were made to contact each of the 111 and to schedule interviews, but only 91 could be accommodated in the time period allotted for interviews (November 1994 through January 1995).

The critical question about this set of people is, of course, how representative are they of the Softmatics population? I have addressed the representativeness of the questionnaire respondents in Appendix A, above. (The questionnaire response rate was just under 40 percent of the total population.) To determine if those agreeing to the interviews differed from the other survey respondents, t-tests were conducted. It is important to note that the interview group exhibited *no* significant differences in attitudes compared to the noninterviewed. The following variables were significantly different, at the five percent level or less, for the interview group versus those who did not agree to an interview.

Gender

Fewer women volunteered to be interviewed. Women comprised 24.8 percent of those surveyed, but were only 17.6 percent of those interviewed. Mitigating this potential bias is the finding in both my survey and the literature that gender has no discernible influence on any of the attitudes measured (Mathieu & Zajac 1990).

Age

Older people were more likely to agree to be interviewed. The means are: noninterviewee: 39.12; interviewee: 42.02. While this could lend some distortion to impressions formed by the interviews, the disproportion of older employees was a boon, since the questionnaires revealed that the older cohort had significantly different views, and more information on this important group was welcome.

Job Code

Managers were more likely to volunteer. The percentage of managers and supervisors in the survey group was 17.9; the group volunteering to be interview included 28.4 percent managers. This is hardly surprising since managerial and supervisory people typically are more interested in the company.

Tenure

The longer tenured were more likely to volunteer. The means are: noninterviewees: 9.3 years; interviewees: 11.8 years. Again, this is far from surprising: tenure is closely correlated with age, and also the longer tenure are probably more interested in the company.

I believe it is quite noteworthy that none of the other variables—preeminently the key attitude variables—showed any statistically significant differences between the interview group and those who declined to be interviewed. Therefore, the group interviewed is representative of the group surveyed in terms of attitudes, but of course, the caution still must be made that both those interviewed and those surveyed selected themselves.

The Interview Process

Before conducting the interviews, a pretest was arranged with a random selection of ten Softmatics employees. This proved valuable from a number of perspectives. I had learned a good deal of the events of the previous twelve months or so from Softmatics management and human resources staffers, but the interviews with pretest people lent a different perspective and provided useful new information. Also, I learned that my proposed technique, requesting the interviewee to complete some forced-rating questionnaires, was too confusing and generated resistance. In the event, I decided to use a few open-ended questions, which are presented below.

All interviews were tape-recorded and subsequently transcribed; all were strictly private: just the subject and myself. The headquarters and California interviews were conducted in company conference rooms on the premises; the remote interviews were conducted over the telephone, except for one person who found himself at HQ at a mutually convenient date.

The subjects ran the gamut of human types: from the loquacious to the reticent, from the angry to the jovial, the disillusioned to the inhabitants of the best of all possible worlds. I did not systematically note my impression of "hidden agendas," but some clearly wanted me to note certain of their opinions of management and the company. By far the majority seemed to be motivated simply by curiosity; in fact one gentleman, I am convinced, agreed to the session because he was under the impression that I was the popular author, *Tom* Clancy. (He had little to say after I disappointed him in that hope.)

The Interview Questions

The following series of open-ended questions was posed to the subjects. In some cases, as noted below, not all questions were asked of all.

1. "Tell me about yourself."[1]

2. "Why did you join this company?"

3. "Why do you stay? What keeps you here?"

4. "What is the most important thing to you about your job?; Why is that so? Does the company give that to you? Why or why not?"

5. "I am going to describe to you the changes that have taken place in Softmatics over the last several years."[2] "Did any of these events affect you personally? Did you agree with the need for these

changes? Did any of these events affect your attitude toward the company? If so, describe your attitude before and after the event(s)."

6. "What does it mean to you to say that you are loyal to something or somebody?"

7. "Do you think you are more or less loyal to this company than you were in the past? When do you think your loyalty changed? Why do you think it changed?"[3]

8. "Do you think that this company, or any company should owe anything to its employees, should have any obligations to them, other than a paycheck?"

9. "It has been said of Sun Microsystems that they tell their employees two things:

A. Your career is your responsibility, not the company's.

B. You have a job here as long as the project you are working on is active, but after that, there is no guarantee.

What do you think about that?"[4]

10. "Mattel Toy Company recently issued a press release. The following was included in the same release:

- We have had our fifth year in a row of record sales and earnings.
- We are increasing the dividend to our shareholders.
- We are laying off 1500 people, four percent of the workforce.

What do you think about that?"[5]

11. "If I were a friend or neighbor and asked you what it is like to work for Softmatics, what would you tell me?"[6]

12. "Is there anything else you would like to tell me?"

Content Analysis

A content analysis was performed on the responses to some of the interview questions, following R. Weber's process (R. Weber 1985, 22–24). It is well known that the results of content analysis can be unreliable due to the ambiguity of the respondent's expression and the arbitrariness of the categories chosen by the analyst (R. Weber 1985, 15). In any event, the attempt was made to review the subjects' responses and judge in an objective way their fit to assigned categories. The variables and their definitions follow.

"SELF"

The value for this variable was constructed from the subject's response to the first question: "Tell me about yourself." The coding was as follows:

"1" if the subject began with a personal description.

"2" if the subject first asked for a context, then gave a personal description.

"3" if the subject first asked for a context and then gave a business description, e.g., "I am a software developer."

"4" if the subject began with a business description.

"LOYDFN" (Loyalty definition)

The value for this variable was constructed from the response to question number 6 above, a request to define loyalty. The coding followed the definitions of Fletcher, i.e., "minimum loyalty" is merely the "demand for maintenance of the relationship, which requires the rejection of alternatives that undermine the bond. . . ." (Fletcher 1993, 5.)

"Maximum loyalty" contains the notion of thoroughgoing devotion. "He that is not with me is against me" (Matthew 12:30 and Luke 11:23). Maximum loyalty demands an emotional, even an irrational, attachment to its object: "There comes a point when logic runs dry and one must plant one's loyalty in the simple fact that it is *my* friend, *my* club . . . In loyalty, as in love, there is not even an illusion of scientific neutrality and intellectual impartiality . . ." (Fletcher 1993, 61.)

The procedure was that an expression of maximum loyalty was coded "4" and minimum loyalty "1," with ambivalent expression coded either "2" or "3" depending on how close they seemed to be to the poles. Examples may clarify this. Here is an expression from subject number 806, a person past retirement age who is explaining why he stays on. This was coded as "maximum," or "4":

> there's a certain loyalty you have to certain people and other people are just kind of equal and I know them, but I'm not loyal to them I don't think. So, but, you know I got this group of family at work and friends that I think that's what loyalty is to me, to do anything that they want done. It just to me whatever they want done. . . . If that group says that "would you do me a favor?," I'd say sure, anything. I don't care what it is. I'm not going to blink about it.

Here is an example coded as "minimum loyalty," from subject number 831:

> So I think that . . . while I would not be disloyal while I'm here and after I left I would honor, you know, any proprietary information . . . But if there was a better opportunity that came along, I wouldn't feel so loyal that I would feel awful about leaving the company, if you know what I mean. . . . My sense of being loyal (is) while I'm here is to do my job well, well, you know, I guess with integrity and to perform the best that I can and to be loyal also would be that if I did leave, that I would not bad-mouth the company or . . . divulge anything that I know that's confidential.

"LOYTRND" (Loyalty trend)

Values for this variable were rather easily coded since the question, number seven, is straightforward and unequivocally calls for an answer of either more loyal, less loyal, or the same.

"OWE"

The value for this variable was constructed from the subject's response to question number 8, which seeks an opinion on the obligations a company should have to its employees. The coding scheme is: "4" for a strongly positive answer, "1" for strongly negative, and "2"and "3" for ambivalence, depending on the shading toward one of the poles. An example of a strongly positive answer is this from subject number 837:

> I definitely think that if people give away a large portion of their lives to an organization that that organization needs to take care of its people. . . . see to it that they get compensation, that they get the respect that they need, that they get the opportunities to grow and to learn and that they have the power to basically set up their lives here at work the way they want it. . . . We are spending a lot of hours here and that's part of our happiness is dependent on the relationships and the environment that we have here at work and it is a very large investment to work at a place like this.

An example of a strongly negative view of a company's obligations is this from subject number 803:

> I don't think a company should owe anything to an employee any more than an employee should owe something to the company. . . . I don't think they owe me anything. You know they've hired me to do a job for them. I will do that job for them and if they don't think I'm doing that job for them, then I don't think they owe me anything but saying we don't think you're doing this job for us and we don't want you working for us anymore.

"SUN" (Reaction to the Sun Microsystems question, number 9)

The value for this variable was constructed from the subject's answer to question number 9, regarding Sun Microsystems' purported statement to its employees. The coding scheme is: "4" for a strongly positive answer, "1" for strongly negative, and "2"and "3" for ambivalence depending on the shading toward one of the poles. Here is an example of a positive response, this from subject number 802:

> I think it's good. I mean they're up-front and they tell you like it is. It's nice to know that up-front when you're going in . . . I think it's an excellent approach.

A strongly negative reaction is the following from subject number 837:

> I would not work at a place like that. We're not just machines working. We are humans and I think Sun should realize that. They're humans . . . these human beings have families . . .

"Mattel" (Reaction to the Mattel Toy press release)

The value for this variable was constructed from the subject's answer to question number 10, his or her reaction to the Mattel Toy Company's press release. Responses were coded in the same manner as the "SUN" variable, above. An example of a strongly positive response is this from subject number 819:

> My personal feeling is you've got some smart businessmen. They're not hatchet men. They don't like layoffs any more than anyone else, but they foresee the future and know exactly how to run a business so as to maintain those profit levels year by year. . . . The reason that it does that is (shows ever better results) not because they're lucky. It's because they have some very sharp financial people that understand exactly what it takes to continually post a profit and to grow every year.

Subject number 837, again, an unusually opinionated and articulate person, gives us an example of a strongly negative reaction.

> I find it ridiculous. Absolutely ridiculous. I think: who's responsible for the success of the company? The people that are responsible for the success of the company are the people that work in the company and to give the benefits of that work to stockholders (it) does not make sense to me because they haven't done anything. It's the people that work there daily that are responsible for the existence of that dividend and they should have it. And they got laid off and that's disgusting.

Statistical Correlations

The variables constructed from content analysis were correlated with one another and with personal characteristics and the subjects' attitudes derived from the survey questionnaire. The correlations were done with the computer program "SPSS for the Macintosh 4.0" (Norusis 1990). The results are presented in Table B-1. A discussion of these results follows.

"Self"

This variable, the subjects' choice of personal or business status in beginning to tell the interviewer about themselves, is associated with the subjects' definition of loyalty. Those who respond with a personal description of themselves are more likely to define loyalty towards the high end of the "maximum" loyalty definition scale.

"LOYDFN" Loyalty Definition

As noted above, the definition of loyalty is associated with SELF, but also with Cohort and with ORGCOM. A "maximum" definition is more likely to come from the older cohorts and from those with higher organizational commitment.

TABLE B-1
Correlations of Interview Variables[7]

INTERVIEW VARIABLE	INTERVIEW VARIABLE	SURVEY VARIABLE
SELF	LOYDFN, SUN	
LOYDFN	SELF	ORGCOM, COHORT
LOYTRND	OWE	ORGCOM, EXTR-C, INTR-C, ORGCOM, JOBSAT, EXR-DEL
OWE	LOYTRND, MATTEL	EI
SUN	MATTEL, SELF	INTR-C, INTR-DEL, EXSOC-C EXSOC-S[8]
MATTEL	SUN, OWE	EXSOC-S, EI

"LOYTRND" (Loyalty trend)

A subject's loyalty trend is associated with a number of the work-values variables and with ORGCOM. A downtrend in loyalty is connected with lowered perception of the company's extrinsic rewards and as well as the company's intrinsic rewards. Not surprisingly, a downtrend goes hand-in-hand with lowered organizational commitment, lowered job satisfaction, and a lower belief in the company's ability to meet extrinsic rewards. Also, those reporting a downtrend in loyalty are more likely to believe that the company owes employees something (OWE), than those whose trend is stable or up.

For cohort 1, the mean is 2.00, that is to say, the trend is flat. For cohort 2, the trend is 1.54, that is, downward. This is a statistically significant difference. Cohort 3's loyalty trend is higher than cohort 2's and is almost flat (1.91). This too is a significant difference. The differences between cohorts 1 and 3 are not significant statistically.

"Owe"

The sense that a company has definite obligations to its employees is associated with relatively lower expressive individualism (EI), with a downward loyalty trend and with low approval of Mattel. (See below).

"SUN" (Reaction to the Sun Microsystems question)

The question on Sun Microsystems was asked of 63 of the 91 subjects. Approval of Sun's statements on their relationship with employees is quite well correlated with approval of Mattel's actions. In other words, there is a clear division between people who accept the modern idea of a company's purpose and functions and people who do not. From this sample of 63 people, I found that 16 percent strongly approved of Sun, 30 percent strongly disapproved. Combining all degrees of approval accounted for 44 percent of those surveyed.

SUN is also correlated with SELF: people who begin self-descriptions with an account of their business life are more likely to approve of Sun's statements. Controlling for age uncovers further correlations. The strongest are with INTRS-C and INTR-DEL, respectively the perception of the company's effectiveness in meeting intrinsic work needs such as autonomy, and the difference between that and one's needs. Those who have lower perceptions of the company's performance are more likely to approve of Sun. And, those who find less disparity in their own needs and their perception of reality are also more likely to approve of Sun. Further, EXSOC-S is correlated with SUN. Those who approve of Sun are more likely to have lower needs for a friendly and cooperative workplace.

"MATTEL" (Reaction to the Mattel Toy press release)

This question was posed to only 30 of the 91 subjects, so the analysis cannot be as rich as with the other variables. But, even so, some definite conclusions are possible.

The strongest correlation is with EXSOC-S, the need for a cooperative workplace. Those expressing a high need for this were the least likely to approve of Mattel. Also, there is a good correlation with expressive individualism: a high degree of this trait was associated with low approval of Mattel. As noted above, a low approval of Mattel was also correlated with disapproval of Sun and with a skepticism about company obligations. Those who believed the company owed the employee little were more inclined to approve of Mattel.

Let us look further at the reactions to Sun and to the Mattel stories, both stories having been chosen to elicit attitudes about current management practices. The reactions, in terms of correlation with other factors and attitudes, are not identical, although they are well correlated one with the other. The reactions to Sun's statement seem to bear more upon the need for intrinsic rewards, and an orientation to the private person, rather than the business person. (The "SELF" variable).

The Sun question is in essence directed at the individual and his fate in a large organization; the Mattel question more toward the equity of management practices in the overall American economy. Those with a high level of expressive individualism seem to have more of an ethical problem with the Mattel practices, as representing a society going in the wrong direction, whereas their approval or disapproval of Sun may be more a matter closely associated with practices that they might encounter in their own company—a matter of individual perception of their own management, rather than a comment on society at large.

Notes

Chapter 1. Introduction

1. All names of individuals and organizations are pseudonyms to protect confidentiality.

2. I separated my subjects into three age cohorts. Cohort 1 comprised those born in 1940 or before; cohort 2, those born 1941 to 1955; cohort 3, born after 1955. See Table 2-1, below.

3. Ronald Dore (1973) coined the term "welfare corporatism" to indicate the methods first used by many large Japanese companies and, increasingly, by large American companies after World War II. Typically, the practices included a variety of employee welfare programs, organizational structures and personnel policies designed to induce employee loyalty. Invariably, welfare corporatist firms made the implicit promise of lifetime employment for good behavior.

4. I will often use the words "generation" and "cohort" interchangeably to denote people born in the same period. As I will explain in chapter 2, the term is also used by Mannheim in a technical sense to distinguish particular age groups which are agents of social change.

5. Women were underrepresented in my interviews, although not in my survey. But my own findings are consistent with the literature in that gender seems to have little correlation with organizational commitment (Mathieu and Zajac 1990).

6. "Instrumental commitment": a relationship with the organization based on an exchange relationship. Members become committed because they see a beneficial or equitable exchange relationship between their contributions and the rewards they receive (Mowday et al. 1982, 21).

7. "Normative commitment": an intense orientation toward the organization based on internalization of the organization's goals values, and norms. The individual identifies with authority (Mowday et al. 1982, 21).

8. Throughout, I will follow Galambos's (1975) usage and refer to the set of values—including loyalty—as "bureaucratic values" and "the corporate culture." I realize that for many "corporate culture" means an individual corporation's ways of doing things, but Galambos intends the term to mean society's embrace of values that enhance the operation of an economy consisting of large corporations. Note that I also refer to this set of values as "the old dispensation."

Chapter 2. The Old Dispensation Speaks

1. All subjects' names are pseudonyms.

2. A pseudonym for the organization's headquarters site.

3. A pseudonym for the former parent of Softmatics.

4. I measured "normative commitment," a type of commitment which does not include the simple desire to stay for instrumental reasons. The instrument used was the the scale developed by Mowday, Porter, and Steers (Mowday et al. 1982), with the questions relating to instrumental commitment removed, as recommended by Shore and Martin (1989). Appendix A has the details of the survey.

5. See note 7 in chapter 1. I repeat that I am employing Galambos's (1975) term and I do not intend the practices of individual companies when I say "corporate culture."

Chapter 3. Social and Historical Conditioning: The Great Depression

1. Elton Mayo did not directly influence welfare capitalism, since his famous Hawthorne experiments were not done until 1924–1927—long after the movement began, and in fact when it was on the wane. But Mayo's work is a systematic exposition of the impulse that led to welfare capitalism in an earlier time. Note also that "welfare capitalism" is a set of management practices quite distinct in kind from "welfare corporatism"; that latter is detailed in chapter 8, below.

Chapter 5. The Heart of all the Virtues: Loyalty

1. In my view, these commentators are referring to a stunted form of loyalty, a condition not really worthy of the name, which is called "instrumental commitment" in the literature of organizational commitment. This form of attachment is purely instrumental and can indeed be generated by a rational cost-benefit calculation of one's own interests.

2. See, for example, Cialdini 1993, 57ff; Kanter 1977, 144; Kiesler 1971, 22; Kiesler, Collins and Miller 1969, 191; McGee and Ford 1987; Lincoln and Kalleberg 1990, 122; Mowday, Porter and Steers 1982, 25; and, Salancik 1977, 2.

3. The statistical analysis is presented in Appendix B.

4. Details of the survey and the statistical analysis are presented in Appendix A.

5. Mathieu & Zajac's (1990) exhaustive literature survey of the antecedents of normative commitment shows little evidence that gender is correlated with commitment. One example from this literature: Chusmir (1986) specifically measured gender effects on *job* commitment and found no relationship between gender and commitment.

Chapter 6. The Baby Boomers: Cohort 2

1. See chapter 2.

2. The interview results are presented in Appendix B.

3. The mean organizational commitment for cohort 1 is 3.90 on a five point scale; cohort 2 is 3.57. The difference is significant at the 1.8 percent

level, i.e., there is one chance in 56 that the difference could be due to chance. See Appendix A for details on the survey and the statistical results.

4. On a scale of 5.0 representing "very satisfied," the mean for cohort 1 was 4.25; for cohort 2 it was 3.7 (3.0 means "neutral"). This difference is significant at the 1.5 percent level. See Appendix A for details on the survey and the statistical results.

CHAPTER 7. "THE LONG UNRAVELING, THE FRESH START"

1. After Nixon's former attorney general, John Mitchell, was convicted for his part in the Watergate affair, he pushed through the crowd gathered outside New York's federal courthouse in Foley Square. A young man in full counterculture regalia stood a few feet away and mocked Mitchell with the chorus from "Like a Rolling Stone": "How does it *feel*?" Everyone under 30 caught the reference and found it apt.

2. The institutions are: financial institutions, major companies, organized religion, education, executive branch of the federal government, organized labor, the press, medicine, TV, the U.S. Supreme Court, the scientific community, the Congress, and the U.S. military.

3. The question asked was: "Generally speaking, would you say that most people can be trusted or that you can't be too careful in dealing with people?" See Appendix B for details of the interviews.

CHAPTER 8. The Sixties: Economy and Management Practices

1. A "throffer" is an offer combined with a threat.

2. Ironically, the conclusions for which the name "Hawthorne" has become so famous have been disproved by later statistical analysis of the data. Over 90 percent of the variance in the observed production rates can be statistically correlated with Taylorian variables such as the quality of inputs and management discipline. Quantitative analysis of the Hawthorne data simply does not support the notion that improvements in human relations yield better economic performance (Franke and Kaul 1978). But, it is probable that as with Freud's work, the details may be wrong, but the overall conclusion is important, and largely correct.

3. "Welfare capitalism" was a movement quite distinct from "welfare corporatism," earlier in time and different in practices and intent. Welfare *capitalism* was discussed in chapter 3 and Welfare *corporatism* is reviewed in this chapter.

4. You may recall our cohort 1 friend Art Merrill from chapter 2, who "walked into RLX Employment one day and said 'I'm here to get a job.' And they said, 'What can you do?' I said 'I can't do anything really.'" But they hired him for the potential they saw in him and in 30 years he had risen to the top.

5. Appendix B gives details of the interviews and the content analysis of the information.
6. See chapter 5.

Chapter 10. The Shipwreck of Welfare Corporatism

1. The wording of the question was "Do you think that this company, or any company, should owe anything to its employees, should have any obligations to them, other than a paycheck?" See Appendix B for details of the interviews and the analysis.
2. Counterintuitive because less staff lowers the denominator; if the numerator—output—can be maintained, productivity must rise.
3. Beth Rubin refers to the relationship as "the Accord" and says it "was characterized by a basic understanding between the employers and workers, a social contract that provided workers with reasonably secure and well-paid jobs and provided employers with reasonably stable and productive workers (Rubin 1996, 27).

Chapter 11. The Old Dispensation Withers Away

1. Charles Pearson's organizational commitment is more than one standard deviation below the mean, and his loyalty trend is down.
2. Source is General Social Survey, (Davis and Smith 1994)
3. Original data is from the General Social Survey. Wood's age categories differ slightly from my cohorts: "Cohort 1" in Figure 11-2 have birth years from 1927 to 1938; "Cohort 2," 1939–56; "Cohort 3," 1957 and after.
4. Appendix B gives details on the interviews and their analysis.
5. Respondents were asked to agree or disagree with the statement: "In spite of what some people say, the lot of the average man is getting worse, not better." (Source: General Social Survey, Davis and Smith 1994).

Chapter 12. The Natural History of Loyalty

1. As Gertrude Himmelfarb has pointed out, "values" is a modern term, replacing what our grandfathers called "virtues." Himmelfarb decries this development, which she attributes to the unfortunate modern belief that all values are relative, that there are no absolute and enduring moral standards (Himmelfarb 1994, 9–11).
2. Appendix A describes the measurement of the Protestant Ethic in my survey, and the correlations of this construct with other variables.
3. With 5.0 meaning "strongly agree," 4.0 "somewhat agree," and 3.0 "neutral," the cohort means were: cohort 1, 3.21; cohort 2, 3.09; cohort 3, 3.05. The differences between cohort 1 and the other two is statistically significant; the difference between cohorts 2 and 3 is not. See Appendix A for details on the survey and the statistical results.
4. Galbraith makes much the same argument in his *The New Industrial State* (1967).

5. Marx said, as is well known, that capitalism's superstructure of private property was inconsistent with its highly organized economic base, and hence capitalism by necessity must fail.

Chapter 13. Consequences: The Old Dispensation's Demise

1. The "Vision Statement" is prominently displayed and refers to employees as the company's most valuable asset.

2. "Ressentiment: Souvenir d'une offense, d'un manque d'égards, *avec intention de vengeance.*" (emphasis added). *Larousse de Poche.* 1979. Paris: Librarie Larousse.

3. The numbers for happiness and financial satisfaction are still quite high, but the downward trend is statistically significant. In 1994, about 28 percent said they were "very happy," down from 38 percent in 1974. And in 1994 a little over 28 percent said they were dissatisfied with their financial position, versus 23 percent in 1974.

4. Stalin saw a similar dilemma in the social character of the German people. He noted an incident in the 1920s when German Communists, on their way by rail to a revolutionary rally, passively stood at the station and waited for the stationmaster to arrive and punch their exit tickets. These self-styled "fire-eating revolutionaries" could not shake off their inbred respect for authority. Stalin said such people would never make a revolution. And in the same way, people sunk into privatism are unlikely to stir themselves and change the conditions they lament.

5. Bill's organizational commitment score is more than one standard deviation below the Softmatics mean, and his loyalty trend is down.

Appendix A

1. All organization names are pseudonyms.

2. Etzioni (1961, 10) describes normative or "moral" commitment as an intense orientation toward the organization based on internalization of the organization's goals, values, and norms. The individual identifies with authority.

3. Note that Softmatics' surveys substituted "overall" for "on the whole."

4. ORGCOM is correlated with these variables at the 5 percent significance level, or better.

5. "1" designates manager; "3" nonmanger, so the correlation coefficient is negative.

Appendix B

1. Frequently, the subjects would ask for clarification of the context: "Do you mean personal, business," etc. I would reply noncommittally, leaving it to them to begin in their own way.

2. Here I recited a series of layoffs, mergers, and acquisitions going back to 1988, when Softmatics was a unit of RLX.

3. In some cases, when people had trouble with the question as posed, I asked them to plot their sense of loyalty as a function of time.

4. This question was not asked of all subjects, since I learned of Sun's purported stance after the interview process was underway.

5. This question was asked only at interviews after I learned of the press release in early January 1995.

6. This question often required further probing, e.g., "Is it a friendly environment?. Is it a fun place to work? Is the atmosphere of Softmatics the same now as it was under RLX?"

7. Significant correlation at the 5 percent level or more.

8. A significant correlation when controlling for age.

Bibliography

Ackoff, R. L. 1986. Profit as a Means. *The New York Times.* August 31, 1986.

Ajzen, I. and Fishbein, M. 1977. *Understanding Attitudes and Predicting Social Behavior.* Englewood Cliffs, N.J.: Prentice Hall.

Alchian, A. A. and Demsetz, H. 1972. Production, Information Costs and Economic Organization. *American Economic Review.* 62:777–95.

Alwin, D. F. 1989. Changes in Qualities Valued in Children in the United States, 1964 to 1984. *Social Science Research.* 18:195–236.

Angeles, P. A. 1981. *Dictionary of Philosophy.* New York: Harper & Row.

Angle, H. L., and Perry, J. L. 1981. An Empirical Assessment of Organizational Commitment and Organizational Effectiveness. *Administrative Science Quarterly.* 26:1–14.

Arnold, M. 1986. *Matthew Arnold.* New York: Oxford University Press.

Aron, R. 1962. *Dix-huit Leçons sur la Société Industrielle.* Paris: Gallimard.

Arrow, K. 1974. *The Limits of Organization.* New York: W. W. Norton and Co.

Barnard, C. I. 1950. *The Functions of the Executive.* Cambridge, MA: Harvard University Press.

Bell, D. 1976. *The Cultural Contradictions of Capitalism.* New York: Basic Books.

Bellah, R. N., Madsen, R., Sullivan, W. M., Swidler, A. and Tipton, S. M. 1985. *Habits of the Heart: Individualism and Commitment in American Life.* New York: Harper & Row.

———. 1991. *The Good Society.* New York: Alfred A. Knopf.

Bendix, R. 1956. *Work and Authority in Industry: Ideologies of Management in the Course of Industrialization.* New York: John Wiley & Sons, Inc.

Bennett, A. 1990. *The Death of the Organization Man.* New York: William Morrow and Company.

Berger, P. L. and Luckman, T. 1966. *The Social Construction of Reality.* Garden City, NY: Doubleday.

Berle, A. A., Jr. and Means, G. C. 1932. *The Modern Corporation and Private Property.* New York: Macmillan.

Bierce, A. 1958. *The Devil's Dictionary.* New York: Dover.

Blackburn, S. 1994. *The Oxford Dictionary of Philosophy.* New York: Oxford University Press.

Blinder, A. S. (ed.) 1990. *Paying for Productivity: A Look at the Evidence.* Washington, D.C.: The Brookings Institution.

Bradach, J. L. and Eccles, R. G. 1989. Price, Authority and Trust: From Ideal Types to Plural Forms. *Annual Review of Sociology.* 15:97–118.

Bradsher, K. 1995. Widest Gap in Incomes? Research Points to U.S. *The New York Times.* October 27, 1995. C-2.

Brandes, S. D. 1976. *American Welfare Capitalism, 1880–1940.* Chicago. University of Chicago Press.

Brockner, J., Grover, S., Reed, T., Dewitt, R. and O'Malley, M. 1987. Survivors; Reactions to Layoffs: We Get by With a Little Help from our Friends. *Administrative Science Quarterly.* 32:526–41.

Brody, D. 1993. *Workers in Industrial America: Essays on The Twentieth Century Struggle.* 2d Edition. New York: Oxford University Press.

Brown, N. O. 1959. *Life Against Death: The Psychoanalytical Meaning of History.* Middletown, CT: Wesleyan University Press.

Bruchey, S. 1988. *The Wealth of the Nation: An Economic History of the United States.* New York: Harper and Row.

Bruyn, S. T. 1991. *A Future for the American Economy: The Social Market.* Stanford, CA: Stanford University Press.

Burawoy, M. 1979. *Manufacturing Consent: Changes in the Labor Process under Monopoly Capitalism.* Chicago: University of Chicago Press.

Business Week. 1986. The End of Corporate Loyalty. August 4, 1986:42–49.

Butler, G. and Vodanovich, S. J. 1992. The Relationship between Work Values and Normative and Instrumental Commitment. *Journal of Psychology.* 126:139–46.

Carroll, P. 1993. *Big Blues: The Unmaking of IBM.* New York: Crown Publishers.

Chandler, A. D., Jr. 1977. *The Visible Hand: The Managerial Revolution in American Business.* Cambridge, MA: The Belknap Press.

———. 1990. *Scale and Scope: The Dynamics of Industrial Capitalism.* Cambridge, MA: The Belknap Press.

Chilton, K. and Weidenbaum, M. 1994. *A New Social Contract for the American Workplace: From Paternalism to Partnering.* Policy Study Number 123. St. Louis: Center for the Study of American Business. Washington University.

Chirot, D. 1986. *Social Change in the Modern Era.* San Diego: Harcourt Brace Jovanovich.

Church, G. J. 1993. Jobs in an Age of Insecurity. *Time.* November 22, 1993:34–39.

Chusmir, L. H. 1986. Gender Differences in Variables Affecting Job Commitment among Working Men and Women. *Journal of Social Psychology.* 126:87–94.

Cialdini, R. B. 1993.*Influence: The Psychology of Persuasion.* 3d Ed., New York: William Morrow.

Clancy, J. J. 1989. *The Invisible Powers: The Language of Business.* Lexington, MA: Lexington Books.

Clecak, P. 1983. *America's Quest for the Ideal Self: Dissent and Fulfillment in the 60s and 70s.* New York: Oxford University Press.

Cochran, T. C. 1985. *Challenges to American Values: Society, Business, and Religion.* New York: Oxford University Press.

Cohen, A. 1993. Age and Tenure in Relation to Organizational Commitment: A Meta-Analysis. *Basic and Applied Social Psychology.* 14:143–59.

Coleman, J. S., 1990. *Foundations of Social Theory.* Cambridge, Harvard University Press.

Conrad, J. 1988. *Chance: A Tale in Two Parts.* New York: Oxford University Press.

Cooper, M. R., Morgan, R. S., Foley, P. M. and Kaplan, L. B. 1979. Changing Employee Values: Deepening Discontent? *Harvard Business Review.* 57:117–25.

Crispell, D. 1993. In Friends, Many See Reflection of Themselves. *The Wall Street Journal.* June 30, 1993, B-1.

Crosland, C. A. R. 1956. *The Future of Socialism.* London: Jonathan Cage.

Dahl, Robert. 1982. *Dilemmas of Pluralist Democracy.* New Haven: Yale University Press.

Davis, J. A. and Smith, T. W. 1994. *General Social Surveys, 1972–1994: Cumulative Codebook.* Chicago: National Opinion Research Center.

Dean, J. W. and Evans, J. R. 1994. *Total Quality Management, Organization, and Strategy.* St. Paul, MN: West Publishing Company.

Deutsch, C. H. 1995. You're Out! Clean out your Office!. Now for Some Nice Parting Gifts. *The New York Times.* June 11, 1995. F-10.

Dore, R. 1973. *British Factory-Japanese Factory: The Origins of National Diversity in Industrial Relations.* London: George Allen and Unwin Ltd.

Dunham, R. G. and Mauss, A. L. 1976. Waves from Watergate: Evidence Concerning the Impact of the Watergate Scandal upon Public Legitimacy and Social Control. *Pacific Sociological Review.* 19:469–90.

Easterlin, R. A. 1987. *Birth and Fortune: The Impact of Numbers on Personal Welfare.* 2d Edition. Chicago: University of Chicago Press.

Economic Report of the President. 1994. Washington, D.C.: United States Government Printing Office.

Economist. 1993. The Death of Corporate Loyalty. April, 3, 1993:63–64.

Edwards, R. 1979. *Contested Terrain: The Transformation of the Workplace in the Twentieth Century.* New York: Basic Books.

Ellul, J. 1990. *The Technological Bluff.* Bromiley, G. W. (translator). Grand Rapids, MI: William B. Erdmans Publishing Company.

Etzioni, A. 1961. *A Comparative Analysis of Complex Organizations: On Power, Involvement and Their Correlates.* New York: Free Press.

Ewin, R. E. 1992. Loyalty and Virtues. *The Philosophical Quarterly.* 42:403–19.

Fallows, J. 1995. The Republican Promise. *The New York Review of Books.* January 12, 1995.

Festinger, L. 1957. *A Theory of Cognitive Dissonance.* Evanston, IL: Row, Peterson and Co.

Filion, F. L. 1976. Estimating Bias Due to Nonresponse in Mail Surveys. *Public Opinion Quarterly*. 39:482–92.

Filoramo, G. 1990. Alcock, A. (translator). *A History of Gnosticism*. Oxford: Basil Blackwell.

Fischer, A. B. 1991. Morale Crisis: Job Satisfaction Among Middle Managers is Hitting Lows. What's an Employer to Do? *Fortune*. November 18, 1991, 70–80.

Fitzgerald, F. S. 1951. *This Side of Paradise*. New York: Charles Scribner's Sons.

Fitzgerald, T. H. 1979. *Harvard Business Review on Human Relations*. New York: Harper & Row.

Flanagan, R. J., Strauss, G. and Ulman, L. 1974. Worker Discontent and Work Place Behavior. *Industrial Relations*. 13:101–23.

Fletcher, G. P. 1993. *Loyalty: An Essay on the Morality of Relationships*. New York: Oxford University Press.

Ford, H. 1923. *My Life and Works*. New York: Doubleday, Page.

Foucault, M. 1990. Hurley, R. (translator).*The History of Sexuality: Volume I, An Introduction*. New York: Vintage Books.

Franke, R. H. and Kaul, J. D. 1978. The Hawthorne Experiments: First Statistical Interpretation. *American Sociological Review*. 43:623–43.

Freud, S. 1922. *Group Psychology and the Analysis of the Ego*. New York: Boni and Liveright.

Fromm, E. 1994. *Escape from Freedom*. New York: Henry Holt and Company.

Furnham, A. 1990. *The Protestant Work Ethic: The Psychology of Work-Related Beliefs and Behaviors*. London: Routledge.

Gaertner, K. N. 1989. Career Experiences, Perceptions of Employment Practices, and Psychological Commitment to the Organization. *Human Relations*. 42:975–91.

Galambos, L. 1975. *The Public Image of Big Business in America, 1880–1949: A Quantitative Study of Social Change*. Baltimore: The Johns Hopkins University Press.

———. 1983. *America at Middle Age: A New History of the United States in the Twentieth Century*. New York: McGraw-Hill Book Company.

Galambos, L. and Pratt, J. 1988. *The Rise of the Corporate Commonwealth: U.S. Business and Public Policy in the Twentieth Century*. New York: Basic Books.

Galbraith, J. K. 1967. *The New Industrial State*. Boston: Houghton Mifflin.

———. 1983. *The Anatomy of Power*. Boston: Houghton Mifflin Company.

———. 1987. *Economics in Perspective: A Critical History*. Boston: Houghton Mifflin.

Galinsky, E., Bond, J. T. and Friedman, D. 1993. *The Changing Work Force*. New York: Families and Work Institute.

Gans, H. J. 1988. *Middle American Individualism: The Future of Liberal Democracy*. New York: Oxford University Press.

Genasci, L. 1994. The Downside of Downsizing. *St. Louis Post-Dispatch*. July 7, 1994, 5C.

Gerlach, L. P. & Hine, V. H. 1973. *Lifeway Leap: The Dynamics of Change In America.* Minneapolis: University of Minnesota Press.

Gitlin, T. 1989. *The Sixties: Years of Hope, Days of Rage.* New York: Bantam Books.

Glenn, N. D. 1977. *Cohort Analysis.* Beverly Hills, CA: Sage Publications.

———. 1987. Social Trends in The United States: Evidence from Sample Surveys. *Public Opinion Quarterly.* 51:S109-S126.

Glenn, N. D. and Weaver, C. N. 1985. Age, Cohort, and Reported Job Satisfaction in the United States. In Blaue, M. (ed). *Current Perspectives on Aging and the Life Cycle.* New York: JAI Press.

Goyder, J. 1987. *The Silent Minority: Nonrespondents on Sample Surveys.* Boulder. CO: Westview Press.

Graff, H. J. 1995. *Conflicting Paths: Growing up in America.* Cambridge, MA: Harvard University Press.

Grosman, B. A. 1989. Corporate Loyalty, Does It Have a Future? *Journal of Business Ethics.* 8:565–68.

Habermas, J. 1968. *Toward a Rational Society: Student Protest, Science, and Politics.* Shapiro, J. J. (translator). Boston: Beacon Press.

Halberstam, D. 1993. *The Fifties.* New York: Villard Books.

Hamilton, R. F. and Wright, J. D. 1986. *The State of the Masses.* New York: Aldine.

Hamori, P. A. 1974. *The Communist Manifesto: A Framework for a Critical Analysis and a Cursory Interpretation.* Muncie, IN: Ball State University.

Harris, Louis. 1989. *Inside America.* New York: Vintage Books.

Haskell, T. L. 1992. Capitalism and the Origins of the Humanitarian Sensibility, Part 1. In Bender, T. (ed.). *The Antislavery Debate: Capitalism and Abolitionism as a Problem in Historical Interpretation.* Berkeley: University of California Press.

Hayek, F. A. 1994. *The Road to Serfdom.* Chicago: The University of Chicago Press.

Heckscher, C. 1995. *White-Collar Blues: Management Loyalties in an Age of Corporate Restructuring.* New York: Basic Books.

Heilbroner, R. L. 1961. *The Worldly Philosophers: The Lives, Times, and Ideas of the Great Economic Thinkers* (revised edition). New York: Simon and Schuster.

Herbert, B. 1995. Out of Work. *The New York Times.* July 31, 1995. A-9.

Hershey, R. D., Jr. 1995. Worker Earnings Post Rise of 2.7%, Lowest on Record. *The New York Times.* November 1, 1995, A-1.

Himmelfarb, G. 1994. *The De-Moralization of Society: From Victorian Virtues to Modern Values.* New York: Alfred A. Knopf.

Hirschman, A. O. 1970. *Exit, Voice, and Loyalty: Responses to Decline in Firms, Organizations, and States.* Cambridge, MA: Harvard University Press.

Hobbes, T. 1988. *The Leviathan.* Amherst, NY: Prometheus Books.

Iaccoca, L. 1986. *Iaccoca.* New York: Bantam Books.

Jacobs, J. 1992. *Systems of Survival: A Dialogue on the Moral Foundations of Commerce and Politics.* New York: Random House.

James, H. 1965. *The Wings of the Dove.* New York: Penguin Books.

Jarrell, R. 1985. *The Lost World.* New York: Collier Books.

Jennings, M. K. 1987. Residues of a Movement: The Aging of the American Protest Generation. *American Political Science Review.* 81:367–82.

Kalb, L. and Hugick, L. 1990. The American Worker: How we Feel about our Jobs. *The Public Perspective.* 1:21–22.

Kamer, P. M. 1988. *The U.S. Economy in Crisis: Adjusting to the New Realities.* New York: Praeger.

Kanter, R. M. 1977. *Men and Women of the Corporation.* New York: Basic Books.

Kerr, C. 1988. The Neoclassical Revisionists in Labor Economics 1940-1960: R.I.P. In Kaufman, Bruce E. (ed.) 1988. *How Labor Markets Work.* Lexington, MA: Lexington Books.

Keynes, J. M. 1963. *Essays in Persuasion.* New York: W. W. Norton & Company.

Kiesler, C. A. 1971. *The Psychology of Commitment.* New York: Academic Press.

Kiesler, C. A., Collins, B. E., and Miller, N. 1969. *Attitude Change: A Critical Analysis of Theoretical Approaches.* New York: John Wiley and Sons.

Kilborn, P. T. 1994. Job Security Hinges on Skill, Not on an Employer for Life. *The New York Times.* March 12, 1994, A-1.

Kissinger, W. 1986. The Word for Takeovers: Pernicious. *The New York Times.* December 5, 1986, 15.

Kleinfield, N. R. 1996. The Company as Family, No More. *The New York Times.* March 4, 1996.

Ladd, E. C. and Lipset, S. M. 1980. Anatomy of a Decade. *Public Opinion.* 3:2–9.

Lee, J. W. 1968. Organizational Loyalty: A Second Look. *Personnel Journal.* 53:461–66.

Lehman, E. W. 1987. The Crisis of Political Legitimacy: What is It; Who's Got It; Who Needs It? *Research in Political Sociology.* 3:202–221.

Leinberger, P. and Tucker, B. 1991. *The New Individualists: The Generation after the Organization Man.* New York: HarperCollins.

Lester, Richard A. 1988. Wages, Benefits, and Company Employment Systems, in Kaufman, Bruce E. (ed.) 1988. *How Labor Markets Work.* Lexington, MA: Lexington Books.

Levinson, H. and Rosenthal, S. 1984. *CEO: Corporate Leadership in Action.* New York: Basic Books.

Light, P. C. 1988. *Baby Boomers.* New York: W. W. Norton & Company.

Lincoln, J. R., and Kalleberg, A. L. 1990. *Culture, Control and Commitment: A Study of Work Organization and Work Attitudes in the United States and Japan.* Cambridge: Cambridge University Press.

Lipset, S. M. and Schneider, W. 1987. *The Confidence Gap: Business, Labor and Government in the Public Mind.* Baltimore: The Johns Hopkins University Press.

Lublin, J. S. 1993. Walking Wounded: Survivors of Layoffs Battle Angst, Anger, Hurting Productivity. *The Wall Street Journal.* December 6, 1993, A-1.

Luthans, F., Baack, D. and Taylor, L. 1987. Organizational Commitment: Analysis of Antecedents. *Human Relations.* 40:219–35.

Maccoby, M. 1988. *Why Work: Leading the New Generation.* New York: Simon and Schuster.

———. 1990. The American Character: The Organization Man. *Current.* October 1990, 4–8.

MacIntyre, A. 1981. *After Virtue.* South Bend: University of Notre Dame Press.

Mailer, N. 1948. *The Naked and the Dead.* New York: The New American Library.

de Mandeville, B. 1724. *The Fable of the Bees: Or, Private Vices, Publick Benefits.* 3rd Edition. London: J. Jonson.

Mannheim, K. 1959. *Essays on the Sociology of Knowledge.* New York: Oxford University Press.

Marcuse, H. 1955. *Eros and Civilization: A Philosophical Inquiry into Freud.* Boston: The Beacon Press.

———. 1969. *An Essay on Liberation.* Boston: The Beacon Press.

Marin, P. 1975. The New Narcissism. *Harper's.* 25:45–56.

Markoff, J. 1993. At Apple, Search for Direction. *The New York Times.* October 1, 1993, C-1.

Marks, M. L. 1988. The Disappearing Company Man. *Psychology Today.* 22:34.

Martin, B. 1981. *A Sociology of Contemporary Cultural Change.* New York: St. Martin's Press.

Marx, K. 1904. Historical Materialism Summarized. In Etzioni, A. and Etzioni-Halevy, E. (Eds.) 1973. *Social Change: Sources, Patterns and Consequences.* New York: Basic Books.

Mathieu, J. E. and Zajac, D. M. 1990. A Review and Meta-analysis of the Antecedents, Correlates, and Consequences of Organizational Commitment. *Psychological Bulletin.* 108:171–94.

Matusow, A. 1984. *The Unraveling of America: A History of Liberalism in the 1960s.* New York: Harper & Row.

Mayo, E. 1946. *The Human Problems of an Industrial Civilization.* (Second Edition). Cambridge, MA: The Murray Printing Company.

McClosky, H. and Zaller, J. 1984. *The American Ethos: Public Attitudes toward Capitalism and Democracy.* Cambridge, MA: Harvard University Press.

McDonnell, J. 1994. The New Employment Contract. *Spirit.* Fall, 1994. St. Louis: McDonnell Douglas Corporation.

McGee, G. W., & Ford, R. C., 1987. Two (or more?) Dimensions of Organizational Commitment: Reexamination of the Affective and Continuance Commitment Scales. *Journal of Applied Psychology.* 72:638–42.

Merton, R. 1968. *Social Theory and Social Structure.* New York: Free Press.

Meyer, J. P., Paunonen, S. V. and Gellatly, I. R. 1989. Organizational Commitment and Job Performance: It's the Nature of the Commitment that Counts. *Journal of Applied Psychology.* 74:152–56.

Mills, C. W. 1953. *White Collar: The American Middle Classes.* New York: Oxford University Press.

Mirels, H. and Garrett, J. 1972. The Protestant Ethic as a Personality Variable. *Journal of Consulting and Clinical Psychology*. 36:40–44.

Moore, W. E. 1972. Organization and Change. In Nisbet, R. (ed). *Social Change*. Oxford: Basil Blackwell.

Moskowittz, M. 1993. Spare the Knife, Spoil the Company. *The New York Times*. May 14, 1993, C-1.

Mottaz, C. J., 1987, An Analysis of the Relationship between Work Satisfaction and Organizational Commitment. *Sociological Quarterly*. 28:541–58.

———. 1988. Determinants of Organizational commitment. *Human Relations*. 41:467–82.

———. 1989. An Analysis of the Relationship between Attitudinal Commitment and Behavioral Commitment. *Sociological Quarterly*. 30:143–58.

Mowday, R. T., Porter, L. W. and Steers, R. S. 1982. *Employee-Organization Linkages: The Psychology of Commitment, Absenteeism and Turnover*. New York: Academic Press.

Niemi, R. G., Mueller, J. and Smith, T. W. 1989. *Trends in Public Opinion: A Compendium of Survey Data*. New York: Greenwood Press.

Nisbet, R. 1972. *Social Change*. Oxford: Basil Blackwell.

North, D. C. 1990. *Institutions, Institutional Change and Economic Performance*. Cambridge: Cambridge University Press.

———. 1993. Institutions, Transaction Costs and Productivity in the Long Run. *8th World Productivity Congress*. May, 1993.

Norusis, M. J. 1990. *SPSS Base System User's Guide*. Chicago: SPSS Inc.

Oldenquist, A. 1982. Loyalties. *Journal of Philosophy*. 89:173–193.

O'Reilly, B. 1994. The New Deal: What Companies and Employees Owe One Another. *Fortune*. June 13, 1994.

Organ, D. W. 1988. *Organizational Citizenship Behavior: The Good Soldier Syndrome*. Lexington, MA: Lexington Books.

O'Toole, J. et al. 1973. *Work In America: Report of a Special Task Force to the Secretary of Health, Education, and Welfare*. Cambridge, MA: MIT Press.

O'Toole, J. 1986. *Vanguard Management: Redesigning the Corporate Future*. Garden City, NY: Doubleday.

Ouchi, W. G. and Price, R. L. 1980. Hierarchies, Clans, and Theory Z: A New Perspective on Organizational Development. In Hackman, J. R., Lawler, E. E. and Porter, L. W. (eds.). 1983. *Perspectives on Behavior in Organizations*. (Second Edition). New York: McGraw-Hill Book Company.

Perrow, C. 1979. *Complex Organizations: A Critical Essay*. Glenview, IL: Scott, Foresman and Co.

Perry, R. B. 1992. The American Cast of Mind. In Wilkinson, R. (ed.). 1992. *American Social Character: Modern Interpretations from the '40s to the Present*. New York: HarperCollins.

Petit, P. 1988. The Paradox of Loyalty. *American Philosophical Quarterly*. 25:163–170.

Polanyi, K. 1944. *The Great Transformation*. Boston: Beacon Press.

Putnam, R. D. 1993. *Making Democracy Work: Civic Traditions in Modern Italy*. Princeton: Princeton University Press.

———. 1994. Bowling Alone: Democracy in America at the End of the Twentieth Century. Harvard University. (Preliminary Draft).

Quint, M. 1993. Change Worries Kodak's Hometown: A Warm Old Relationship Seems Threatened by Hard-nosed Values. *The New York Times*. August 9, 1993, C-1.

Rapoport, C. 1994. Charles Handy Sees the Future. *Fortune*. October 31, 1994. 155–68.

Reynolds, L. G. 1988. Labor Economics Then and Now. In Kaufman, Bruce E. (ed.) 1988. *How Labor Markets Work*. Lexington, MA: Lexington Books.

Riesman, D. 1950. *The Lonely Crowd: A Study of the Changing American Character*. New York: Doubleday & Company.

Romzek, B. S. 1990. Employee Investment and Commitment: The Ties that Bind. *Public Administration Review*. 50:374–82.

Rosenthal, A. M. 1995. The Real Revolution. *The New York Times*. January, 6, 1995. A-17.

Roszak, T. 1969. *The Making of a Counter Culture: Reflections on the Technocratic Society and its Youthful Opposition*. Garden City, NY: Doubleday & Company.

Rousseau, D. 1989. Psychological and Implied Contracts in Organizations. *Employee Responsibilities and Rights Journal*. 2:121–39.

Royce, J. 1908. *The Philosophy of Loyalty*. New York: Macmillan.

Rubin, B. A. 1996. *Shifts in the Social Contract*. Thousand Oaks, CA: Pine Forge Press.

Russell, C. H. and Megaard, I. (eds.). 1988. *The General Social Survey, 1972–1986: The State of the American People*. New York: Springer-Verlag.

Salancik, G. R. 1977. Commitment and the Control of Organizational Behavior and Belief. In B. M. Staw and G. R. Salancik (eds.). *New Directions in Organizational Behavior*. Chicago: St. Clair Press.

Sanchez, R. 1995. Survey Finds Maturity, Cynicism Among High-Achieving Teens. *The Washington Post*. June 15, 1995. A-3.

Sanger, D. E. 1993. Layoffs and Factory Closings Shaking the Japanese Psyche. *The New York Times*. March 3, 1993, A-1.

Schellhardt, T. D. 1993. Fewer Good Deeds Go Unpunished in '90s Corporate Climate. *The Wall Street Journal*. October 6, 1993, B-1.

Schumpeter, J. A. 1950. *Capitalism, Socialism, and Democracy*. (3d Edition). New York: Harper & Brothers Publishers.

Selznick, P. 1969. *Law, Society, and Industrial Justice*. New York: Russell Sage Foundation.

Shore, L. M., and Martin, H. J. 1989. Job Satisfaction and Organizational Commitment in Relation to Work Performance and Turnover Intentions. *Human Relations*. 42:625–38.

Shore, L. M. and Wayne, S. J. 1993. Commitment and Employee Behavior: Comparison of Affective Commitment and Continuance Commitment with Perceived Organizational Support. *Journal of Applied Psychology*. 78:774–79.

Sigband, N. B. 1974. What's Happened to Employee Commitment? *Personnel Journal.* 53:131–35.

Simon, H. 1961. *Administrative Behavior.* New York: Macmillan.

Sloan, A. P., Jr. 1965. *My Years with General Motors.* McDonald, J. (ed.). New York: McFadden Books.

Smith, A. 1974. *The Wealth of Nations: Books I–III.* Introduction by Andrew Skinner. New York: Penguin Books.

Smith, T. W. 1980. *A Compendium of Trends on General Social Survey Questions.* NORC Report No. 129. Chicago: National Opinion Research Center.

Stevens, J. M., Beyer, J. M. and Trice, H. M. 1978. Assessing Personal, Role, and Organizational Predictors of Managerial Commitment. *Academy of Management Journal.* 21:380–96.

Stewart, J. B. 1993. Taking the Dare. *The New Yorker.* July 16, 1993.

Stivers, R. 1994. *The Culture of Cynicism: American Morality in Decline.* Oxford. Blackwell.

Strom, S. 1995. This Year's Wave of Mergers Heads Toward a Record. October 31, 1995. *The New York Times.* A-1.

Sussman, B. 1988. *What Americans Really Think.* New York: Pantheon Books.

Taylor, F. W. 1914. A Piece Rate System: Being a Step Toward Partial Solution of the Labor Problem. In Thompson, C. B. (ed.) 1914. *Scientific Management: A Collection of the More Significant Articles Describing the Taylor System of Management.* Cambridge, MA: Harvard University Press.

Terkel, S. 1970. *Hard Times: An Oral History of the Great Depression.* New York: Pantheon Books.

———. 1984. *'The Good War': An Oral History of World War Two.* New York: Pantheon Books.

Thomas, D. M. 1981. *The White Hotel.* New York: Pocket Books.

Tipton, S. M. 1982. *Getting Saved from the Sixties.* Berkeley, CA: University of California Press.

de Tocqueville, A. 1988. *Democracy in America.* Lawrence, G. (translator). New York: HarperCollins.

Trigg, R. 1973. *Reason and Commitment.* Cambridge: Cambridge University.

Uchitelle, L. 1994. Job Losses Don't Let Up Even as Hard Times Ease. *The New York Times.* March 22, 1994, A-1.

Usanler, E. M. 1993. *The Decline of Comity in Congress.* Ann Arbor, MI: The University of Michigan Press.

Vecchio, R. P. 1980. The Function and Meaning of Work and the Job: Morse and Weiss (1955) Revisited. *Academy of Management Journal.* 23: 361–67.

Veroff, J., Douvan, E. and Kulka, R. 1981. *The Inner American: A Self-Portrait from 1957 to 1976.* New York: Basic Books.

Vonnegut, K. 1963. *Cat's Cradle.* New York: Dell Publishing Company.

Vroom, V. H. 1964. *Work and Motivation.* New York: John Wiley and Sons.

Watkins, T. H. 1993. *The Great Depression: America in the 1930s.* Boston: Little, Brown and Company.

Weber, M. 1947. *The Theory of Social and Economic Organization.* Parsons, T. and Henderson, B. (translators). New York: Oxford University Press.

———. 1958. *The Protestant Ethic and the Spirit of Capitalism.* Parsons, T. (translator). New York: Scribner's.

———. 1966. *Basic Concepts in Sociology.* Secher (translator). New York: Citadel Press.

Weber, R. P. 1985. *Basic Content Analysis.* Beverly Hills, CA: Sage Publications.

Weiner, R. and Stillman, D. 1979. *Woodstock Census: The Nationwide Survey of the Sixties Generation.* New York: The Viking Press.

Whyte, W. H., Jr. 1956. *The Organization Man.* New York: Simon and Schuster.

Wiebe, R. H. 1967. *The Search for Order: 1877–1920.* New York: Hill and Wang.

Wiener, Y. 1982. Commitment in Organizations: A Normative View. *Academy of Management Review.* 7:418–28.

Williams, G. C. 1966. *Adaptation and Natural Selection: A Critique of Some Current Evolutionary Thought.* Princeton, NJ: Princeton University Press.

Williamson, O. E. 1975. *Markets and Hierarchies.* New York: Free Press.

Wilson, J. Q. 1993. *The Moral Sense.* New York: Free Press.

Wood, F. W. (ed.) 1990. *An American Profile: Opinions and Behavior, 1972–1989.* Detroit: Gale Research, Inc.

Wright, R. 1994. *The Moral Animal: The New Science of Evolutionary Psychology.* New York: Pantheon Books.

Yankelovich, D. 1975. The Status of *Ressentiment* in America. *Social Research.* 42:760–77.

———. 1979. Work, Values and the New Breed, in Kerr, C. and Rostow, J. M. (eds.) 1979. *Work in America: The Decade Ahead.* New York: Van Nostrand.

———. 1994. Corporate Logic in the 1990s. Address to the 1994 Arthur W. Page Society. Spring 1994.

Yates, R. E. 1993. Downsizing's Bitter Pill. *Chicago Tribune Magazine.* November 21, 1993:15–41.

Yinger, J. M. 1982. *Countercultures: The Promise and the Peril of a World Turned Upside Down.* New York: Free Press.

Zuckerman, L. 1994. Shades of the Go-Go 80's: Takeovers in a Comeback. *The New York Times.* November 3, 1994, A-1.

Zunz, O. 1990. *Making America Corporate: 1870–1920.* Chicago: University of Chicago Press.

Index